Born on the Links

Born on the Links

A Concise History of Golf

John Williamson

ROWMAN & LITTLEFIELD

Lanham · Boulder · New York · London

Published by Rowman & Littlefield
An imprint of The Rowman & Littlefield Publishing Group, Inc.
4501 Forbes Boulevard, Suite 200, Lanham, Maryland 20706
www.rowman.com

Unit A, Whitacre Mews, 26-34 Stannary Street, London SE11 4AB

British Library Cataloguing in Publication Information Available

Library of Congress Cataloging-in-Publication Data

Names: Williamson, John Harvey, 1937-
Title: Born on the links : a concise history of golf / John Williamson.
Description: Lanham, Maryland : Rowman & Littlefield, [2018] | Includes
  bibliographical references and index.
Identifiers: LCCN 2018002017 (print) | LCCN 2018003471 (ebook) | ISBN
  9781538114537 (electronic) | ISBN 9781538114520 (hardcover : alk. paper)
Subjects: LCSH: Golf—History.
Classification: LCC GV963 (ebook) | LCC GV963 .W55 2018 (print) | DDC
  796.352—dc23
LC record available at https://lccn.loc.gov/2018002017

Printed in the United States of America

Contents

Acknowledgments

Much of the information set forth in this book came from reliable written and internet sources. Foremost among the written sources was Herbert Warren Wind's classic, _The Story of American Golf_, which should be required reading for anyone interested in the history of golf in the United States. Other useful written sources were Curt Sampson's _The Eternal Summer_ (for information related to the golfing events of 1960), Ramona Harriet's _A Missing Link in History_ (for information related to the early African American professional golfers), and Kenneth C. Chapman's _The Rules of the Green_ (for information related to the history of the rules of golf). Foremost among the internet sources was ScottishGolfHistory.org, a website registered in Scotland that provides information related to early Scottish golf and the courses it was played on.

Completing this book would not have been possible without the help of my wife, Beth. The proofreading, research, and editorial assistance she provided improved the quality and readability of this writing immeasurably. Christen Karniski, the sports and recreation acquisition editor at Rowman & Littlefield, also contributed much to the undertaking of getting this book in print.

Author's Note

The word *links* is a descriptive Scottish term for coastal grasslands. In Scotland, the links are strips of flat, grass-covered land between the seashore and the farmland. The sandy soil of the links is not suitable for farming and the links are said to be the lands that link the seashore to the farmland. It was on the links in Scotland that the game of golf was invented and first played in the fifteenth century.

Introduction

𝒯he first three chapters of this book deal with the history of golf in Scotland and England during the first 400 years of its existence. The rest of the book deals with the history of the game in the United States. It is hoped that this writing will deepen the reader's appreciation of the game by making the reader aware of the incredible history of the sport, beginning with its origins on the links in Scotland in the 15th century and concluding with the era of Tiger Woods in the 21st century. Accounts of the evolution and development of the equipment, playing fields, and rules of the game are given, together with accounts of the important players and events of the game as it changed from a pastime of the rich to a game that today is played and followed throughout the world by people of all classes, ages, and backgrounds.

The history of the ball used in the game is traced from the small leather ball stuffed with animal hair that was used during the early years of the game to the inventions of the feathery golf ball in the early 1600s, the gutta-percha golf ball in the 1850s, the rubber-wound golf ball in the early 1900s, and the solid-core golf balls of today. The history of the clubs used in the game is traced from the crude thorn-wood clubs with ash shafts used by the Scots in the 15th and 16th centuries to the spoons, mashies, and niblicks of the 17th, 18th, and 19th centuries, the numbered woods and irons of the 20th century, and the metal woods, perimeter-weighted irons, and oversized drivers of today.

The history of the playing fields of the game is traced from the unimproved fields of the early years of golf to the development of distinct putting and teeing areas in the 18th and 19th centuries to the manicured greens, groomed fairways, and multiple tee boxes of today's golf courses. The history of the rules is traced from the unwritten local rules of the first three hundred

1

years of the game to the first written rules in 1744 to the uniform rules governing the game that are in effect today throughout the world.

The persons who play the game are traced from the ordinary Scots who invented the game on the links in Scotland in the 15th and 16th centuries to the establishment of the first membership golf clubs by aristocrats and affluent British merchants in the 18th century, to the early golf clubs in the United States established by well-to-do Americans in the late 1800s, to the popularization of the game following Francis Ouimet's historic victory in the 1913 US Open, and finally to the phenomenal growth of golf in the United States beginning with the arrival of Arnold Palmer and televised golf in the 1960s. Separate accounts are given of the African American experience in the game and the history of women's golf in the United States.

Accounts of the great players and events of the game are given, mostly through descriptions of golfing events, beginning with Old Tom and Young Tom Morris in the 1800s and continuing to Harry Vardon and Walter Travis in the early 1900s; Walter Hagen, Gene Sarazen, and Bobby Jones in the 1920s and 1930s; Byron Nelson, Ben Hogan, and Sam Snead in the 1940s and 1950s; Arnold Palmer, Gary Player, Lee Trevino, and Jack Nicklaus in the 1960s through the 1980s; and Tiger Woods in the 1990s and early 2000s.

• 1 •

The Origins of Golf in Scotland

ost scholars and golf historians believe that the game of golf had its origins in the Dutch game of *het kolven*. Popular in the Netherlands in the 14th century, *het kolven* was a stick-and-ball game derived by the Dutch from the Belgian game of *chole* and the French game of *jeu de mail*, both of which were games wherein players used heavy wooden or iron mallets to strike a wooden ball about the size of a melon and propel it from a starting point to a target, with the player doing so in the fewest strokes prevailing.

The Dutch replaced the melon-sized wooden ball used in *chole* and *jeu de mail* with a smaller ball made of tightly wound wool or cow's hair encased in a leather covering. It is believed that the ball used by the Dutch was slightly larger than a modern-day golf ball. The Dutch replaced the heavy mallets used in the Belgian and French games with a bladed wooden club that looked much like a modern-day hockey stick. The Dutch played *het kolven* on public streets and roads with multiple players each hitting a small leather-covered ball from a starting point to a series of targets, with the player doing so in the fewest stokes prevailing. The targets were trees, poles embedded in the ground, or any other convenient local landmark. During the winter months, the Dutch played the game on frozen lakes and canals and called it *kolf*. Scenes of the Dutch playing *kolf* on frozen lakes were featured in paintings made by Dutch artists during this period.

Early in the 15th century, the game of *het kolven* crossed the North Sea to Scotland. The game was most likely introduced to the Scots by Dutch merchants, who were carrying on a significant trading business with the Scots during this period. However, some historians believe the game was introduced to the Scots around the turn of the 15th century when the Scottish ship *Good Hope* ran aground off the Zuider Zee in the Netherlands. It is thought that several of the Scottish crew members began playing *het kolven* while convalescing in the Netherlands and brought the game with them when they returned to Scotland. Either way, the Dutch game of *het kolven* was introduced to the Scots in the early 1400s.

Instead of playing the imported game on public streets and roads, as the Dutch had done, the Scots played it on the links. The word *links* is a descriptive Scottish word for coastal grasslands. In Scotland, the links (or linksland, as it is sometimes called) are strips of flat, grass-covered land between the seashore and the farmland. The links were not suitable for farming and were said to be the lands that linked the seashore to the farmland. The word *links* is thought to have been derived from the 10th-century Anglo-Saxon word *hlinc*, meaning a ridge. Although the word *links* was originally used to denote any rough grassy area between the sea and the farmland, the word later came to denote any common, flat, grassy area. Today, the word is most often used as a synonym for golf course.

In the 12th century, King David I of Scotland had set aside the links for the common use of his subjects. From that time on, the links were treated as public lands, not subject to private ownership, and were reserved for the recreational use of all Scots, regardless of class. It was only natural that the Scots would play the imported game on the links. The open, level topography of the land, the hardy wild grasses that grew there, and the public status of the lands made the links an ideal playing field for the game.

The Scots adopted the small, leather-covered ball used by the Dutch in *het kolven* as the ball for their game on the links. The assertion by some golf historians that the balls used by the Scots during the early years of golf were made of wood has been discredited in recent years. According to the British Golf Museum in St. Andrews, the evidence supporting the use of wooden golf balls by the Scots is flimsy at best. The museum reports that there is no substantiated evidence of a wooden golf ball ever being used, not a single wooden golf ball has ever been found, and there is no mention in any written record or document of anyone ever having played golf using a wooden ball.

It appears that from the very beginning the ball used by the Scots was composed of a leather casing stuffed with animal hair. The Scots called the ball the "hairy." Balls of this size and type were being manufactured in great numbers in the Netherlands in the 15th century for use in the Dutch games of *het kolven* and *kolf*, and it has been documented that balls of this type were exported to Scotland by the Dutch in significant numbers during the 15th and 16th centuries.

Another reason for believing that the Scots used the hairy during the early years of golf was that it could be driven farther than a wooden ball. Recent tests have shown that the maximum distance a wooden golf ball could have been driven with the clubs then available was about 80 yards. The same tests show that a hairy could have been driven nearly twice that far. Because golfers will invariably choose the ball that gives them the greatest distance, it only stands to reason that the hairy was the ball used by the Scots during the early years of golf.

Strangely, while the Scots changed the imported game into a spacious game on their links playing fields, in the Netherlands *het kolven* evolved in the opposite direction. At about the time that *het kolven* was introduced to the Scots, cities and villages in the Netherlands started banning the playing of the game on public streets and roads, primarily because of the damage to buildings and windows caused by errant shots. Forbidden from playing on public streets and roads and there being no other public areas on which to play the game, the Dutch reverted to playing *het kolven* on the smaller courses on which they had earlier played *maliespel*, which was the Dutch version of *chole* and *jeu de mail*.

Most of the *maliespel* courses adjoined cafes and inns, were short, and required the use of a larger and heavier ball. Over time, the courses were increasingly shortened and roofed over until a new game evolved that was played entirely indoors. The new game, whose name was shortened to *kolven*, became very popular in the Netherlands in the 17th and 18th centuries. Records show that in 1769 there were over 200 *kolven* courses in the city of Amsterdam alone. The game is still played in a few cities in Holland on indoor courts that are about twenty yards long and five yards wide.

Over time, the Scots significantly changed the imported game. Most of the changes in the game were made to accommodate the links playing fields used by the Scots. The targets were changed from poles, trees, and other stationary objects to holes in the ground. Lofted clubs were invented and the use of multiple clubs was initiated. Over time, the Scots also devised a unique playing field for the game and developed a comprehensive set of rules governing its play.

One of the first changes to the Dutch game made by the Scots was to devise a club that would work on the grass of their links playing fields. The bladed club used by the Dutch just didn't work on the links. Although it was possible, with practice, to hit a ball into the air consistently off of the smooth surface of a road or frozen canal with the bladed club used by the Dutch, it was impossible to do so consistently on the wild grasses of the links. Mechanical grass cutters had not yet been invented and the Scots had to rely on sheep and rabbits to keep the grass short. Consequently, the grass on the early playing fields was often long and uneven, and the bladed club used by the Dutch more often than not got caught up in the grass before getting to the ball. What was needed was a club with a head that was thin and heavy enough to slice through the grass, strike the ball forcibly, and propel it out of the grass and into the air.

In the early 1400s, the Scots invented a club with a narrow, heavy head made of thorn wood that would slice through the grass and strike the ball in such a way as to propel it up out of the grass and into the air. The club was what we call a lofted club. The first lofted clubs developed by the Scots had banana-shaped, shallow-faced wooden heads made of thorn wood that were attached to thin wooden shafts made of ash. The hitting surfaces of the club heads were slanted or beveled in such a way as to propel the ball on an upward trajectory when struck properly. The invention of the lofted club added a distinctly Scottish feature to the game.

Once lofted clubs were invented, it was not difficult to vary the degree of loft on the club head so that different clubs would produce different trajectories and distances. In doing this, the Scots invented the concept of using multiple clubs and added another distinctly Scottish feature to the game.

The targets used by the Scots when the game first arrived in Scotland were most likely poles embedded in the ground. There weren't many trees or other large stationary objects on the links so the Dutch practice of using such objects as targets wasn't feasible on the links playing fields in Scotland. During the very early years of golf in Scotland, there were no permanent golf courses and players had to install a series of targets before playing the game. Although the first targets might have been poles embedded in the ground, it wasn't long until the poles were replaced with holes in the ground. It is not known when a hole in the ground was first used as a target or who came up with the idea. It could have been that sometime in the early 1400s a player's ball rolled into a rabbit hole and it dawned on the player that a hole in the ground would make a target that could be easily made and relocated. Conceivably, his fellow golfers liked the idea and discovered that rolling a ball into a hole requires significantly more skill and finesse than banging a ball against a pole or tree. The concept of using holes in the ground as targets added another distinctly Scottish feature to the game.

There being no rules governing the number of holes on a course, those preparing the targets had to decide how many holes they wanted to play. If they wanted to play three holes of golf, they made three targets; if they wanted to play ten holes, they made ten targets.

Perhaps the most important change the Scots made to the imported game was to devise a playing field for the game on their links habitat. Once again, there are no recorded accounts that shed any light on how or even when the Scots first devised a playing field for the game. There is no record as to when, where, and by whom the first rudimentary golf course was established. Most likely it was early in the 15th century. Given its reputation as being the cradle of golf, one would think that the first golf course would have been the Old Course at St. Andrews. It may have been, but there are no records to substantiate it because the origins of the Old Course are shrouded in mystery. No one knows with any degree of certainty how, when, or by whom the Old Course was first laid out and built. The first recorded account of golf being played on the links at St. Andrews was in 1450, but it is likely that an early form of the game was played there decades earlier.

Because staking out a course before playing was burdensome and inconvenient, it is likely that communal targets were established on at least some of the links playing fields during the first half of the 15th century and were used by all who played there. Over time it is likely that standard distances between the targets were adopted by the common consent of those who played there, and one-shot, two-shot, and three-shot holes were established. Of course, the lay of the land on a particular links also had a lot to do with where the targets were established and how far apart they were. The targets had to fit the natural landscape because the only earth-moving equipment available in those days was a man with a shovel. It is known that the holes on the early links golf courses were played in no set or particular order.

Precisely when and where the first communal playing grounds for the game were established on the links playing fields and who designed and built them is not known. However, it must have occurred fairly early in the 15th century because in 1457 the Parliament of King James II of Scotland issued a proclamation stating, "It is ordanyt and decretyt that ye fute bawe and ye golfe be utterly cryit doune and nocht usyt." Translated, the proclamation reads, "It is ordained and decreed that football and golf be utterly condemned and not practiced."

It seems that by 1457 the Scots were playing so much golf that the good monarch and the members of his Parliament were of the opinion that Scottish soldiers were neglecting their archery practice to play golf. The ban on golf was repeated in 1471 by the Parliament of King James III and again in 1491 by the Parliament of King James IV. It appears that the ban was largely ignored by the general population and it was lifted by James IV in 1502 when the Treaty of Glasgow temporarily ended hostilities between Scotland and its traditional enemy, England, and archery practice became less important to the national defense. James IV, a Stuart whose great-grandson would later become King James I of England, celebrated the lifting of the ban by purchasing a set of golf clubs. To combat the high prices that Dutch manufacturers were charging for golf balls, James IV appointed an official ball maker and set a ceiling on the price of golf balls.

During the formative years of golf, the game was played extensively during the winter months because that was when the grass on the links playing fields was the shortest and easiest to play on. We find this surprising today because we think of golf as a warm-weather game. However, before the advent of mechanical grass cutters in the 1850s, it was often difficult to play golf during the warmer months because of the length and condition of the grass, which was kept in check primarily by rabbits and sheep. It is known that during the early years of golf, golf balls were painted red for winter play and white for warm-weather play.

From the Dutch game of *het kolven* the Scots acquired the small leather-covered ball, the concept of multiple players each hitting a ball with a club from a starting point to a series of targets in successive strokes, and a scoring system whereby the player doing so in the fewest strokes prevailed. To this game the Scots added the concepts of using holes in the ground as targets, playing with lofted clubs, and using multiple clubs. They also devised a unique playing field for the game and adopted rules that are unique to the game. It is clear that the game of golf, as we know it, was born on the links in Scotland during the 15th and 16th centuries.

It should be understood, however, that the Scots did not invent the game of golf overnight. It took the efforts of countless generations of unknown Scotsmen to develop the game into one that resembles the game we play today. Most of the changes to the imported game were made incrementally over time by persons whom history has neither recorded nor recognized.

The changes made by the Scots to the imported game changed the very nature of the sport and produced a game that was infinitely more complex and challenging than the simple stick-and-ball game from which it originated. It is ironic that the Dutch game, as played in the Netherlands, has morphed into an indoor game that today is played only in a few cities in the Netherlands, while the Scottish game has spread around the world and become one of the most popular and widely played games of our time.

• 2 •

The Evolution of Golf during the 17th and 18th Centuries

*S*ituated on St. Andrews Bay on the east coast of Scotland between the Firth of Forth on the south and the Firth of Tay on the north is the town of St. Andrews. In the 15th century, St. Andrews was the center of Scottish Catholicism. It was said that the bones of the apostle Andrew were entombed in the St. Andrews Cathedral and pilgrims came from all over Europe to pay homage. In 1410, St. Andrews University, the third-oldest university in the English-speaking world, was established in the town by Pope Benedict XIII.

St. Andrews was also an early hotbed of golf. There are records indicating that an early form of golf was played on the links at St. Andrews as early as 1450. It is apparent that golf had become a popular pastime in St. Andrews by the middle of the 16th century because in 1553 the archbishop of St. Andrews recorded an edict inviting his parishioners to use the links at St. Andrews "for golff, futeball, schuteing and all other manners of pastime."

When Scotland became a Protestant country in 1560, the importance of St. Andrews declined and its population dropped from about 14,000 in 1560 to fewer than 2,000 a hundred years later. It would be golf, along with its historic university, that would put St. Andrews back on the map.

From the beginning, the hairy had its shortcomings as the ball for the Scottish game. The firmness and overall quality of the balls varied considerably; even the good ones were not very hard and did not putt well. The hairy also did not fare well in water, where it quickly became waterlogged and ruined. Most importantly, perhaps, when hit it didn't go far enough. Like all golfers, then and now, the Scots wanted a golf ball that they could hit farther than the one they were playing with. However, they would have to wait 200 years before a better golf ball became available: a ball they called the "feathery."

The old course at St. Andrews. Old, flat, and of uncertain origin, but one of the great golf courses of the world.
© iStock / JByard

It is not known who invented the feathery or who first hit a feathery with a golf club, but both events occurred early in the 17th century. Some reports say the feathery was invented in 1618. Once introduced, the feathery caught on quickly and became the ball of choice of well-to-do golfers everywhere for the next 250 years. Made of a leather casing stuffed with feathers, the feathery had several advantages over the hairy. Because it was harder than the hairy, it could be hit farther and it putted better. It also flew straighter than the hairy and was easier to control in the air. The feathery was slightly larger than today's golf ball, but at three-quarters of an ounce, it was about half the weight of today's ball.

The feathery's biggest shortcoming was its cost. The cost of a top-quality feathery was about five shillings, which is the modern-day equivalent of about twenty dollars, while a hairy cost a shilling or less. The feathery was too expensive for ordinary Scotsmen, and many of them continued using the hairy well into the 17th century.

The feathery was expensive because of the amount of time and skill it took to make one. To make a feathery, a craftsman first had to cut three precisely measured pieces of tough leather. Using a fine, waxed thread, he then stitched the pieces together in such a manner as to form an empty round casing. Using an awl, he stuffed boiled breast feathers from a goose or chicken into the empty casing through a small hole in the leather. When no more feathers could be forced into the casing, he closed the hole with a couple of stitches and painted the ball with several coats of lead paint. The final procedure was to soak the ball in alum, which caused the leather to shrink and harden. The feathers expanded as they dried and the leather casing shrank as it dried, the combination of which produced a ball that, when new, was nearly as hard as today's ball. Making a feathery was a time-consuming and tedious undertaking, and a typical craftsman could make only four or five balls a day.

The feathery had detriments other than its expense. Because it was difficult to make a feathery that was perfectly round, many were not—and those did not fly or putt well. Like the hairy, the feathery did not fare well in water and became waterlogged if not quickly removed from the water and dried. Because it was harder than the hairy, the feathery was more susceptible to being cut if not hit properly, especially with an iron club. If the cut was wide and deep enough, some of the feathers would emerge through the cut and the ball would be ruined.

During the 17th and 18th centuries, a typical golfer carried about a half-dozen golf clubs. The clubs were carried by the golfer or his caddie in his hands, as golf bags were yet to be invented. Most golf clubs had heads made of wood. The only iron club used extensively during this period was a rut iron, which had a small iron head shaped like a doctor's probe and was used for hitting balls out of wheel ruts and other narrow crevices that could not be reached with a wooden club. After the arrival of the feathery in the 17th century, iron clubs became unpopular because of the damage they inflicted on the expensive ball if it was not struck properly.

The woods used by a typical golfer during this period included a slightly lofted play club (or driver) used for hitting balls off of tees, a couple of lofted spoons for fairway shots, a baffing spoon for pitch shots, and a putting club for rolling the ball the final few feet to the hole. The heads of the clubs were typically made of thorn wood and were attached to the shaft by a long splice that was glued, coated with pitch, and held firm with tightly wound fishermen's twine. The grips were made of strips of sheepskin or calfskin glued to the shaft. The shafts were made of ash. Hickory did not grow in Europe and hickory shafts were not used until the 19th century. The first shipment of hickory from the United States to Britain arrived in 1826. The best clubs were made by bow makers, but cabinet makers, shipwrights, and just about anyone skilled in woodworking could produce a set of clubs.

Even though the Parliaments of three Scottish kings had banned the playing of the game, once the ban was lifted golf quickly became a favorite pastime of

Scottish royalty, who were of the Stuart clan. When King James IV lifted the ban in 1502, he promptly purchased a set of golf clubs from a bow maker in Perth and took up the game in earnest. In 1567, his daughter, Mary, Queen of Scots, was reportedly seen playing golf with the Earl of Bothwell a few days after the murder of her husband, an indiscretion and lack of concern that later contributed to her imprisonment and demise. When Mary played golf, she was assisted by cadets who carried her clubs. It is believed that the term *caddie* originated from this arrangement.

In 1603, Mary's son, James, as King James I of England, took his golf clubs to London and five years later arranged the building of the first golf course outside of Scotland—a five-hole layout at Blackheath, near London. Legend has it that in 1641, Mary's grandson, King Charles I of England, was playing golf at Leith Links in Edinburgh when he was informed of the Irish rebellion. It is said that he finished his round before taking up the matter of the rebellion.

Forty years later, in 1681, Mary's great-grandson, the future King James II of England, while he was still the Duke of York, engaged two English noblemen in a high-stakes money match at Blackheath. As his playing partner, he chose John Patersone, a shoemaker from Edinburgh who played a lot of golf. James and Patersone won the match handily and when they split up their winnings, Patersone pocketed enough to build a house in Edinburgh upon which he mounted a plaque bearing the words "Far and Sure."

During its formative years, there were no written rules governing the game of golf and for three centuries it was essentially a local game. Each community and golfing group had its own thoughts on how the game should be played and followed its own unwritten rules on most aspects of the game. Penalties, for example, varied significantly from course to course, both as to the infractions for which penalties could be imposed and the type and severity of the penalties. The sizes of the putting holes varied significantly from course to course, as did the number of holes on a course. The course at Leith Links, for example, had five holes, while the Old Course at St. Andrews, 30 miles away, had 22 holes.

Organization and standardization in the game of golf began with the formation of membership golf clubs in the 18th century. The first membership golf club was the Burgess Golfing Society of Edinburgh, which was founded in 1738 by a group of Edinburgh golfers who played at Bruntsfield Links in Edinburgh, near the Edinburgh Castle. A few years later, another group of Edinburgh golfers who played at nearby Leith Links founded a golf club called the Gentlemen Golfers of Leith. In 1744, the Gentlemen Golfers of Leith sponsored a golf tournament at Leith Links, open to all golfers, for the purpose of determining the champion golfer of the land. The winner of the tournament would be called the "Captain of Golf." In March of that year, several members of the Gentlemen Golfers of Leith, representing themselves as being "skillful in the ancient and healthful exercise of golf," petitioned the Edinburgh Town Council to purchase a silver cup to be awarded to the winner of their tournament.

Hoping to attract golfers from all over Scotland to their tournament and aware that golfers from other courses would not be familiar with the rules governing play at Leith Links, the Gentlemen Golfers of Leith prepared a written set of rules governing play at their tournament. In the spring of 1744, the Gentlemen Golfers of Leith drew up a set of 13 rules that would govern play in their tournament at Leith Links.

As translated from the archaic English used by the Scots at the time, the rules drawn up by the Gentlemen Golfers of Leith provided as follows:

Articles and Laws in Playing at Golf

1. You must tee your ball within a club's length of the hole.
2. Your tee must be upon the ground.
3. You are not to change the ball which you strike off the tee.
4. You are not to remove stones, bones, or any break club for the sake of playing your ball, except upon the fair green, and that only within a club's length of your ball.
5. If your ball comes among water or any watery filth, you are at liberty to take out your ball and bringing it behind the hazard and teeing it; you may play it with any club and allow your adversary a stroke for so getting out your ball.
6. If the balls be found anywhere touching one another, you are to lift the first ball until you play the last.
7. At holing you are to play your ball honestly for the hole, and not to play upon your adversary's ball not lying in your way to the hole.
8. If you should lose your ball by its being taken up or any other way, you are to go back to the spot where you struck last and drop another ball and allow your adversary a stroke for the misfortune.
9. No man at holing his ball is to be allowed to mark his way to the hole with his club or anything else.
10. If a ball is stopped by any person, horse, dog, or anything else, the ball so stopped must be played where it lies.
11. If you draw your club in order to strike and proceed so far with your stroke as to be bringing down your club, if then your club should break in any way, it is to be accounted a stroke.
12. He whose ball lies farthest from the hole is obliged to play first.

13. Neither trench, ditch, nor dyke made for the preservation of the links, nor the Scholars' Holes, nor the Soldiers' Lines shall be accounted a hazard, but the ball is to be taken out, teed, and played with any iron club.

A brief discussion of each of the Gentlemen Golfers' 13 articles follows.

Article 1. *You must tee your ball within a club's length of the hole.* Accustomed as we are to manicured greens and spacious tee boxes, it is hard to comprehend teeing off within a club-length of the hole. It must be understood, however, that in 1744 the type, quality, and condition of the grass in the areas around the holes (the putting areas) differed little from the rest of the course. The grass in the putting areas around the holes was cut and maintained in the same manner and by the same means as the grass on other parts of the course—usually by sheep that were let onto the course at night. It would be another 110 years before mechanical grass cutters were invented.

Article 2. *Your tee must be upon the ground.* This article has puzzled many a golf historian. Bearing in mind that in those days a "tee" consisted of a small pile of wet sand placed under the ball, the rule was probably meant to prohibit a player from placing anything between the sand and the ground.

Article 3. *You are not to change the ball which you strike off the tee.* The featheries and hairies used as golf balls in those days were very susceptible to being cut, split open, waterlogged, or otherwise damaged. It was apparently thought that damage to a ball was usually caused by the misplay of the person hitting it and that to allow such a player to replace a damaged ball would be unfair to an adversary who had not misplayed and damaged his ball.

Article 4. *You are not to remove stones, bones, or any break club for the sake of playing your ball, except upon the fair green, and that only within a club's length of your ball.* This article deals with what we now refer to as loose impediments, like leaves and twigs. The "stones, bones, and break clubs" referred to in the article give us an idea of the primitive conditions endured by golfers at that time.

Article 5. *If your ball comes among water or any watery filth, you are at liberty to take out your ball and bringing it behind the hazard and teeing it, you may play it with any club and allow your adversary a stroke for so getting out your ball.* Because this article doesn't distinguish between water hazards and casual water, it apparently applied to both and a penalty was assessed for lifting a ball out of casual water as well as out of a water hazard. The term *watery filth* refers to soggy or sloppy ground that golfers today get relief from without penalty. Relief without penalty was hard to come by during the early days of golf, and a golfer unfortunate enough to hit his ball into casual water or wet grounds was assessed a penalty if he chose to move his ball to playable ground.

Article 6. *If the balls be found anywhere touching one another, you are to lift the first ball until you play the last.* While in today's game two balls rarely come to rest touching one another, the featheries and hairies used in those days behaved differently, especially if the balls were wet and two of them happened to be in the same small depression or rut. In 1775, the Gentlemen Golfers of Leith amended this article to read, "If your balls be found anywhere touching or within six inches of one another, you are to lift the first ball until the other is played." Because the "first ball" is the ball closest to the hole, this amendment gave birth to the stymie. If the first ball was more than six inches from the other ball, it did not have to be lifted; if it blocked the path of the other player's ball to the hole, the other player was stymied.

Article 7. *At holing you are to play your ball honestly for the hole, and not to play upon your adversary's ball not lying in your way to the hole.* This article makes it clear that a player must play his ball to the hole and may not play an adversary's ball. This article was necessary because apparently on some courses at that time a player was allowed to play on his adversary's ball and hit it with his ball without penalty. This is an example of the differences in the rules of play in effect at that time on various golf courses throughout Scotland.

Article 8. *If you should lose your ball by its being taken up or any other way, you are to go back to the spot where you struck last and drop another ball and allow your adversary a stroke for the misfortune.* This article imposes a stroke and distance penalty on a player whose ball is either lost or picked up by another person. It should be remembered that the links were public areas and persons other than golfers were often present and occasionally picked up a golfer's ball. This is a broader penalty than under today's rules, which permit a player to replace without penalty a ball that has been "taken up."

Article 9. *No man at holing his ball is to be allowed to mark his way to the hole with his club or anything else.* This article prohibits a player from making a line or track of any kind in the grass or dirt from where the ball lies to the hole, a practice that was apparently allowed on some courses at that time. The rule makes us aware of the primitive conditions of the putting areas in those days.

Article 10. *If a ball is stopped by any person, horse, dog, or anything else, the ball so stopped must be played where it lies.* The wording of this article again makes us aware of the obstacles that golfers had to put up with at that time. It should again be remembered that the links were public lands where people could engage in all sorts of activities, many of which interfered with the playing of golf. This article basically provides that interference by outside entities is a rub of the green and a player must bear the risk of it.

Article 11. *If you draw your club in order to strike and proceed so far with your stroke as to be bringing down your club, if then your club should break in any way, it is to be accounted a stroke.* This article deals with the tendency of ash shafts to break—remember, hickory shafts did not exist at that time. Under this rule, if the shaft of a club broke during a player's backswing, it was not counted as a stroke—but if it broke during the downswing, it was counted as a stroke, whether or not the ball was struck.

Article 12. *He whose ball lies farthest from the hole is obliged to play first.* This article establishes the order of play. The rule that the ball farthest from the hole shall be played first has remained unchanged throughout the years.

Article 13. *Neither trench, ditch, nor dyke made for the preservation of the links, nor the Scholars' Holes, nor the Soldiers' Lines shall be accounted a hazard, but the ball is to be taken out, teed, and played with any iron club.* This article is believed to be the first written local rule in the history of golf. It deals with obstacles and conditions unique to Leith Links.

In 1984, the City of Edinburgh erected a monument in the city park that now encompasses the original Leith Links. The inscription on the monument reads:

Leith Links—The Home of Golf

Historical Home of the Honourable Company of Edinburgh Golfers.
    The game was played over a five-hole course, each hole being over 400 yards long. In 1744 the first official rules were drawn up for a tournament on Leith Links and these rules, 13 in all, formed the basis for the modern game of golf.

The tournament sponsored by the Gentlemen Golfers of Leith, who later changed the name of their club to the Honourable Company of Edinburgh Golfers, turned out to be a disappointment. Only twelve golfers, all local, signed up for the tournament and only ten played in the event, which was played in match play—the only form of play known for the first three hundred years of golf. The winner of the tournament, and the first Captain of Golf, was John Rattray, an Edinburgh surgeon.

Unfortunately, Dr. Rattray's fortunes took a turn for the worse after the tournament. The British Civil War broke out in 1744 when the Hanovers, who were English, tried to unseat the Stuarts, who were of Scottish ancestry, from the English throne (King James II and his golfing lineage were Stuarts). In 1745, Dr. Rattray was impressed into service as a medical officer by the Stuarts' army during its occupation of Edinburgh. A year later he was captured and imprisoned by the Hanoverian army when it defeated the Stuarts' army in the Battle of Culloden Moor. He was awaiting a possible death sentence in an English prison when his release was arranged by Duncan Forbes, a fellow Gentlemen Golfer who happened to be the lord president of the Court of General Sessions. Dr. Rattray celebrated his release by winning the Silver Cup at Leith Links again in 1751.

Even though their 1744 tournament didn't turn out to be much of an event, the actions of the Gentlemen Golfers of Leith were noteworthy for two reasons: First, their tournament was the first tournament ever held that was open to all golfers and played under a set of written rules. Second, the rules they drew up were the first written rules governing the game of golf.

Following the lead of the Burgess Golfing Society of Edinburgh and the Gentlemen Golfers of Leith, during the last half of the 18th-century golfers throughout Scotland began forming membership clubs and adopting written rules governing play on the golf courses they played on. The most notable of the new clubs was founded in May 1754 when a group of 22 "noblemen and gentlemen" who played on the links at St. Andrews formed a membership golf club and named it "the Society of St. Andrews Golfers." Wishing to hold a tournament of their own and award their own silver cup, the Society of St. Andrews Golfers adopted a set of 13 written rules that were very similar to, and obviously patterned after, the 13 articles that had been drawn up by the Gentlemen Golfers of Leith in 1744. The St. Andrews tournament, which was also open to all golfers, turned out to be a bit of a bust as only four golfers showed up. The winner was Bailie William Landale, a local merchant.

As the names suggest, membership golf clubs were typically established by noblemen, the gentry, and well-to-do merchants and professionals. This did not mean, however, that the sport at that time was limited to golfers of that sort. The courses used by the early membership golf clubs were built on the links, which were public lands open to all Scots and were not subject to private ownership. Because the membership golf clubs did not own the golf courses on which their members played, they could not prevent other golfers from playing on the courses that they built and maintained. Therefore, any golfer who could afford the expense of golf balls and clubs could play on the same links courses that the club members played on. An unknown, but probably substantial, number of ordinary Scotsmen (like John Patersone, for example) played golf on the links courses that were built and maintained by the membership golf clubs. In hindsight, such an arrangement seems only fair because it was the ordinary Scots who, prior to the advent of membership golf clubs, had spent three centuries inventing and developing the game on the links.

During the last half of the 18th century, about a dozen membership clubs were founded in Scotland. In 1776, the first membership golf club outside of Scotland was established at Blackheath in England, and in 1818 a membership club was founded at Old Manchester in northern England. Most clubs adopted written rules of play that were similar to the rules adopted by the Gentlemen Golfers of Leith and the Society of St. Andrews Golfers, and the game took its first steps toward standardization. However, the rules adopted by the various clubs were not comprehensive and there was much they did not cover. For example, the size of the putting hole was not covered by the rules and hole sizes continued to vary significantly from course to course. The number of holes on a golf course also was not covered by the rules and continued to vary greatly from course to course, as did penalties for lost balls and balls hit into hazards or out of bounds.

The tournament held by the Society of St. Andrews Golfers became more popular in subsequent years. As the number of competitors grew, it became apparent that holding large tournaments in match play was not workable because of the number of rounds and the amount of time it took to determine a winner. A large tournament could take a week to complete in match play.

On May 9, 1759, the Society of St. Andrews Golfers addressed the problem and adopted the following resolution:

> In order to remove all disputes and inconveniences with regard to the gaining of the Silver Cup, it is enacted and agreed by the captain and the gentlemen golfers present, that in all time coming whoever puts in the ball at the fewest strokes over the field, being 22 holes, shall be the declared and sustained victor.

With this resolution, stroke play was born. Because golf had evolved as a match-play game, for the next century or so most tournaments and competitions continued to be held in match play. In time, however, as golf became more popular and golf tournaments attracted more and more players, stroke play replaced match play as the preferred method of scoring in most tournaments of any size. Even in match-play tournaments, a couple of rounds of stroke play were often held to determine the qualifiers for the match-play portion of the event.

Prior to 1764, the Old Course at St. Andrews was composed of twelve fairways, ten of which were played twice, for a total of 22 holes. There were twelve putting greens for the 22 holes, ten of which contained two putting holes and were played to twice. The putting greens for the 11th and 22nd holes were played to but once and contained one hole apiece. The ten other putting greens contained two holes, one of which was played to on the way out of town and the other on the way back into town. The teeing ground for the first hole was next to the putting green for the 22nd hole.

In 1764, the town of St. Andrews took the land that included two of the putting greens on the Old Course. The elimination of the two putting greens reduced the number of putting greens on the course from twelve to ten. At about the same time, the Society of St. Andrews Golfers combined the first four short holes into two longer holes. The combined effect of the two revisions was to reduce the number of holes on the course from 22 to 18, although there were still only ten fairways and ten putting greens, eight of which were played twice. After the revisions, nine holes of golf were played on the way out of town and nine were played on the way back into town, for a total of 18 holes in a full round of golf.

During the 19th century, St. Andrews became the dominant club in British golf. As such, it became the rule-making authority for British golf, and 18 holes eventually became the standard for the number of holes in a full round of golf. Standardization didn't happen overnight, however, because in 1890 it was reported that there were still fewer than twenty golf courses in the world with an 18-hole layout.

The advent of membership golf clubs also led to improvements in the playing fields of golf. The most notable improvements were in the putting areas, which on many courses were trimmed and kept free of impediments. In addition, the one-club-length-from-the-hole requirement for teeing off on the next hole was either lengthened or eliminated by most clubs. For example, in 1773 the Society of Golfers at Bruntsfield Links adopted a rule preventing a golfer from making a tee within 10 yards of a hole. As the 18th century drew to a close, the game of golf and the fields upon which it was played were beginning to resemble the game and courses we play today.

· 3 ·

The Proliferation of
Golf during the 19th Century

*D*uring the 19th century, golf spread beyond its Scottish homeland, going first to England and then to the United States and the rest of the world. The 19th century would also see phenomenal increases in the numbers of golfers and membership golf clubs, as well as continued improvement in the rules, equipment, and playing fields of the game as it evolved into what is essentially the game we play today.

In 1800, there were six membership golf clubs in the world, all but one of which were in Scotland. The membership clubs in Scotland were the Burgess Golfing Society of Edinburgh, whose members played at Bruntsfield Links; the Honourable Company of Edinburgh Golfers (formerly the Gentlemen Golfers of Leith), whose members played at Leith Links; the Society of St. Andrews Golfers, whose members played on the Old Course at St. Andrews; the Society of Golfers at Aberdeen, whose members played at Aberdeen Links; the Crail Golfing Society, whose members played at Crail Links; and the Glasgow Golf Club, whose members played at Glasgow Green. The only membership golf club outside of Scotland was the Blackheath Golf Club in England.

Golf was being played on other links courses in Scotland as well, but membership golf clubs had not been established there. The links at Dornock, for example, did not host a membership golf club at the beginning of the 19th century, even though golf had been played there since 1621. Similar situations existed on the links at Perth, Burntisland, Musselburgh, Montrose, and Penmure.

Fueled by the Industrial Revolution that started in England in the 1760s, the number of membership golf clubs in both Scotland and England grew steadily during the early 1800s; by 1834 there were 14 membership golf

The birthplaces of golf. This map of Scotland shows the locations of the early Scottish golf courses.

clubs in Scotland, two in England, and one in India, established by British colonists.

During the early 1800s, the most influential golf clubs in Scotland in terms of prestige and rule-making were the Honourable Company of Edinburgh Golfers and the Society of St. Andrews Golfers. Around 1830, however, the Honourable Company of Edinburgh Golfers encountered financial difficulties and went out of existence for several years. When it resolved its financial problems and reestablished itself in 1836, it moved its golfing location from Leith Links to Musselburgh, citing overcrowding at Leith Links as the reason.

While the Honourable Company of Edinburgh Golfers floundered, the Society of St. Andrews Golfers continued to prosper and grow in prestige. In 1834, King William IV of England bestowed royal patronage on the Society of St. Andrews Golfers by decreeing it a "Royal and Ancient Golf Club." From that time on, the Society of St. Andrews Golfers became known as the Royal and Ancient Golf Club of St. Andrews (the R&A).

The R&A was not the first golf club to receive royal patronage—that honor, unaccountably, was bestowed upon the Perth Golfing Society in 1833, even though it had been in existence for only nine years. Although royal patronage was bestowed upon the Perth Golfing Society, it was not accorded royal and ancient patronage, which meant that while it could thereafter call itself the Royal Perth Golfing Society, it could not refer to itself as a royal and ancient club. Royal patronage has since been bestowed upon some sixty-four golf clubs around the world, but only the R&A has been accorded royal and ancient status.

The bestowing of royal and ancient patronage upon the R&A in 1834, coupled with the temporary disappearance of the Honourable Company of Edinburgh Golfers, established the R&A as the most influential golf club in Great Britain. From that time on, the rules and practices adopted by the R&A would be adopted by golf clubs throughout Great Britain and most of the world. A principal source of the prestige of the R&A was the status and personal influence of its members, many of whom were members of other golf clubs as well and wished to have the same rules in effect wherever they played.

King James I had introduced golf to the English in 1603 and had established a five-hole course at Blackheath in 1608. However, for more than 200 years the English did not take to the game. The sporadic wars between England and Scotland during the 17th century probably had a lot to do with the lack of enthusiasm by the English for the Scottish game. Even after the unification of the two countries (into Great Britain) in 1707, the English did not take to the game. Conceivably, after warring with the Scots for 500 years, the distaste of the English for anything Scottish did not disappear simply because the two countries had been unified by an act of Parliament. During the early 1800s, however, the English started playing golf and several membership golf clubs were founded in England.

While golf grew in popularity in both Scotland and England during the first half of the 19th century, most of those taking up the game were from the upper classes. Most commoners could not afford the expense of the game and few took it up. In 1848, however, an event occurred that would enable ordinary people to take up the game as never before. That event was the invention of the gutta-percha golf ball.

Robert Adams Paterson of Scotland is credited with inventing the gutta-percha golf ball in 1848. Molded out of gutta-percha (the milky, rubberlike sap of the Malaysian sapodilla tree), the gutta-percha golf ball was the first new golf ball since the invention of the feathery in 1618. The "gutty," as the new ball was called, was superior to the feathery in several respects. Most importantly, the gutty was easier to manufacture than the feathery and it cost but a shilling. It was also tougher and more durable than the feathery and, unlike the feathery, it was not damaged by water. In addition, when it was chipped, cracked, or otherwise damaged, the gutty could be heated and reshaped to look and play like a new ball. The distance golfers got from a gutty was comparable to that of a good feathery and, because it held its shape better, the gutty was easier to putt than the feathery.

However, the gutty was not without its shortcomings. The rock-like hardness of the gutty gave the golfer who mishit one, especially with an iron club on a cold day, a discomforting sting in his hands and arms. The gutty would also occasionally split into fragments, especially in cold weather. This happened often enough to prompt the R&A to adopt a rule in 1851 providing that "if a ball should split into two or more pieces a fresh ball shall be put down at the spot of the largest fragment." Generally, however, the gutty was a big improvement over the feathery, and by 1860 it had replaced the feathery as the ball of choice of most golfers. It would retain that status until the invention of the rubber-wound golf ball in the early 1900s.

The original gutties had a smooth surface and poor aerodynamic qualities. However, golfers soon discovered that gutties flew better after they had been nicked up a little. By the 1850s ball makers were using tools to create grooves on the gutties' smooth surface. By 1860, gutties were being made with molds that gave them a textured surface and their aerodynamic qualities improved even more. The patterns imprinted on the surfaces of gutties were known as "brambles" because of their resemblance to the surface of a brambleberry.

The advent of the gutty brought about changes in the clubs that golfers used. The hard thorn-wood heads of the drivers and spoons used to play the feathery tended to crack or split when used to hit the rock-hard gutty. Conversely, the iron clubs that had been so damaging to the feathery did little damage to the tough gutty. Consequently, a demand for iron clubs sprang up in the 1850s and metalworkers (cleek makers, they were called) joined bow makers as the primary makers of golf clubs.

The type of wood used in golf clubs also changed with the arrival of the gutty. The hard thorn-wood club heads that had been used to play the feathery were replaced with heads made of beech, a softer wood that better absorbed the shock of hitting the hard gutty. The wood used in the shafts of golf clubs changed at about the same time, with Tennessee hickory, imported from the United States, replacing ash in the shafts of golf clubs. It took a few years for hickory shafts to catch on, but by the middle of the 19th century they had become the shafts of choice of golfers everywhere. Serious golfers were particular about their hickory shafts, with most preferring shafts made with hickory from halfway up the mountain, as opposed to either swamp hickory or mountaintop hickory.

The clubs used by a typical golfer during the last half of the 19th century included two or three woods, three or four irons, and a putter. The woods included a driver for hitting off tees and a spoon and sometimes a brassie for fairway shots. The irons included a rut iron for hitting out of ruts and crevices, a cleek for long fairway shots, a mashie for medium-length fairway shots, and a couple of niblicks of varying degrees of loft for pitch shots. A cleek was the equivalent of a modern-day three iron, a mashie was the rough equivalent of a modern-day five iron, and a niblick was the equivalent of a modern-day nine iron or pitching wedge.

The first great figure in the long history of golf whose name we are aware of is Old Tom Morris. He was called Old Tom Morris by the Scots to distinguish him from his son of the same name, whom they called Young Tom Morris. The son of a hand-loom weaver, Old Tom Morris was born in St. Andrews in 1821. When he was 14 and had attended school long enough to learn how to read and write and add simple sums, he was apprenticed to Allan Robertson, the resident professional and keeper of the green at St. Andrews. Most of Robertson's income came from the sale of featheries, which he made in his kitchen and sold at his golf shop in St. Andrews.

Robertson was known throughout Scotland as the champion golfer of the land because of his many tournament victories. He loved to gamble at golf and supplemented his income with winnings from golf matches with R&A members and anyone else willing to take him on for a few shillings a hole.

Old Tom Morris spent most of his teenage years caddying for R&A members and making featheries in Allan Robertson's kitchen. However, he managed to play enough golf to improve his game to the point where, late in his apprenticeship, he defeated Robertson in a tournament sponsored by the R&A. The defeat did not sit well with the temperamental Robertson and he accused his apprentice of cheating.

Because it threatened his livelihood as a feathery maker, Robertson hated the gutta-percha golf ball. He made his apprentices promise never to use a gutty and paid local boys to find gutties, which he would burn in his stove. In 1851, Robertson caught Old Tom using a gutty in a match at St. Andrews and fired him on the spot.

Old Tom's prospects did not look good after being fired by Robertson—he was thirty years old with a pregnant wife and no source of income. Fortunately, Colonel James Fairlie, an R&A member, liked Old Tom and found him a job as the keeper of the green at a new golf course that was being developed by the Earl of Eglinton in Prestwick, on the Firth of Clyde, ninety miles west of St. Andrews on the west coast of Scotland.

Old Tom's first assignment at Prestwick was to design, lay out, and build the Prestwick golf course. Lord Eglinton, it seems, had purchased fifty acres of dunes, brush, and wild grasses in Prestwick and wanted to put a golf course on it. Old Tom, whose only experience in golf-course design had come when he assisted Allan Robertson in laying out a few holes at Carnoustie several years earlier, began laying out and building Lord Eglinton's golf course at Prestwick in the spring of 1851.

Lord Eglinton wanted an 18-hole course built on the Prestwick property, but Old Tom quickly determined that the parcel was too small to support a course of that length. Only by using cross-routing, where a single fairway is used for more than one hole, was he able to squeeze 12 holes onto the parcel. He ultimately designed, laid out, and built a 3,800-yard, 12-hole, classic links golf course on the Prestwick property. Lord Eglinton's golf club at Prestwick adopted the St. Andrews rules of play and opened its course for play in the autumn of 1851. Thirty years later, in 1882, the Prestwick Golf Club acquired more land and Old Tom, who had left Prestwick by then, returned and redesigned the course, expanding it to 18 holes and eliminating the cross-routing.

During his lifetime, Allan Robertson was recognized by everyone as the champion golfer of Scotland. He was the first golfer to break 80 in a tournament on the Old Course at St. Andrews when he shot a 79 in a tournament in 1858. When he died of jaundice in 1859, it wasn't clear who should be recognized as the champion golfer of the land. Hoping to establish the Prestwick Golf Club as a club of importance in Scottish golf, the Earl of Eglinton sponsored a tournament at Prestwick in 1860, open to all professional golfers, for the purpose of determining the champion of golf in Scotland.

To attract professional golfers to his tournament, Lord Eglinton offered a challenge belt made of silver and red Moroccan leather that he claimed was worth twenty-four pounds. The winner would get to keep the belt for a year and anyone winning the championship three years in a row could retain the belt permanently. So that their crude attire wouldn't offend the ladies at his club, Eglinton gave hunting coats to the eight professional golfers who entered the event.

Old Tom Morris and seven other professional golfers showed up for Lord Eglinton's stroke-play event, which consisted of playing the 12-hole course at Prestwick three times in a single day. The winner was Willie Park of Musselburgh, who edged Old Tom by two strokes, shooting a 174 in the 36-hole event.

Noting the high scores posted by the professional golfers in the 1860 tournament, several amateur golfers asked to be included in the next event. To accommodate the amateurs, when the second tournament was held in 1861 it was declared to be "open to all the world." This time twelve golfers entered the event and Old Tom won what the Prestwick Golf Club called "the Open Championship." He shot a 163 in the 36-hole event. Old Tom won the Open Championship again in 1862 and 1864, and in 1867 he won the event for the last time at age 46, a feat that makes him to this day the

Professional golfers at a golf tournament at Leith Links in Edinburgh, Scotland in 1867.
Library of Congress

oldest player ever to win the Open Championship. In the United States, the Open Championship is usually referred to as the British Open.

In 1868, Young Tom Morris, 17 years old and strong enough to snap a hickory shaft with a waggle of his club, won his first Open Championship. Still the youngest player ever to win the Open Championship, he shot a 154 in the 36-hole event and broke the tournament record by eight strokes. He finished three strokes ahead of Old Tom Morris, the runner-up. Young Tom won the Open Championship again in 1869, this time shooting a 157 and winning the event by eleven strokes. In 1870, Young Tom won the Open Championship for the third straight year, shooting a 149 and winning the event by 12 strokes. His 149 was 13 strokes lower than the score posted by any previous winner of the event other than himself.

His three consecutive Open Championships entitled Young Tom to permanent possession of Lord Eglinton's challenge belt. When Young Tom elected to retain the belt permanently, Lord Eglinton canceled the tournament in 1871 because he couldn't afford to purchase another belt. Additional sponsors were found and the Open Championship was resumed at Prestwick in 1872. When Young Tom won the event again in 1872 (giving him four consecutive Open Championships), he was given a silver claret jug, the trophy that is still awarded to the winner of the British Open.

Beginning in 1872, the R&A and the Honorable Company of Edinburgh Golfers were added as sponsors of the Open Championship, and for the next 20 years the event was rotated among the courses at St. Andrews, Musselburgh, and Prestwick. The Open Championship continued to be a 36-hole event despite the differing number of holes on each of the three courses on which the tournament was played. When the tournament was played at St. Andrews, which had 18 holes, two rounds were played; when it was played at Musselburgh, which had 9 holes, four rounds were played; and when it was played on the 12-hole Prestwick course, three rounds were played. The practice of rotating the Open Championship among the three courses continued until 1892, when it was changed to a 72-hole event and played at Muirfield Links.

Tragically, on September 2, 1875, Young Tom Morris's wife and newborn baby both died at childbirth. On Christmas Day of that same year, Young Tom was found dead in his bed, the victim of an aneurysm. The best golfer of his generation, and perhaps of any generation, died at age 24.

Old Tom outlived his son by 37 years. In 1865, he left Prestwick and returned to St. Andrews, where he was the keeper of the green and the resident professional of the R&A. An icon of the game, he lived above his famous golf shop near the 18th green on the Old Course for the rest of his life.

The game's first great golf course architect, Old Tom traveled the length and breadth of Scotland and south into England designing and laying out golf courses. During his lifetime he created or substantially improved some four dozen golf courses throughout the British Isles. Some were simple nine-hole courses, while others, like Muirfield, were masterpieces. At Muirfield, he introduced the concept of double-loop routing, so common today, where each nine starts and finishes at the clubhouse. At Prestwick, he improved the grass of the putting areas by periodically covering the grass with sand for a short period. In so doing, he developed the first authentic putting greens. In 1875, he created the first separate teeing areas by building a tee box for each hole on the Old Course at St. Andrews. Old Tom Morris, perhaps more than any other person, transformed golf courses from the unimproved fields of the early years of golf to the courses we have today with manicured greens, separate teeing areas, man-made hazards, and strategic playing options.

Since the earliest days of golf, the size of the hole had always been arbitrary, varying from three inches in diameter on some courses to five inches or more on others. In 1891, the R&A adopted a rule requiring the hole to be "4-1/4 inches in diameter and at least 4 inches deep." The 4-1/4-inch-diameter requirement is said to have been chosen because that was the diameter of the uniform hole cutter then being used at St. Andrews. The four-inch depth requirement was adopted because that was the length of the metal hole liner then being used at St. Andrews. The uniform hole cutter had been invented by a greenskeeper at Musselburgh Links in 1829 and the first metal hole liner had been used at Crail Links in 1874.

During the 1850s and 1860s, there was a tenfold expansion in the number of miles of rail line in the Scottish railroad system. In 1852, Queen Victoria purchased Balmoral Estates in Scotland, a happening that drew Scotland and Scottish golf to the attention of English golfers. The expanded rail lines made it easier for English golfers to travel north to Scotland and play the historic Scottish golf courses, and Scottish golfing holidays became a fad in England. Scottish golfing centers from Dornock and Aberdeen in the north to Troon and Prestwick in the south began catering to English golfers during this period. Many an Englishman caught the golf bug while on a Scottish golfing holiday. Hundreds of Englishmen, made affluent by the Industrial Revolution and given a taste of golf in Scotland, established golf clubs in England during the last half of the 19th century.

The invention of the mechanical grass cutter in the 1850s also did much to increase the popularity of golf during the last half of the 19th century. Prior to the arrival of mechanical grass cutters, the primary grass cutters were rabbits and sheep. During the early years of golf, the hardy Scots played a lot of golf during the winter months because that was when the grass was short and easier to play on. The longer grass during the summer months often made finding and hitting golf balls difficult and kept many golfers away from the course during those months. The invention of the mechanical grass cutter and the resulting improvement in the playability of the links courses during the warmer months did much to make golf the enjoyable warm-weather game we know today.

The 19th-century British golfing boom was brought about by a combination of the Industrial Revolution, the invention of the gutta-percha golf ball, the expansion of the Scottish railroad system, and the invention of the mechanical grass cutter. The Industrial Revolution created a class of people with wealth and leisure time, while the gutta-percha golf ball reduced the cost of playing the game. The expansion of the Scottish railroad system enabled the English to travel to Scotland, where they developed a fondness for golf, while mechanical grass cutters greatly improved the playability of golf courses during the warmer months.

The amount of golf played in England increased exponentially during the last half of the 19th century; by the end of the century, there were more golfers in England than there were in Scotland. The first British Amateur Championship was held at Royal Liverpool in 1885. The 30-year stranglehold of Scottish professional golfers on the Open Championship was broken in 1890 when John Ball, an English amateur, won the event at Prestwick. Two years later, Harold Hilton, another English amateur, won the Open Championship at Muirfield, and in 1894, in the first Open Championship held outside of Scotland, English professional J. H. Taylor won at Royal St. George's. In 1895, Taylor won the event again, this time on the Old Course at St. Andrews, and in 1897 Harold Hilton won the event at Royal Liverpool in England.

According to the British Golf Museum in St. Andrews, 62 new membership golf clubs were founded in Scotland between 1850 and 1880, eighty were founded in the 1880s, and 362 in the 1890s. A comparable growth occurred in England, where more than 500 membership golf clubs were founded during the last half of the 19th century. The Pau Golf Club, the first golf club on the continent of Europe, was founded in the South of France in 1856, and in 1875 the first two university golf clubs were founded at Cambridge and Oxford. In 1873 the first golf club in North America was founded in Montreal, Canada, and in the 1880s a number of golf clubs were founded in the United States. As the 19th century drew to a close, golf was well on its way to becoming an international sport.

Golf Comes to America

The First Clubs and Courses

In 1786, a club known as the South Carolina Golf Club was founded in Charleston, South Carolina. Despite its name, the club appears to have been a social club as there is no record of a golf course in the area at that time and there is nothing to indicate that any of the members actually played golf. In 1794, a club called the Savannah Golf Club was founded in Savannah, Georgia, but it, too, appears to have been a social club as there is no record of either a golf course or the playing of golf in the area at that time. There is no record of the existence of either club after the War of 1812. (The present Savannah Golf Club was founded in 1899 by persons who were apparently unaware of the existence of the earlier Savannah Golf Club.)

In the middle 1880s, the British golfing boom finally made it across the Atlantic, and a number of golf clubs and courses were established at about the same time. The Montreal Golf Club was established in 1873, when it opened a nine-hole course at Fletcher's Field on the outskirts of the city. The club changed golf courses several times before settling on its current 45-hole layout in L'Ile-Bizard. The club was granted royal patronage by Queen Victoria in 1884 and is now known as the Royal Montreal Golf Club. It was the first and is now the oldest golf club in North America.

After the disappearance of the South Carolina and Savannah golf clubs, there is no record of golf in the United States until 1881, when Andrew Bell, a young Scottish immigrant, built a four-hole golf course on his father's farm near Burlington, Iowa. The course has long since disappeared, but it must have sparked an interest in golf by the residents of Burlington because the Burlington Golf Club was founded in 1899 and now claims to be the oldest continuously operating golf club west of the Mississippi River.

The Edgewood Club of Tivoli in Tivoli, New York, about 60 miles north of New York City, opened a two-hole golf course in 1884 that was later expanded. The club still exists as a privately owned golf club whose course is open to the public. It claims to be the oldest golf club in the United States with continuous golf at the same location.

In 1886, a group of golfers from Troy, New York, who liked to spend their summers in Vermont, founded the Dorset Field Club in Dorset, Vermont. They built a nine-hole golf course that was later expanded to 18 holes. The Dorset Field Club still exists and claims to have the oldest continuously operating golf course in the United States.

In 1887, Alexander Findlay, a Scottish immigrant, brought his golf clubs to the Merchiston Ranch in rural Nance County, Nebraska, where he was employed as a ranch hand. Shortly after arriving, he laid out a rudimentary six-hole golf course on ranch property where he improved his golfing skills to the point where he was able to quit his job as a ranch hand and become a professional golfer. He later became a well-known professional golfer and golf course designer and was instrumental in establishing golf as a viable sport in his adopted country. He apparently failed to convince any of his fellow ranch hands to take up the game, however, because the golf course he built on the Merchiston Ranch reverted back to grazing land shortly after he left.

John Mickle Fox lived on his family's estate in Foxburg, a small town in western Pennsylvania about 50 miles north of Pittsburgh. In 1884, while in Britain for a cricket match, he visited St. Andrews and struck up a friendship with Old Tom Morris, who persuaded him to take up golf and sold him a set of golf clubs. Fox liked the game and brought his golf clubs with him when he returned to Foxburg, where he built an eight-hole golf course on land owned by his family. In 1887, he founded the Foxburg Golf Club, which later became the Foxburg Country Club. In 1888, the course was expanded to nine holes. The club still exists and its course is open to the public. The club claims to have the oldest continuously used golf course in the United States.

In 1887, the Quogue Field Club opened a 12-hole golf course in Quogue, New York, on Long Island. In 1938, the course was reduced to nine holes when a storm ruined three of its holes. The club still exists as a privately owned club with a nine-hole course. In 1888, the Kebo Valley Golf Club was founded in Bar Harbor, Maine, a favorite watering hole of well-to-do New Yorkers and Bostonians. The club opened a six-hole golf course in 1891 that was expanded to nine holes in 1896 and to 18 holes in 1920. The club still exists and claims to be the eighth-oldest golf club in the United States.

The most written-about early golf club was founded in 1888 in Yonkers, New York, a few miles north of New York City. In February of that year, John Reid, a Scottish immigrant, and four of his friends laid out a primitive three-hole golf course in a cow pasture in Yonkers and played a few holes of golf. A few months later, Reid and his friends founded a golf club that they named the St. Andrew's Golf Club, hoping the name would attract members. The "apostrophe s" in the name distinguishes it from the Scottish club. In 1892, the club built a six-hole layout in a nearby apple orchard. A year later it moved to a nine-hole layout at Grey Oaks, a few miles away. In 1897, it moved to an 18-hole layout at Mt. Hope in nearby Hastings-on-Hudson, New York, where it has since remained. The club still exists and claims to be the oldest continuously existing golf club in the United States.

The Tuxedo Club in Tuxedo Park, New York, a few miles west of New York City, was founded as a hunting and fishing club in 1886. In 1889, the club built a six-hole golf course for its members. Before they could play on their new course, however, the members had to send to Montreal for golf clubs. Golf became a popular sport at the club, and a nine-hole course was opened in 1892, followed by an 18-hole course a few years later. The Tuxedo Club still exists as a privately owned club with golf as its primary sport.

Russell Montague was a wealthy Boston lawyer with a vacation home in Oakhurst, West Virginia, near the resort town of White Sulphur Springs. In the summer of 1887, one of Montague's neighbors at Oakhurst was expecting a Scottish visitor who had sent word that he was bringing his golf clubs with him to Oakhurst. When the neighbor mentioned that he was in a quandary as to how to entertain his visitor, Montague, who had played a few rounds of golf when he was studying law in London, suggested that they build a golf course that they could all use after the visitor left. His neighbor liked the idea and a short time later he and Montague, assisted by a few other neighbors, laid out and built a nine-hole golf course on Montague's property and founded the Oakhurst Links Golf Club.

In 1888, the Oakhurst Links Golf Club sponsored a golf tournament called the Oakhurst Challenge. It also had a medal struck, called the Challenge Medal, that was awarded to the winner of the event. Both the tournament and the medal were the first of their kind in the United States. The tournament was held annually until the club ceased operations in 1912, after which the golf course fell into disuse and eventually became a pasture. In 2012, the Oakhurst property was purchased by the Greenbrier Sporting Club of White Sulphur Springs, West Virginia, and the original nine-hole golf course was restored and put back into use. Greenbrier now operates Oakhurst Links and claims it to be the oldest golf course in the United States.

In 1890, a few prominent men in upscale Southampton, New York, on Long Island, hired Willie Dunn, a professional golfer from Musselburgh, Scotland, to design and build a golf course on a tract of land they had purchased on Great Peconic Bay on Long Island Sound, near Southampton.

Using horse-drawn dirt scrapers and 150 Native Americans from the nearby Shinnecock Reservation as laborers, Dunn designed and built a 12-hole seaside links golf course that opened for play in 1891. The organizers also hired architect Stanford White to design and build a clubhouse. In 1891, the organizers founded the Shinnecock Hills Golf Club. In 1893, a nine-hole women's course was added to the complex.

When the golf course and clubhouse were completed, many Long Islanders and other New Yorkers were enthralled by the club and wished to join. However, the organizers decided to limit membership in the club to residents of suitable social standing in the Southampton area. They also decided to admit women members. In 1894, Willie Dunn added six more holes to the original twelve, giving the club a full 18-hole layout.

Shinnecock Hills, with its seaside links golf course and elegant clubhouse, was the first golf club in the United States that was comparable to the elite British clubs. It was also the first American golf club to have an architecturally designed clubhouse, the first to admit women members, and the first to have a membership waiting list. In 1896, Shinnecock Hills hosted the second US Open Golf Championship. When low scoring in the tournament led to criticism of its course, the club closed the popular nine-hole women's course and used it to lengthen the 18-hole course.

In 1892, the Palmetto Golf Club was established in Aiken, South Carolina, by Thomas Hitchcock, who lived in New York City and had a vacation home in the Aiken area. The club's original golf course was a four-hole layout with sand greens. The course was lengthened to 18 holes in 1894, but the sand greens were not converted to grass until the 1930s. The club still exists as a privately owned club and claims to be the second-oldest golf club in the United States with an 18-hole golf course that has been in continuous operation at its original location. The Glen Arven Country Club in Thomasville, Georgia, was also established in 1892. It still exists as a privately owned club and claims to have the oldest golf course in the state of Georgia.

The Country Club in Brookline, Massachusetts, was established in 1882 as a riding club and did not initially have a golf course. In the summer of 1892, Florence Boit came to Boston to spend the summer with her aunt and uncle. She had spent a year in France, where she had played golf at the Pau Golf Club and had taken to the game. Assuming that there would be a golf course in the Boston area, she brought her golf clubs with her when she came to visit her aunt and uncle. When she learned that there were no golf courses in the area, she convinced her uncle and two of his neighbors to pool their lawns and create enough room for seven short golf holes. She then introduced the game to her uncle and his neighbors and had little trouble convincing them that golf was a game that should be played in the Boston area. One of her uncle's neighbors happened to be a member of the Country Club in nearby Brookline and was able to persuade the club to build a golf course on its property for the use of its members.

In March 1893, a rudimentary six-hole golf course was built on the Country Club's property in Brookline by three club members. When the course opened, enough club members took to the game to convince the club to hire Willie Campbell, a professional golfer from Scotland, as its golf professional. Over the next five years, Campbell and his successor, Alex Campbell, another Scot, supervised the revision and gradual lengthening of the golf course to 18 holes. The Country Club's golf course turned out splendidly and is still one of the premier courses in the United States.

Another prominent golf club founded in 1893 was the Chicago Golf Club, which was a creation, almost single-handedly, of Charles Blair Macdonald. Macdonald, who was also known as C. B. Macdonald and Charlie Macdonald, was born in November 1855 in Niagara Falls, Ontario, Canada. His father was a Scotsman and his mother a Canadian. He was blessed with athletic ability, considerable size and strength, a sizeable personal fortune, and a belief that he alone was divinely appointed to decide how golf should be played in the United States.

When he was 16, Macdonald was sent to Scotland to study at St. Andrews University. Upon his arrival in St. Andrews, his paternal grandfather, who lived in St. Andrews and was a member of the R&A, took him to Old Tom Morris's golf shop and fitted him out to take up golf, a game he had never before played. Macdonald took to the game wholeheartedly and, under the guidance of Old Tom Morris and others, soon became an accomplished golfer—good enough to play an occasional round with Young Tom Morris. It was in St. Andrews, playing on the Old Course, that Macdonald's beliefs as to how and by whom golf should be played were formed.

When he returned home in 1875, Macdonald was disappointed to find that there were no golf courses in the Chicago area. For the next 18 years (which he later called the dark ages and during which he worked as a very successful stockbroker), he was able to play golf only during business trips to England, where he played at Coldham Common, Wimbledon, and Royal Liverpool. For years, he was unable to persuade anyone in Chicago to join him in building a golf course. In 1892, assisted by some golfers from New York who had come to Chicago to work temporarily at the World's Fair and needed a golf course to practice on while in they were in Chicago, Macdonald build a seven-hole course in nearby Lake Forest, on the estate of the father-in-law of one of the New York golfers.

When the course was completed, Macdonald invited his Chicago friends to join him for a few rounds of golf. His friends liked the game and urged

Macdonald to build a bigger and better golf course. A few months later, Macdonald and a few of his friends purchased a small farm in Belmont, Illinois, about 20 miles west of Chicago, where Macdonald laid out and built a nine-hole golf course. Unhappy with the nine-hole course, in the spring of 1893 Macdonald and a few others founded the Chicago Golf Club and added nine holes to the Belmont course, making it the first 18-hole golf course in North America. Later that year, Macdonald raised more money and purchased a 200-acre farm in nearby Wheaton, Illinois, where he laid out and built the second 18-hole golf course in North America. He used the inland courses he had played on in England as guides in designing and building the 6,500-yard Wheaton course.

After the Chicago Golf Club moved to Wheaton, the Belmont course was converted back to a nine-hole course. It is still operated as a public course by the Downers Grove Golf Club. Once they were exposed to the game, Chicagoans took to golf in a big way and by the turn of the twentieth century there were 26 golf courses operating in the Chicago area.

The Town & Country Club of St. Paul in St. Paul, Minnesota, was founded as a social and athletic club in 1887. In 1893, the club built a golf course for its members and hosted the first round of golf ever played in the state of Minnesota. The course was designed and laid out by George McCree, a Scottish immigrant who asked to be allowed to participate in the design and building of the course after reading a newspaper article suggesting that the club was considering building a golf course.

The most notable golfing event among the rich and famous in 1893 occurred in Newport, Rhode Island, the richest and most socially prominent resort in North America. The event was the founding of the Newport Country Club by John Jacob Astor IV, Cornelius Vanderbilt II, Perry Belmont, Theodore Havemeyer, and others. Theodore Havemeyer was a wealthy sportsman whose family owned the American Sugar Company. Called "the Sugar King" by the newspapers, Havemeyer had learned to play golf while vacationing at Pau in the South of France in 1889 and was the driving force behind the founding of the Newport club.

When he returned to his summer home in Newport in 1890, Havemeyer convinced a few of his Newport neighbors that they should try the game and arranged to have a nine-hole golf course built in nearby Benton's Point. When his neighbors joined him in playing the Benton's Point course, they liked the game and concluded that golf was not a passing fad and was a game that should be played in America.

In 1893, Havemeyer convinced John Jacob Astor IV, Cornelius Vanderbilt II, Perry Belmont, and a few others to join him in purchasing a 140-acre tract of farmland in Newport called Rocky Farm for the purpose of building an 18-hole golf course and a suitable clubhouse. Later that year they founded the Newport Country Club and arranged to have a golf course and a classic Beaux Arts–style clubhouse built on the Rocky Farm property. The club's first golf professional was Willie Davis, a Scottish immigrant who laid out and built a nine-hole golf course on the Rocky Farm property that opened for play in 1894. The course was expanded to 18 holes in 1899, and the clubhouse, which overlooked Bailey's Beach and was called "High Tide" by the members, was completed in 1900.

In 1894, Leslie Pell-Clark and Henry Wardell founded the Otsego Golf Club in Springfield Center, New York, and built a 12-hole golf course on some land they owned near the north end of Lake Otsego, about nine miles north of Cooperstown. The club still operates the nine-hole golf course, which it calls one of the oldest golf courses in the United States. Also in 1894, the Tacoma Golf Club, the first golf club on the West Coast, was founded in Lakewood, Washington, near Tacoma. The club now operates its 18-hole course as the Tacoma Country and Golf Club and claims to be the oldest private golf club west of the Mississippi River.

In 1894 the Tuxedo Club in Tuxedo Park, New York, celebrated the opening of its new 18-hole golf course by hosting the first interclub golf tournament held in the United States. Joining the players from the Tuxedo Club in the tournament were players from the Shinnecock Hills Golf Club, the Country Club in Brookline (Massachusetts), and the St. Andrew's Golf Club. The Country Club's players prevailed in the tournament and were presented with a trophy, which was later donated to the US Golf Association (USGA) and is now the trophy awarded to the winner of the US Senior Open.

Because golf was predominantly a pastime of the affluent during its early years in the United States, it only followed that hotels and resorts that catered to the affluent would build golf courses. The first resort golf course in the United States was built in 1890 by the Lake Champlain Hotel near Plattsburgh, New York, which at the time was one of the most famous and elegant hotels in the country. It was used as the Summer White House by President William McKinley in the late 1890s. The hotel's golf course, an impressive, 18-hole layout along the shores of Lake Champlain, was designed by noted golf course architect A. W. Tillinghast. The Lake Champlain Hotel no longer exists, but its golf course has survived and is now operated as a public course by the Bluff Point Golf Resort. Bluff Point claims its golf course to be the third oldest in the United States.

On the other end of golf's social structure, and as an indicator of things to come in American golf, the first municipal golf course in the United States was opened at Van Cortland Park in North Bronx, New York, on July 6, 1895. Owned by the city of New York, "Vanny," as the locals call it, is still in operation and is the oldest of the 2,500 publicly owned golf courses in the United States today.

At the close of the 19th century, there were an estimated 1,000 golf courses in the United States, all but one of which were owned and operated by privately owned membership golf clubs. Of the estimated quarter-million golfers in the United States at that time, all but a handful were members of golf clubs. At this juncture, golf in the United States was controlled by membership golf clubs and the sport was unavailable to most Americans. Unlike in Scotland, where the links courses were built on publicly owned land and were open to all golfers, whether or not they belonged to a golf club, in the United States golfers who could not afford the expense of joining a private membership golf club, or for any reason chose not to or could not join one, had no place to play and were effectively frozen out of the sport.

· 5 ·

Golf Takes Root in the United States

To celebrate the opening of their new nine-hole golf course on Rocky Farm, in 1894 the members of the Newport Golf Club invited golfers from other clubs to come to Newport in September for a competition to determine the country's champion amateur golfer. Twenty amateur golfers entered the 36-hole, two-day, stroke-play event. The leader after the first day was Charlie Macdonald of the Chicago Golf Club, whose 18-hole score of 89 gave him a four-stroke lead over runner-up W. G. Lawrence of the Newport Golf Club.

On the second day, Macdonald was leading the tournament when he hit his ball into a stone wall that course designer Willie Dunn had left on the course as a hazard. The ball was unplayable in the stones and under the rule at the time Macdonald was assessed a two-stroke penalty for lifting his ball out of the stones. When he subsequently lost the tournament to W. G. Lawrence by one stroke, he refused to recognize Lawrence as the champion, claiming that the stone wall was not a legitimate hazard and that he should not have been assessed a two-stroke penalty for lifting his ball from it. He also argued long and loud that stroke play was not a proper method of determining the winner of an amateur golf championship because, as anyone who knows anything about golf knows, in Britain amateur championships are always held in match play. He demanded that the Newport tournament be ruled "no contest" and that it be replayed in match play. Not surprisingly, his arguments fell on deaf ears in Newport, and W. G. Lawrence was declared by the Newport Golf Club to be America's champion amateur golfer.

A few weeks later, in October 1894, the St. Andrew's Golf Club held a match-play tournament on its nine-hole course at Grey Oaks in Yonkers, New York, again to determine the national amateur champion. Charlie

Macdonald and 26 other amateur golfers showed up for the event. The long-hitting Chicagoan won his first two matches easily and in the third round defeated W. G. Lawrence, his nemesis at Newport, 2 and 1 to reach the finals, where his opponent was Laurence Stoddart, also of the Newport Golf Club. Macdonald and Stoddart finished 18 holes all square, but on the first extra hole Macdonald sliced his tee shot into a ploughed-ground hazard. It took him three strokes to get out of the hazard and Stoddart won the hole and the tournament.

Macdonald again refused to recognize the man who had defeated him as the national amateur champion, blaming his loss on an ill-advised lunch of steak and champagne and arguing that a single golf club could not determine a national champion. To be a true national championship, he argued, a tournament must have the approval of and be sponsored by every golf club in the country, which would require the establishment of an official organization representing all golf clubs. Again, Macdonald's arguments fell on deaf ears and Stoddart was declared by the St. Andrew's Golf Club to be America's champion amateur golfer. There were now two national amateur champions, both from the Newport Golf Club.

Aware of the folly of having two national champions and acknowledging the logic of Macdonald's argument about who should be permitted to hold a tournament to determine a national champion, the golfing establishment decided to do something about it. Consequently, on December 22, 1894, representatives from the five most prominent golf clubs in the United States met in New York City for the purpose of establishing a governing body for American golf. The golf clubs represented at the meeting were the Shinnecock Hills Golf Club; the Country Club from Brookline, Massachusetts; the St. Andrew's Golf Club; the Newport Golf Club; and the Chicago Golf Club.

At the meeting, the clubs, through their representatives, agreed to unite and invite other clubs to join them in forming the Amateur Golf Association of the United States, whose purpose was to promote the interests of golf, share and publicize a code of rules for the game, hold annual meetings, and conduct competitions for the amateur and open championships of the United States. The association later changed its name and became the United States Golf Association (the USGA), the organization that is today the governing body of golf in the United States, its territories, and Mexico. The governing body of golf for the rest of the world is the Royal and Ancient Golf Club of St. Andrews (the R&A).

Theodore Havemeyer of the Newport Golf Club was elected president of the new association. Charlie Macdonald attended the meeting as a representative of the Chicago Golf Club and reportedly lobbied hard for the presidency but had to settle for second vice-president. One of Havemeyer's first acts as president was to donate a handsome trophy to be awarded to the US Amateur Champion. The trophy bears his name and is still awarded each year to the winner of the US Amateur. The Sugar King also personally paid any bills that the association didn't have the funds to cover.

The first US Amateur Golf Championship sponsored by the USGA was held at the Newport Golf Club during the first three days of October 1895. Anxious for the tournament to be a success at his home club, Havemeyer personally paid the expenses of the 32 amateur golfers who entered the event and sponsored a lavish party for them. The runaway winner of the match-play event was—you guessed it—forty-year-old Charlie Macdonald. He won the final match 12 and 11 and became the first official US Amateur Champion.

Almost as an afterthought, the first US Open Championship was held the next day, also at the Newport Golf Club. Eleven professional golfers and no amateurs entered the 36-hole, stroke-play event. Horace Rawlins, a 21-year-old Englishman, shot a 173 to win the event and collected $150 in prize money for doing so. The superior status of the amateur championship reflects the elevated status given amateur golf at that time by the golfing establishment.

In 1896, both the US Amateur and the US Open were held at the Shinnecock Hills Golf Club in Southampton, New York. Jim Whigham, an Englishman who was Charlie Macdonald's son-in-law, won the US Amateur. Macdonald played in both events and was defeated in the second round of the US Amateur.

The 35 entrants in the US Open included John Shippen Jr., a 16-year-old African American, and Shippen's friend Oscar Bunn, a 19-year-old Native American from the Shinnecock nation. The youngest competitor in the tournament, Shippen had spent most of his life in Washington, D.C., where his father was a Presbyterian minister. In 1889, his father was assigned to a ministry on the Shinnecock Indian Reservation in Southampton. Shortly after arriving in Southampton, young Shippen began working as a caddie at the Shinnecock Hills Golf Club, where he learned to play golf.

Oscar Bunn's father was killed in a shipwreck when he was an infant and he lived with his mother on the nearby Shinnecock Reservation. To help his mother support her family, Bunn worked as a caddie at Shinnecock Hills, where he learned to play golf and became a friend of John Shippen Jr. Both boys became quite good at the game and in 1896 several Shinnecock Hills members urged them to enter the US Open and offered to pay their entry fees. The boys accepted the offer and registered to play in the event. They were not eligible to play in the US Amateur because they were not club members.

When it became known that Shippen and Bunn had registered to play in the US Open, several entrants complained about having to play with "that colored boy Shippen and his Indian friend" and threatened to withdraw from the tournament if the boys were allowed to play. USGA president Theodore Havemeyer responded by announcing that the tournament would go on even if Shippen and Bunn were the only competitors. No one withdrew and Scottish-born American Jim Foulis won the 36-hole, stroke-play event with a score of 152, three strokes ahead of runner-up Horace Rawlins.

Shippen, who was paired with an unhappy Charlie Macdonald in the first round of the tournament, opened with a 78 and was tied for the lead at that point. He remained in contention until he had trouble getting out of a sand trap on the 13th hole in the second round and took an 11 on the hole. He wound up shooting a 159, which tied him for fifth place, the highest finish among the few American-born players in the event. His fifth-place finish in the event earned him ten dollars and he became the first African American to play in the US Open and the first to win prize money. Oscar Bunn, the first Native American to play in the US Open, shot an 89 in the first round and was never in contention.

Charlie Macdonald, who at the time was a member of the Shinnecock Hills Golf Club, was so unhappy about being paired with Shippen in the first round that he withdrew from the event and gave up his membership in the club. It turned out that Charlie's skills as a golf course architect exceeded his considerable golfing skills and he later designed and built the National Golf Links of America, a links-style golf course on the shore of Great Peconic Bay virtually next door to the Shinnecock Hills Golf Club. Charlie's masterpiece opened in 1911 and was called America's first spectacular golf course.

John Shippen Jr. pursued a career in professional golf. He competed in four more US Open Championships, where his best finish was another tie for fifth place in 1902. He spent most of his life as a club pro at various golf clubs and courses. In the early 1930s, he became the club pro at the Shady Rest Golf and Country Club in Scotch Plains, New Jersey, the first African American–owned golf club in the United States. He held that position for 30 years. He died in 1968 at age 88. The epitaph on his tombstone reads, "John Shippen 1879–1968 The First American Born African American Golf Professional."

Oscar Bunn also pursued a career in golf. He later served as a club pro at golf courses in Lake Placid, New York; Jacksonville, Florida; and New Britain, Connecticut. He was also an accomplished artist, specializing in wood carvings. He died of pneumonia in 1918 at age 42.

Willie Anderson was born in North Berwick, Scotland, in 1879. Like many Scots, he started playing golf at an early age. In 1896, at age 16, he immigrated to the United States with his father and brother. In 1897, at age 17, he entered the US Open at the Chicago Golf Club and was the runner-up in the event to Joe Lloyd, who eagled the final hole to defeat him by a stroke. He subsequently won US Open Championships in 1901, 1903, 1904, and1905. Since then, Bobby Jones, Ben Hogan, and Jack Nicklaus have matched his total of four US Open Championships, but only he has won three consecutive titles. His brilliant career was cut short by his untimely death from epilepsy in 1910 at age 31.

For the first 400 years of the game, there were no base, target, or par scores for holes or rounds of golf. The concept of what we now call *par* did not exist until the early 1900s. Strangely, it began with the concept of bogey devised by the British. In 1890, Hugh Rotherham of the Coventry Golf Club in England conceived the idea of establishing the number of shots a good golfer should take on each hole of a golf course. He called that number a "ground score" for the hole.

A few years later, the Great Yarmouth Golf Club, also in England, became the first club to assign a ground score to each hole on its golf course. Its members then began playing match-play rounds against an imaginary opponent called "the bogey man," whose score on each hole was the ground score for that hole. The name "bogey man" is thought to have originated from a song called "Hush! Hush! Here Comes the Bogey Man," which was popular in music halls at the time. Within a few years, so-called bogey competitions were being held by golf clubs throughout Great Britain wherein golfers played match-play rounds against the bogey man, with the player winning the most holes from the bogey man being deemed the winner of the event. In time, the ground score for a hole became known among British golfers as the bogey score and, when achieved, was called a bogey.

The word *par* was first used with respect to golf in 1870, when A. H. Doleman, a golf writer for a British newspaper, asked a couple of professional golfers to determine the score that should win the Open Championship at Prestwick that year. The professionals determined that mistake-free play should produce a score of 49 on each round of the 12-hole Prestwick course. Doleman referred to this score as the par score for the Prestwick course. Young Tom Morris won the Open Championship that year with a 149, a score that was two strokes over Doleman's par for the 36-hole event. Doleman is thought to have borrowed the word *par* from stock-exchange terminology, where certain stocks and bonds have a base value that is referred to as a par value.

The idea of having a base or ground score for each hole and round of golf caught on among golfers on both sides of the Atlantic and in the early 1900s golf courses began posting such scores for their holes and rounds of golf. In the United States, where the so-called bogey competitions never caught on, these scores were called par scores, while in Britain they were called bogey scores. American golfers later adopted the term *bogey* for a score of one-over-par on a hole. The American terminology was eventually adopted everywhere.

In 1911, in an attempt to standardize par scores on golf courses in the United States, the USGA adopted distance standards for determining par scores on holes. Holes up to 225 yards in length were deemed to have a par of three, holes from 225 yards to 425 yards in length were deemed to have a par of four, holes from 426 yards to 600 yards in length were deemed to have a par of five, and holes more than 600 yards in length were deemed to have a par of six.

The term *birdie* for a score of one under par on a hole was reportedly first coined at the Atlantic Country Club in Plymouth, Massachusetts, in 1898. It was derived from the word *bird*, an American slang expression at the time meaning anything excellent. Phrases like "that was a bird of a shot" were common at the time. The use of the term *eagle* for a score of two under par on a hole is an extension of the theme of using bird-related terms for good golf scores. It was adopted in the United States, where the eagle is a national symbol. The term *albatross* is a British term for a score of three under par on a hole and is another extension of the theme of using bird-related terms for good golf scores. Most American golfers use the term *double eagle* for a three-under-par score on a hole. The term customarily used for a hole-in-one is *ace*, which was derived from the playing card of that name bearing a single spot. There are no one-word terms for scores of two or three over par on a hole—they are just double or triple bogeys. Anything higher is said to be a "blow up" or a "disaster."

Coburn Haskell was a businessman from Cleveland, Ohio, who played a lot of golf. Like many golfers in the 1890s, he was not at all satisfied with the gutta-percha golf ball. In 1898, while visiting a business associate at a B. F. Goodrich Rubber Company plant in Cleveland, he was given a tour of the facility. During the tour he noticed that B. F. Goodrich manufactured rubber thread for commercial purposes and it dawned on him that thread of this type might be wrapped tightly around a solid rubber core and made into a golf ball. During the next few months, he and Bertram Work, a B. F. Goodrich employee, worked on the idea and developed an experimental golf ball composed of rubber thread wrapped tightly around a solid rubber core and covered with a sheath of gutta-percha.

In August 1898, Haskell and Work filed a patent application for the ball, which was granted in 1899. With the help of John Gameter, another

B. F. Goodrich employee, they devised a machine that would mechanically wrap rubber thread around a solid rubber core and cover it with a layer of gutta-percha. Haskell and his friends tried playing the new ball, liked it, and a few months later B. F. Goodrich began mass-producing them. B. F. Goodrich called the new ball the Haskell.

The first Haskells were made with a smooth cover and had a tendency to dive while in flight. This defect was corrected by impressing a bramble pattern similar to that used on the gutties onto the cover of the ball. It was eventually discovered that a pattern of dimples impressed onto the covering of the ball made it fly and spin even better. In the early 1900s, the gutta-percha covering was replaced with a thin covering of balata, a rubber-like material made from the sap of the balata tree, which is native to Central and South America. The soft balata covering gave the Haskell a better feel and made it easier to spin, but the balata covering cut more easily and made the ball less durable.

Called "bounding Billies" by golfers at the time, the lively Haskell was a little harder to control around the green than the gutty, but this shortcoming was more than made up for by the extra twenty yards the average golfer got off the tee with the Haskell. Also, the Haskell did not break into fragments like the gutty occasionally did and, with dimples impressed on its cover, it flew better than the gutty. The Haskell had a better feel than the rock-hard gutty, was more forgiving, and did not have to be struck perfectly to produce a reasonably good shot. The down side of the Haskell was that it cut easily and had to be replaced more often than the durable gutty. Everything considered, the Haskell outperformed the gutty and the two balls sold for about the same price. Not surprisingly, it wasn't long before the Haskell replaced the gutty as the ball of choice of golfers on both sides of the Atlantic.

The clincher for the Haskell in the United States came in 1901, when short-hitting Walter Travis used it while winning the US Amateur. In Great Britain, the clincher came a year later when Sandy Herd won the 1902 British Open using a Haskell while the rest of the field used gutties.

The advent of the Haskell brought about changes in golf clubs. The Haskell was softer than the gutty and it played better and could be hit farther with club heads made of hard wood. Consequently, persimmon replaced beech as the wood used in the heads of drivers, spoons, and other wood clubs. With the advent of the Haskell, woods made with hickory shafts and persimmon heads became the woods of choice of discriminating golfers. The club faces of irons were enlarged and fitted with deeper groves to make them more forgiving and impart more spin on the softer Haskell.

At about the same time that the Haskell came along, another change took place that added to the enjoyment of the game. This change was the invention of the golf tee. In 1899, George Grant, an African American dentist from Boston, who, like many golfers, didn't like to get his hands dirty pouring wet sand every time he teed up a golf ball, was granted a patent on the wooden golf tee. Grant made some wooden tees and gave them to his friends, but didn't try to market them commercially. It took a few years, but wooden tees eventually replaced sand and water as the tees used by golfers everywhere.

Most golfers today have never heard of Walter Travis, but during the early 1900s he was one of the biggest names in American golf. Born in Maldon, Australia, in 1862, Travis came to New York City in 1885 as a 23-year-old representative of an Australian exporter and never went back. In 1890, he married an American woman and became a naturalized citizen of the United States. What makes Travis unique among great golfers is that he did not hit his first golf ball until he was 34 years old. Blessed with great eye-hand coordination but not great strength, he purchased some instruction manuals, practiced relentlessly, and became an exceptional ball striker with phenomenal chipping and putting skills. Within a year he was the best golfer in the Long Island golf club he belonged to. A year later he entered the US Ama-

Walter Travis. The grand old man of golf and the first American winner of the British Amateur.
Library of Congress

teur and got to the semifinals. Two years later, in 1900, he won his first US Amateur Championship at age 38.

An incredible putter but not a long hitter, he won the US Amateur again in 1901 and 1903, and finished third overall and was the low-scoring amateur in the 1902 US Open. What really put him on the golf map, however, was his performance in the prestigious British Amateur in 1904, an event that had never been won by an American. After qualifying for the match-play portion of the event, the 42-year-old naturalized American took on the best of the English amateurs, head to head. In the quarterfinals, he defeated four-time British Amateur champion and two-time British Open champion Harold Hilton, 5 and 4. In the semifinals, he defeated four-time British Amateur champion Horace Hutchinson, 4 and 2. In the 36-hole final match, he was paired against Ted Blackwell, a powerful man who had once driven the 18th green on the Old Course at St. Andrews. On that day, however, Blackwell's driver was no match for Travis's center-shafted Schenectady putter and Travis prevailed 4 and 3 to become the first American winner of the British Amateur.

Known as "the Grand Old Man of Golf," Travis was also a prolific writer who wrote articles for leading sports magazines and a book entitled *Practical Golf*, which was well received and widely read. In 1908, he founded and published the *American Golf Magazine*, which for many years was the most respected and influential golf magazine in the country. He was also a noted golf-course architect. Working mostly in the New York City area, his creations included golf courses for the Garden City Golf Club in Garden City, New York, and the Westchester Country Club in Rye, New York. The Grand Old Man of Golf did much to make golf a viable sport in his adopted country.

In 1910, the R&A banned the use of the center-shafted Schenectady putter that Travis had used in winning the 1904 British Amateur on the grounds that it was a mallet and not a golf club. The USGA refused to ban the putter and a dispute arose between the two rule-making bodies that lasted for 42 years. The dispute ended in 1952 when the R&A lifted its ban on the putter. Leading the charge for the USGA during the early years of its dispute with the R&A was our old friend Charlie Macdonald. The center-shafted putter was called the Schenectady putter because it was reportedly invented and first used by a golfer in Schenectady, New York. Center-shafted putters are common today and are used by millions of golfers.

In 1911, Johnny McDermott, a brash young pro from Philadelphia who was addicted to gambling at golf, ended the foreign and foreign-born dominance of the US Open by becoming the first American-born winner of the event. At age 19 years, 10 months, and 14 days, he is still the youngest player ever to win the US Open and the second-youngest ever to win any of the four modern majors; only Young Tom Morris, who won the British Open in 1868 at age 17, was younger. As if to prove that his victory in 1911 was no fluke, McDermott won the US Open again in 1912 at the Country Club of Buffalo, where he shot a two-under-par 294 on a par-74 course and became the first player to shoot a subpar score in the US Open. Unfortunately, he disappeared from the golfing scene as quickly as he had appeared. In 1914, at age 23, he collapsed and suffered a nervous breakdown in the clubhouse of the Atlantic City Country Club, where he was the club pro. He never recovered from the incident and spent the rest of his life in mental hospitals, rest homes, and living with family members in Philadelphia, suffering from a mental illness.

Harry Vardon was born in 1870 on the English Channel Island of Jersey. The son of an English father and a French mother, his family was not well off and he did not play golf as a youth. During his teens, he worked as a caddy at a couple of golf clubs on Jersey and learned to play golf, for which he had an obvious natural talent. In 1890, he left the island and moved to England proper, where he worked first as a greenskeeper at an English golf club and later as a club pro. His talent was such that by the middle 1890s he was being touted as the best British golfer since Young Tom Morris. In 1896, he won the first of his record six British Open Championships.

He is perhaps best known today as the inventor of the so-called Vardon grip, which he popularized but did not actually invent. Reportedly, he liked the grip because it prevented his right hand from dominating his swing. Also called the overlapping grip, it is a grip wherein the little finger of the right hand of a right-handed golfer overlaps the index finger of the left hand. It is the grip used by most golfers today. Vardon also wrote a very popular instructional book on golf that was first published in 1905. Tommy Vardon, Harry's brother, was also an accomplished golfer and finished second to Harry in the 1903 British Open

In 1900, the A. G. Spalding Company paid Harry Vardon the unheard-of sum of 900 pounds to promote the "Vardon Flyer," its brand-new gutta-percha golf ball, on a tour of the United States and Canada. During the tour, Vardon played a series of exhibition matches against local professionals. He interrupted the tour long enough to play in the 1900 US Open at the Chicago Golf Club, which he won with a record low 72-hole score of 313. Unfortunately for the A. G. Spalding Company, Vardon's tour came on the eve of the introduction of the Haskell golf ball and its investment in Vardon's tour was largely wasted. Nevertheless, Vardon's exhibitions drew large crowds and did much to promote golf in an increasingly golf-conscious United States.

Harry Vardon made another tour of the United States in 1913, this time sponsored by the *Times of London*. Accompanying Vardon on the tour

Harry Vardon. England's greatest golfer and the only six-time winner of the British Open.
Library of Congress

was Ted Ray, who had won the 1912 British Open at Muirfield, defeating Vardon, the runner-up, by four strokes. Ray customarily played in a long, loose-fitting tweed jacket and a crushed felt hat. A large, drooping black mustache gave his face a sinister appearance and he was seldom seen without a large pipe in the corner of his mouth. A big, slope-shouldered man and a prodigiously long hitter of the ball, Ray was a fitting complement to Harry Vardon's smooth, graceful swing and effortless power. Their tour was a resounding success, with record crowds appearing at just about every exhibition.

Ted Ray. The winner of the 1912 British Open in his customary golfing attire.
Library of Congress

Vardon and Ray interrupted their tour long enough to play in the 1913 US Open at the Country Club in Brookline, Massachusetts. The USGA was so eager to have Vardon and Ray play in its tournament that year that it moved the tournament from its usual date in early June to mid-September to accommodate their exhibition schedule.

In addition to Vardon and Ray, appearing in the 1913 US Open were Jerry Travers, a four-time winner of the US Amateur, and Johnny McDermott, the winner of the last two US Open Championships. Other entrants included Scottish American Alex Smith, a two-time winner of the event, and a cocky, 21-year-old assistant pro from Rochester, New York, named Walter Hagen, who announced that he would show up at Brookline to help take care of Vardon and Ray. Also in the tournament were Wilfred Reid, a veteran English professional; diminutive Louis Tellier, France's premier professional golfer; and Francis Ouimet, a 20-year-old hometown amateur who had honed his golfing skills while working as a caddy at the Country Club. A record 165 players entered the event, giving the US Open its largest and most prestigious field ever. The USGA was hoping for a great tournament, and it would succeed beyond its grandest expectations.

Because of the large number of entrants, a 36-hole qualifying round was held in which the players were divided into three groups that would play separately over a two-day period. Harry Vardon's 151 led the first-day qualifiers, followed by unknown Francis Ouimet at 152. Ted Ray's 148 led the second-day qualifiers. Young Walter Hagen, playing in his first national tournament, shot a 157 on the second day and barely qualified.

Louis Tellier. France's premier golfer in the early 1900s.
Library of Congress

All of the notable golfers qualified and the 72-hole tournament proper started on the third morning. Each qualifying golfer would play two 18-hole rounds (36 holes) on each of two consecutive days on the Country Club's demanding par-71 layout. Under fair skies, a large gallery showed up for the opening round. Because of its prestigious field and the United States versus England aspect of the event, the tournament was given broad coverage by newspapers throughout the country. Never had so much interest been shown in an American golf tournament.

The first day ended with the English golfers in firm control. After 36 holes, Harry Vardon and Wilfred Reid were tied for the lead at 147, followed by Ted Ray at 149. American youngsters Walter Hagen and Francis Ouimet were next at 151, while France's Louis Tellier was a stroke back at 152. No one else was in contention. The next day under cloudy skies, Ouimet shot a 74 in the morning round to pull even with Vardon and Ray at 225 at the 54-hole mark. Hagen shot a 76 and was two strokes behind at 227. Reid blew sky-high in the morning round and dropped out of contention.

As the final 18-hole round was about to begin, it commenced to rain and the ensuing downpour soaked the course. When the rain let up, the final round got underway. Among the leaders, Ray was the first to finish. His 79 on the soggy course gave him a 304 for the tournament and the early lead. Vardon encountered putting difficulties during the final round, had to scramble to match Ray's 79, and was tied for the lead at 304. As for the

Walter Hagen. He played in his first U.S. Open in 1913.
Library of Congress

Francis Ouimet. The 19-year-old former caddy had to be persuaded to enter the 1913 U.S. Open in his home town of Brookline.
Library of Congress

Americans—Walter Hagen played well on the front nine and was tied for the lead at the turn. However, he lost his momentum after taking a double-bogie seven on the 14th hole and wound up shooting an 80 for the round and finished in a four-way tie for fourth place, three strokes behind the leaders. Defending champion Johnny McDermott's 308 tied him for eighth place, while Alex Smith finished tied for 16th place and Jerry Travers, who never got it going, finished in 27th place.

By midafternoon it had become evident that the only American player with a chance of catching Vardon and Ray was young Francis Ouimet. His 43 on the front nine of the afternoon round tied him with Vardon and Ray at the turn, but when he started the back nine with bogeys on ten and twelve, his chances of catching the Englishmen, who were playing several holes ahead of him, did not look good. His prospects improved, however, when he chipped in for a birdie on 13 and pulled within a stroke of Vardon and Ray. He stayed within a stroke of the leaders by parring the tough, par-five 14th hole, the hole that had done Walter Hagen in.

On the par-four 15th hole, Ouimet mishit his approach shot and the ball wound up in some heavy rough about ten feet short of the green. Retaining his composure and gauging the resistance offered by the long, wet grass correctly, he hit a superb chip shot that rolled to a stop three feet from the cup. A minute later he sank the three-footer for a par and was relieved to have survived the hole and stayed within a stroke of the leaders.

On the par-three 16th hole, a pulled tee shot and a poor chip left him nine feet from the cup. With many in the large gallery thinking the pressure was getting to the young amateur, he walked calmly to his ball, glanced at the hole, studied the green briefly, and stroked the ball firmly in what his experience in having played the hole countless times told him was the correct line. Seconds later the roar of the gallery informed everyone on the course that the young amateur had holed the tough nine-footer. He had again survived a bad shot without losing ground, but he still trailed the Englishmen by a stroke with but two holes to go. By then Vardon and Ray had finished their round and were waiting in the clubhouse, expecting the inexperienced local amateur to crack under the pressure.

Ouimet knew from experience that it was best to play the dogleg-left, par-four 17th hole conservatively. Electing not to cut the dogleg, he hit a decently long drive down the center of the fairway and selected a spoon for his lengthy approach shot. The persimmon head of his hickory-shafted spoon struck the Haskell ball squarely and sent it flying on a line straight toward the pin. The ball landed short of the green, rolled onto the green, and stopped well short of the pin, leaving him with a difficult, downhill, 20-footer for his much-needed birdie. Again he walked calmly to his ball, studied the green briefly, took a couple of phantom strokes, and stroked the ball firmly in what his intimate knowledge of the green told him was the correct line. He and everyone in the huge gallery watched the ball roll slowly down the hill, break to the left, strike the back of the cup, and disappear into the hole. The roar of the gallery informed Ray and Vardon in the clubhouse that the hometown lad had caught them on 17.

Needing a par on the long, par four 18th hole to tie the Englishmen, or a birdie to overtake them, Ouimet hit his drive in the fairway, but on the soggy turf the ball didn't roll as far as he had hoped and he had to use a brassie for his long and difficult approach shot. Again he struck the ball cleanly and it landed several yards short of the green. However, instead of rolling onto the green as it would normally have done, it was slowed by some mud and stopped in some soggy grass several feet short of the green. His chip shot off of the heavy, wet grass was on line but died five feet short of the hole. Knowing he had to make the five-footer to tie Ray and Vardon, Ouimet walked to the ball, studied the green briefly to get his line, and stroked the ball softly but firmly toward the hole in what he hoped was the right line. Again, the roar of the gallery informed those in the clubhouse that the young amateur had sunk the clutch five-footer and had remained tied with Vardon and Ray. The winner of the 1913 US Open would be determined the next day in an 18-hole playoff.

Sports fans throughout the country followed accounts of the tournament in their local newspapers. They were intrigued by the prospect of an ordinary American, who, like themselves, was not wealthy and did not belong to a golf club, taking on the famous English professionals. Who is this kid, they asked, and how did he learn to play golf?

From newspapers accounts, American sports fans learned that Ouimet (pronounced "Wee-met") came from a working-class family, that his father was a French Canadian with no interest in golf, that his mother was Irish, and that a few years earlier his family had moved into a small house in a sparsely populated section of Brookline, directly across the street from the 17th fairway of the Country Club's golf course. They learned that Ouimet had started working as a caddy at the Country Club when he was 11 and had started playing golf in his early teens using golf balls he had found and a few golf clubs given to him by club members. He had practiced by coming to work early and using the club's facilities before the members arrived. In time he had become quite good at the game.

Newspaper accounts of the event reported that when Ouimet was a freshman at the local high school, he had convinced the school to field a golf team and two years later had led the team to a high school championship. In 1910, at age 17, he wanted to enter the US Amateur, which was being played at the Country Club that year. To enter, he had to be a member of a USGA-approved golf club, so he borrowed twenty-five dollars from his mother and applied for a junior membership at the golf club on whose course his high school team had played. The club granted him a junior membership, but he failed to qualify for the US Amateur. After failing to qualify again in 1911 and 1912, he entered the Massachusetts State Amateur in 1912 and lost in the finals of the match-play event. In 1913, he won the state amateur championship and qualified for the US Amateur, where he got to the semifinals before losing a close match to Jerry Travers, the eventual winner.

While Ouimet was virtually unknown in the rest of the country, in his home state and among those involved in amateur tournament golf, he was a well-thought-of player. Initially, he had not planned on entering the 1913 US Open but was persuaded to do so by members of the Country Club and by USGA president Robert Watson, who was bent on getting a record number of players in the tournament that year.

After finishing the final round tied with Vardon and Ray, Ouimet walked home, had dinner with his family, took a bath, and went to bed at 9:30. He arose at daybreak the next morning, had a light breakfast, and walked to the Country Club, where he hit practice balls to his caddy, ten-year-old Eddie Lowery. At 10:00, he joined Vardon and Ray on the first tee. A day-and-a-half of intermittent rain had soaked the course and a light drizzle was still falling, but the weather did not dampen the enthusiasm of the gallery, estimated at 3,500, that had gathered to watch the event.

The soggy fairway made the first hole play even longer than its 430 yards. Only the powerful Ray had a realistic chance of reaching the green in two, but he pushed his second shot into some mounds to the right of the green. No one was able to get down in two and each player recorded a bogey five on the hole. They all recovered and parred the short, par-four second hole, but Ray needed three putts to get down from forty feet on the third hole and dropped a stroke behind Vardon and Ouimet, both of whom parred the hole.

They all carded fours on the fourth hole and got off the tee well on the 420-yard, par-four fifth hole, where Ouimet mishit his approach shot. It was his first mistake of the day and it was a bad one as his ball flew over the rough on the right side of the fairway and faded out of bounds. Showing no emotion, he dropped another ball over his shoulder and proceeded to hit a solid brassie to the edge of the green, from where he got down in two, giving him a bogey five under the distance-only penalty in effect at that time for balls driven out of bounds.

Fortunately for Ouimet, neither Vardon nor Ray was able to hit the fifth green with their lengthy approach shots and when they both needed three strokes to get down, Ouimet survived his mistake without losing ground. The failure of Vardon and Ray to take advantage of his mistake gave Ouimet a valuable psychological boost. He realized that the veteran English professionals were not infallible and could be beaten if he hit good shots.

On the short, uphill, par-four sixth hole Vardon pitched his approach shot to within two feet of the pin and picked up a stroke with his first birdie of the day. On the par-three seventh hole, no one hit the green off the tee box and only Ray, with a good chip, was able to get down in two and he picked up the stroke he had lost on the third hole. They all hit the fairway with their drives on the par-four eighth hole. Ouimet, hitting first, stuck his approach shot 18 inches from the pin and a few minutes later sank the short putt for a birdie three. Ray matched him by rolling in a 35-footer, while Vardon carded a two-putt par. When they each recorded a five on the 520-yard, par-five ninth hole, there was a three-way tie at 38 and the US Open had become a nine-hole event.

Both Vardon and Ray started the final nine with three-putt bogeys on the 140-yard, par-three 10th hole. Ouimet got down in two for a par and took his first lead of the day. Vardon and Ray both missed opportunities to get the stroke back on the 390-yard, par-four 11th hole by missing makeable birdie putts and matching Ouimet's four on the hole. Ouimet outdrove both Englishmen on the par-four 12th hole and followed it up by hitting a superb mashie to within 10 feet of the pin. Vardon and Ray both came up short of the green with their approach shots and neither was able to get down in two. Ouimet's 10-foot birdie putt stopped just short of the hole, but his tap-in par gave him a two-stroke lead over both Englishmen with six holes to go.

On the short par-four 13th hole, they were all on the green in two, with Ray 30 feet from the hole near the left edge of the green and Vardon and Ouimet each about nine feet from the hole. Ray's long putt didn't drop, but Vardon's straight-in nine-footer did. When Quimet's side-hiller wouldn't drop, his lead shrunk to a stroke over Vardon and two strokes over Ray with five difficult holes left to play. On the long par-five 14th hole, Ouimet topped his second shot badly and the ball traveled less than 100 yards before getting caught up in some heavy rough about two hundred yards from the green. It was his first mishit since the fifth hole and many in the gallery thought the pressure might be getting to the young amateur. Fortunately, he had a decent lie in the rough and was able to hit a superb brassie to the center of the green, from where he got down in two to match the fives recorded by Vardon and Ray.

Ray snap-hooked his tee shot on the par-four 15th hole and his ball was headed for some bushes to the left of the fairway when it hit a spectator and bounced back onto the short grass. He failed to capitalize on the break, however, and under-clubbed his second shot into a fairway bunker, where his ball plugged into the wet sand. It took him two strokes to get out of the bunker and another to get to the green; only by sinking a lengthy putt was he able to card a double-bogie six on the hole. Vardon and Ouimet both parred the hole and Ray found himself four strokes behind Ouimet and three behind Vardon with three holes to go. Ray followed up his debacle on 15 by carelessly three-putting the 16th green. Vardon and Quimet carded pars on the hole and the tournament became a two-man affair with Vardon, the five-time winner of the British Open, trailing the hometown amateur by only a stroke with two holes to go.

Vardon elected to gamble with his tee shot on the 360-yard, dogleg-left 17th hole. Trying to cut the dogleg, he hooked his drive into a fairway bunker. He didn't have a shot to the green from his lie in the bunker and had to pitch out onto the fairway. He managed to hit the green with his third shot, but it took him two putts to get down. Ouimet, who could see his house from the 17th tee box, hit his drive on 17 down the middle of the fairway and followed it up by hitting a mashie to within 18 feet of the cup. When he sank the 18-footer, his lead over Vardon grew to three strokes with but one hole remaining.

Determined not to give Vardon any room, Ouimet hit his tee shot on the tough par-four 18th hole in the fairway with enough distance to give himself a realistic chance of reaching the green with his second shot, which he did. His two-putt par made Vardon's six on the hole meaningless, as was Ray's birdie three. What would come to be known as the most significant tournament in the history of American golf had come to an end. The local lad had defeated the great Harry Vardon by five strokes and Ray by six. He had also become the first amateur and the second American-born player to win the US Open.

The huge gallery had endured wet grounds and cold drizzle for over four hours to watch their native son defeat the best of the English professionals and it was now celebrating loudly. It quieted down long enough to listen to their young champion when he was presented with the winner's cup by the USGA secretary.

"I am as much surprised and pleased as anyone here," Ouimet said, after accepting the cup. "Naturally, it always was my hope to win out. I simply tried my best to keep this cup from going to our friends across the water. I am very glad to have been the agency for keeping the cup in America."[1]

More than any other single event, Ouimet's historic victory over Vardon and Ray in the 1913 US Open democratized golf in the United States and led to its becoming a viable sport for ordinary Americans. The match later became the subject of a Walt Disney film entitled *The Greatest Game Ever Played*.

• 6 •

The Explosion of Golf
in the United States after 1913

*F*rancis Ouimet's incredible victory over Harry Vardon and Ted Ray in the 1913 US Open struck a chord with the American public and initiated a new era of golf in the United States. The sport had produced a champion that ordinary Americans could identify with—someone, like themselves, who had to work for a living and didn't belong to a snobbish golf club. Countless thousands of Americans who had previously considered golf a pastime of the wealthy became interested in the game and sought to take it up. Statistically, in 1913 there were 350,000 golfers in the United States. A decade later the number had grown to two million and there were more people playing golf in the United States than in the rest of the world combined.

In the years following Ouimet's victory, there was a widespread demand for golf courses that were open to the public. Local governments and private developers took notice of the demand and the number of public golf courses in the United States increased sharply during those years. Hundreds of publicly owned golf courses and privately owned daily-fee courses open to the public were built during this period. For the first time, there were golf courses for ordinary Americans to play on and they were no longer frozen out of the sport.

Thousands of athletically gifted Americans who in the past would not have considered playing golf, took up the game in the years following Ouimet's victory, and the quality of American tournament golf improved markedly. In 1924, a record 319 players signed up for the US Open, and the USGA had to implement sectional qualifying to whittle the number down to a starting field of 85. American tournament golfers surpassed their British counterparts during the 1920s and began their long domination of tournament golf, both professional and amateur.

By 1922, public golf had become so popular in the United States that the USGA created the US Amateur Public Links Championship to give public-course golfers a national championship of their own. However, the prestigious US Amateur remained open to golf-club members only and would remain so for another 57 years.

After his much-acclaimed victory over Vardon and Ray, Francis Ouimet received offers of endorsements and contracts that would have netted him thousands of dollars. Realizing that accepting money for these golf-related ventures would jeopardize his standing as an amateur golfer, he turned the offers down. He loved amateur golf and had no desire to play as a professional. Playing as an amateur, he followed up his 1913 US Open victory by winning the 1914 US Amateur at Ekwanok Country Club in Manchester, Vermont, defeating Jerry Travers 6 and 5 in the finals. Later that year, the members of the small golf club he had joined as a junior member in 1910 paid for his trip to England so he could play in the British Amateur. Unfortunately, he lost in the second round of the British Amateur to a golfer of little repute, after which he traveled to France, where he won the French Amateur Championship. He then returned to Brookline and resumed his job as a sporting goods salesman.

In 1916, Ouimet gave up his job and opened a sporting goods store of his own. Shortly after the store opened, the USGA, in one of its most controversial and unpopular acts, revoked Ouimet's amateur status and barred him from playing in USGA-sponsored amateur golf tournaments. The USGA determined that Ouimet was using his golfing popularity to enhance his sporting goods business and was therefore making money from playing golf, which, in their view, made him a professional golfer. Under the USGA's definition of professional golf at that time, any person engaged in a business that was in any way related to the game of golf was considered a professional golfer. Even caddies over the age of 16 were considered professional golfers and were barred from playing in amateur golf tournaments because they made money from the game of golf.

The USGA's revocation of Ouimet's amateur status was very unpopular with the golfing public. One of the most outspoken critics of the USGA's action was Walter Travis, the Grand Old Man of Golf. In a column in the *American Golfer*, he lambasted the USGA as not being representative of the country's golfers and for its intense conservatism. In 1917, Ouimet enlisted in the US Army for service in World War I, during which he served admirably and rose to the rank of lieutenant. After the war, the USGA quietly reinstated his amateur status.

The first great American-born professional golfer was Walter Hagen. He was born to parents of German ancestry in Rochester, New York, on

December 21, 1892. His father worked as a millwright and blacksmith in the Rochester railroad yards and had no interest in golf. To help his father support his family, young Walter started working as a caddie at the Country Club of Rochester at an early age, earning 10 cents a round with an occasional nickel tip. While working as a caddie, he developed a fondness for the game. Using the club's facilities during off-peak hours, he improved his golfing skills to the point where, during his mid-teens, he was hired by the club as an assistant pro.

Hagen made his debut as a professional tournament golfer at age 19 in the 1912 Canadian Open, where he played well and finished a respectable eleventh. In 1913, he played in the historic US Open at the Country Club in Brookline, Massachusetts, and finished tied for fourth place. At Brookline, he was treated poorly by the British professionals. "They pushed me off the tee and told me I couldn't practice until they were through," he complained.

Athletically gifted, young Hagen was also a talented baseball player (pitcher and shortstop) and for a couple of years couldn't decide whether to pursue a career in professional baseball or professional golf. When the editor of a Rochester newspaper offered to cover his expenses in August 1914 to play in the US Open, he canceled a baseball tryout with the Philadelphia Phillies and went to Midlothian Country Club in suburban Chicago.

At Midlothian, he qualified with a 152 and then birdied four of the last five holes and set a course record with a 68 in the first round. In the second round, played in the afternoon of the first day, he shot a 74 to post a 142 for the day and take a three-stroke lead over amateur Frances Ouimet, the defending champion. The next day, he shot a 75 in the morning round and a 73 in the afternoon round and finished the tournament at 290, a score that tied the US Open 72-hole record and earned him a one-stroke victory over Chick Evans, a 24-year-old amateur from Chicago, who, two years later, would become the first player to win both the US Open and the US Amateur in the same year.

A cocky, dashing man-about-town, Walter Hagen was a perfect fit for the Roaring Twenties and just what professional golf needed at that time. Known for his exquisite golfing attire, he spurned the traditional tweeds for tailored clothing in bright colors and expensive fabrics. He was attracted to the bright lights, the good times, and the ladies. He didn't want to be a millionaire, he often said, he just wanted to live like one.

What Walter Hagen didn't like was the status of professional golfers in the golfing establishment. In most golf clubs in the United States at that time, professional golfers were looked upon as servants or hired help by club members, a practice that had been followed by golf-club members in Britain for centuries. Most of the early professional golfers in the United States were

Walter Hagen. Sir Walter was the first great American-born professional golfer.
Library of Congress

Scottish immigrants who were hired by golf clubs to lay out golf courses, repair golf clubs, and give golf lessons to club members. They were treated as servants and employees and were not allowed to enter the clubhouses of the clubs where they worked through the front door. In both the United States and Britain, it was common for a club hosting a golf tournament to deny professional golfers playing in the tournament the use of their dressing room and clubhouse facilities during the tournament.

The low status of professional golfers at that time seems strange to us now, given the popularity of professional golf and the status of professional golfers today, but that's the way it was when Walter Hagen arrived. Called "Sir Walter" by sportswriters, the cocky pro from Rochester had no intention of using the servants' entrance. When he was not allowed to use the club's dressing room during the 1920 British Open at Deal in England, he rented a Pierce-Arrow automobile to use as his personal dressing room and parked it in the club's driveway. On another occasion, he refused to enter the clubhouse to claim his trophy after winning a tournament because he had earlier been denied admission. During the 1920 US Open at the Inverness Club in Toledo, Ohio, he and several other professionals purchased a large grandfather clock and donated it to the club in appreciation for the use of their clubhouse facilities during the tournament.

Sir Walter was popular with the golfing public and attracted large crowds at golfing events. He was in great demand for golf exhibitions and actually made more money at exhibitions than he did in tournament golf. He was the first professional golfer to endorse golf clubs and was paid handsomely for doing so. In 1919, he became the first touring professional not affiliated with a golf club. He did much to improve the popularity and status of professional golf.

Walter Hagen's efforts to improve the status of professional golfers were aided by his incredible golfing talents—he was one of the greatest ever. In 1919, he won the US Open for the second time, in 1921 he became the first American-born winner of the PGA Championship, and in 1922 he became the first American-born winner of the British Open.

During his 28 years in professional golf, Hagen won the British Open four times, the PGA Championship a record-tying five times, and the US Open twice. The Masters did not exist until 1934, when he was in his forties and well past his prime, so he did not have a realistic chance of posting a career Grand Slam. However, his 11 modern majors are the third-most ever—exceeded only by Jack Nicklaus with 18 and Tiger Woods with 14. He won the Western Open five times before the Masters came into existence and the Western Open was considered by many to be a major championship.

It can be argued, therefore, that Sir Walter actually has 16 major champion-ships to his credit. When he died in 1969, Arnold Palmer was a pallbearer at his funeral.

Convinced that the club-dominated, amateur-golf-oriented USGA was not serving their interests, Walter Hagen and several other professional golfers met in New York City on February 1, 1916, to look for answers. The meeting was arranged by Rodman Wanamaker, the owner of Wanamaker Department Stores. The meeting produced the Professional Golfers Associa-tion of America (the PGA of America). The founding purposes of the PGA of America were to promote the game and business of golf, set standards for golf professionals, match golf professionals with job openings at golf clubs, give golf professionals a say in the selection of sites for their golf tournaments, and create and manage a golf tournament sponsored by the organization. From the beginning, however, there was a conflict within the organization between the touring professionals and the club professionals over the organi-zation's priorities and the allocation of its revenues.

In 1916 the PGA of America organized and sponsored the first PGA Championship, which was held in match play in the autumn of that year at the Siwanoy Country Club in Bronxville, New York, a few miles north of New York City. The winner was Jim Barnes, an English professional, who collected $500 and was awarded a handsome trophy donated by Rodman Wanamaker and bearing his name. The tournament was not held in 1917 and 1918 because of America's involvement in World War I, but it was resumed in 1919. From the outset, the tournament was considered a major profes-sional championship by sportswriters and professional golfers. It was held in match play until 1958, when it was converted to stroke play.

The other great professional golfer during the Roaring Twenties was Gene Sarazen. Named Eugenio Saraceni at birth, he was born on February 27, 1902, in Harrison, New York, about twenty miles north of New York City. His parents were Sicilian immigrants who knew nothing about golf ex-cept that it provided a way for their young son to help put bread on the family table. At age 10, young Saraceni started working as a caddie at the nearby Larchmont Country Club, earning nickels and dimes for carrying golf clubs. He later caddied at several other golf clubs in the area and while doing so de-veloped his own considerable golfing talents. He changed his name to Gene Sarazen when he was a teenager competing in local golf tournaments because he thought it sounded more American and looked better in the newspapers.

During World War I, his family moved to Bridgeport, Connecticut, where, in his middle teens, he dropped out of school and worked in a muni-tions factory. After the war he worked briefly at a couple of local golf courses before being hired as an assistant club pro at a country club in Fort Wayne,

Indiana. At the urging of club members in Fort Wayne, he signed up for the 1920 US Open at the Inverness Club in Toledo, Ohio. He qualified for the event but fared poorly, finishing about 20 strokes behind Englishman Ted Ray, who redeemed himself from his failures in the 1913 US Open by winning the event at age 43, which made him the oldest golfer ever to win the US Open. One stroke behind Ray was 50-year-old Harry Vardon. Ray's age record lasted until 1990, when Hale Irwin won his third US Open Championship at age 45.

In 1921, Sarazen again qualified for the US Open and again he fared poorly, finishing 22 strokes behind Englishman Jim Barnes, the tournament winner. After the tournament he was hired as a club pro by the Highland Country Club near Pittsburgh, Pennsylvania. In 1922, at age 20, he again qualified for the US Open. This time his ship came in, as he shot a final round 68 and came from four strokes behind after the third round to edge amateur Bobby Jones by a stroke for the championship. Five weeks later, he established himself as a force in professional golf by winning the PGA Championship at Oakmont Country Club, near Pittsburgh. He won the PGA Championship again the following year, defeating Walter Hagen, one-up in the finals.

Called "the Squire" by sportswriters, the smooth-swinging, five-foot-five-inch, 160-pound former caddie always wore plus fours (knickers) when competing, as they were the fashion when he began playing professional golf. He later became the first golfer to achieve a career Grand Slam by winning each of the four modern professional majors at least once during his career. He won the US Open twice, the PGA Championship three times, and the Masters and the British Open once apiece.

In 1932 while practicing for the British Open, he invented the sand wedge by soldering a piece of lead to the back of the blade of a pitching wedge to create a flange that was wide enough so that when soled the flange would set lower than the leading edge of the clubface. Such a configuration enabled him to strike the sand a couple of inches behind the ball and blast it out of the sand, instead of chipping it out with a niblick or pitching wedge, as had always been the custom. He unveiled his weapon at the 1932 British Open, which he won with a record low 72-hole score of 283. "I was trying to make myself a club that would drive the ball up as I drove the club head down," he explained at the time.[1] He called his new club a sand iron. It was later approved by both the USGA and the R&A and today is one of the most important clubs in the bags of most golfers.

The Squire's greatest moment in golf came in the final round of the 1935 Masters. After 14 holes in the final round, he trailed Craig Wood, the leader, by three strokes. On the par-five 15th hole, he hit a decently long

Gene Sarazen. The first player to win all four of the modern majors.
Library of Congress

drive that left him 235 yards from the hole. For his second shot he chose a three-wood and struck it well. He and his African American caddy, Thor "Stovepipe" Norwall, watched the ball land short of the green, role onto the green, and then disappear into the hole for a double-eagle two that made up the three strokes he needed to catch Wood. He finished the round tied with Wood and defeated him by five strokes in a 36-hole playoff the next day. Called "the Shot Heard around the World" by the sportswriters at the time, it remains one of the most famous shots in the long history of golf. In 1955, the Sarazen Bridge at the Augusta National golf course was named to commemorate the twentieth anniversary of the event.

The incredible growth of golf in the United States during the 1920s created an ever-increasing demand for golf clubs, all of which needed hickory for their shafts. In the mid-1920s, club makers began complaining of a shortage of good hickory and started looking for a replacement. An obvious choice was steel. The first steel-shafted golf clubs had been produced in England in the 1890s, but at that time the technology in tubular steel manufacturing had not reached the point where steel shafts could be manufactured at a competitive price. Because there was still plenty of hickory, the manufacture of steel-shafted clubs was not pursued at that time. In 1910, American Arthur Knight was granted a patent on the seamed, tubular golf club shaft and a few American companies began manufacturing and marketing them, even though they had not been approved by the USGA and could not be used in USGA-sanctioned events. By the mid-1920s, steel-shafted clubs had become so popular with recreational golfers in the United States that the USGA had to decide whether to approve them.

Aware of the complaints of club makers about the shortage of good hickory and of the widespread use of steel-shafted clubs by recreational golfers, in 1924 the USGA approved the use of steel-shafted golf clubs in USGA-sanctioned events. Five years later, the R&A also approved them. By then, American golfers were using steel-shafted clubs in big numbers.

Steel-shafted clubs had several advantages over their hickory-shafted predecessors. First of all, because steel-shafted clubs could be manufactured and assembled in great numbers in factories, they were less expensive than hickory-shafted clubs, which were assembled one at a time by craftsmen. In addition, steel shafts were stronger and more durable than hickory shafts and were less likely to snap or crack. The clincher for steel-shafted clubs was the extra 15 yards the average golfer got off the tee by using them.

The preference of steel-shafted clubs was not unanimous, however. Some golfers preferred the feel and control they got with the flexible hickory shafts and continued using them for several years. Their dislike of steel shafts began to disappear in 1931 when Billy Burke won the US Open using steel-shafted clubs. By the mid-1930s, steel-shafted golf clubs had largely replaced their hickory-shafted predecessors. In 1936 Johnny Fischer became the last player to win a national championship using hickory-shafted clubs when he won the US Amateur.

The advent of steel-shafted clubs brought about changes in how and by whom golf clubs were made. Hickory shafts were created one at a time from tree parts by craftsmen, who attached the club head and grips and assembled clubs one at a time by hand. Steel shafts, on the other hand, were manufactured in factories and steel-shafted clubs were mass-produced by large sporting goods companies like Wilson, Spalding, and MacGregor.

The use of steel shafts resulted in some rather drastic changes in the number of clubs that golfers carried with them on the course. It didn't take golfers long to realize that the rigid steel shafts could not be made to work like the flexible hickory shafts they were used to. The rigidity of steel shafts made it necessary for golfers to use more clubs to produce the same results they had been getting with their hickory-shafted clubs. A hickory-shafted mashie, for example, could be swung and controlled in such a manner as to produce the same results as a steel-shafted four, five, or six iron.

Prior to the advent of steel-shafted clubs, it was common for golfers to carry only five or six hickory-shafted clubs. Because there weren't many of them and they didn't weigh much, hickory-shafted clubs were often carried by golfers in their hands without a bag. When steel-shafted clubs arrived, golfers were known to carry two dozen or more clubs in their bags. Lawson Little claimed to have carried 31 clubs in his bag when he won back-to-back US Amateur Championships in 1934 and 1935. The number of clubs was obviously getting out of hand, and in 1938 the USGA imposed a limit of 14 on the number of clubs a player could carry in a USGA-sanctioned event. After much discussion, the R&A imposed a similar limit in 1939.

Shortly after the USGA approved the use of steel-shafted clubs in 1924, manufacturers started producing matched sets of numbered clubs with graduated lofts. Because manufacturers didn't want to alienate traditional golfers, who were used to having names for their clubs, the early sets of numbered clubs had the traditional name of each iron and wood stamped on the club head. Over time, however, golfers got used to the idea of numbered clubs and the practice of identifying golf clubs by their names was discontinued. With the exception of wedges, drivers, putters, and rescue clubs, most golfers today identify golf clubs only by their number and the type of club (e.g., three wood, five iron, etc.).

The advent of matched sets of numbered clubs with graduated lofts changed the club-acquisition practices of golfers. For hundreds of years golfers had acquired their clubs, often one at a time, from craftsmen on the basis of what they needed and what worked for them. When matched sets of numbered clubs with graduated lofts came along, golfers began acquiring all or most of their clubs at the same time from commercial vendors. It wasn't long before golf-club craftsmen were limited to club repair.

The third great golfer of the Roaring Twenties was Bobby Jones. The son of an Atlanta attorney, Bobby Jones was born in Atlanta, Georgia, on March 17,

1902. He battled health issues as a boy and golf was prescribed as an exercise to strengthen his endurance. Encouraged by his father, who was a member of the Atlanta Athletic Club's East Lake Golf Club, he started playing golf at his father's club as a boy and was taught by instructors at the club. A prodigy, he made it to the quarterfinals of the US Amateur at age 14. He was educated at Georgia Tech, Harvard, and the Emory University Law School, and joined his father's law firm after graduating from law school. Although he became one of the best and most famous golfers in the world, he disliked professional golf and remained an amateur throughout his career.

Bobby Jones was the best and most famous amateur golfer in the history of American golf. Not a big man at five feet, ten inches, and 165 pounds, it was the rhythm and perfection of his swing that set him apart. To veteran observers, his swing was reminiscent of that of the great Harry Vardon. Ironically, in 1920 when he qualified for his first US Open at age 18, he was paired with 50-year-old Harry Vardon in the first two rounds.

In 1923, Jones won his first US Open Championship at age 21. During his ten-year career in tournament golf, he won the US Open four times, the British Open three times, the US Amateur five times, and the British Amateur once. In 1926, after becoming the second American to win the British Open, his popularity was such that he was given a ticker-tape parade in New York City when he returned from England. It was an honor that had not been bestowed upon professional golfer Walter Hagen when he became the first American to win the event in 1922.

Jones's greatest year in tournament golf came in 1930, when he won what sportswriters at the time called the "Grand Slam of Golf" by winning the US Open, the US Amateur, the British Open, and the British Amateur. At that time, these tournaments were thought to constitute the four "major" golf tournaments, and Jones is the only golfer ever to have won all four of them in the same year. In hindsight, it is hard to see how the amateur tournaments could have been deemed major tournaments when their entrants were limited to golf-club members and the best golfers in the world (the professionals) weren't allowed to play in them.

The first leg of Jones's Grand Slam was the British Amateur, a tournament he had never won. The match-play event was held on the Old Course at St. Andrews, a course with which he had had a love-hate relationship since 1921, when, after shooting a 46 on the front nine and taking a double-bogie six on the 10th hole in the third round of the British Open, he had disqualified himself by tearing up his scorecard and walking off the course.

In 1930, however, his relationship with the Old Course was nothing but love as he started the first round by sinking an 18-foot putt to win the first

Bobby Jones, the greatest and most acclaimed amateur golfer ever.
Library of Congress

hole and holing a 150-yard approach shot to win the fourth hole. His fourth-round match against Englishman Cyril Tolley, the defending champion, went to an extra hole, which Jones won by laying a stymie on Tolley. (He putted his ball to a spot more than six inches from Tolley's ball that blocked the path to the hole of Tolley's short, match-tying putt.) In the semifinals, he was one hole down to American George Voigt with two holes to go when he sank an 18-footer to win the 17th hole and then watched Voigt miss a six-footer to lose the 18th hole and the match. In the finals, he defeated Englishman Roger Wethered 7 and 6. In that match, only a missed two-foot putt on the 17th green kept Jones from becoming the first golfer in the long history of the Old Course to complete a round in tournament play with nothing higher than a four on his scorecard.

The second leg of Jones's Grand Slam was the British Open, which was held in mid-June at Royal Liverpool in Hoylake, England. He made himself a three-time winner of the event by coming back from a one-stroke deficit after 54 holes to claim a two-stroke victory over Scotsman Macdonald Smith and American Leo Diegel. When he returned to the United States on July 2

Bobby Jones at his ticker-tape parade in New York City in 1930.
Library of Congress

as the first American golfer to have won both the British Open and the British Amateur in the same year, he was given his second ticker-tape parade in New York City.

The third leg of Jones's Grand Slam was the US Open, which was held in mid-July at Interlachen Country Club in Hopkins, Minnesota. Trailing by two strokes after the second round, he shot a 68 in the third round to take a four-stroke lead into the final round and then held on to win the event by two strokes over Macdonald Smith. The final leg of his Grand Slam was the US Amateur at Merion Cricket Club in Ardmore, Pennsylvania, a match-play event he had won four times in the past six years. His domination of the event continued as he won all of his matches without difficulty, including a 6 and 5 victory in the semifinals and an 8 and 7 triumph in the finals.

In August 1930, shortly after winning his much-acclaimed Grand Slam, 28-year-old Bobby Jones stunned the golfing world by announcing his retirement from tournament golf. He wanted to devote more time to his law practice, he explained at the time. However, there were reports that early in the year, prior to the British Amateur, Jones, or someone on his behalf, had placed a bet on himself to win the Grand Slam with a British bookmaker at odds of 50 to 1 and that he had recently collected $60,000 on the wager. Such a happening, if reported to the USGA, would undoubtedly cost him his amateur standing.

Jones was also aware that the acclaim and popularity he had achieved in winning the Grand Slam could bring him a small fortune in endorsements and contracts. He knew, however, that accepting money from these sources would cost him his amateur standing. If the USGA had revoked the amateur standing of Francis Ouimet in 1916 for making a few dollars in his sporting goods business, it would surely have to revoke Jones's amateur standing, given the hundreds of thousands of dollars he stood to make on the proposed endorsements and contracts.

In essence, then, Jones had three options: He could forgo the endorsement and contract money that he knew was there for the taking and continue playing tournament golf as an amateur, he could take the contract and endorsement money and continue playing tournament golf as a professional, or he could take the contract and endorsement money and retire from tournament golf.

A product of golf clubs whose members did not have a high regard for professional golfers, he could not very well become one at this stage of his career. Realistically then, if he wanted to take the endorsement and contract money he would have to retire from tournament golf. If the reports of his $60,000 wager collection were true, taking that money might also have influenced his decision to retire, as he was not a wealthy man and had reportedly looked to his father for financial assistance from time to time during his career in tournament golf.

After retiring from tournament golf, Jones cashed in on his status as a celebrity golfer. He signed a contract with Warner Brothers to make a series of 18 instructional golf films for which he was reportedly paid a total of $180,000. That was a lot of money in the Depression years of the 1930s. He also signed a contract with the A. G. Spalding Company to design and develop a set of steel-shafted Bobby Jones golf clubs. The clubs were well designed and well received by the golfing public and Jones profited handsomely from them for the rest of his life. Spaulding ultimately sold over two million sets of his golf clubs.

After retiring from tournament golf, Jones became seriously interested in building a golf course of his own and began looking for a parcel of land upon which to build it. Clifford Roberts, a New York investment broker and a friend of Jones, knew of Jones's interest in obtaining land for his golf course. In 1930, Roberts became aware of a 365-acre indigo plantation in Augusta, Georgia, that the owner was seeking to sell. Roberts informed Jones of the availability of the Augusta property and a few months later Jones purchased it for $70,000.

With financial assistance from Roberts, Jones set out to design and build a golf course on the Augusta property. To assist him in designing the course, he hired Alister MacKenzie, a British surgeon turned golf course architect. MacKenzie had designed great golf courses all over the world, including Royal Melbourne in Australia and Cypress Point, a spectacular course on the Monterey Peninsula in California that Jones much admired. Born in England of Scottish parents, MacKenzie was thought to be the best British golf-course architect since Old Tom Morris.

Employing a design that was heavily influenced by the Old Course at St. Andrews, Jones and MacKenzie designed and built Jones's golf course on the Augusta property. While to the casual observer the newly created course in Augusta looked nothing like the ancient, windswept links course on St. Andrews Bay in Scotland, there were important similarities. Both courses had long, open fairways with little rough; large, fast greens; and a few strategically placed bunkers and hazards.

Jones called his course the Augusta National and it opened for play in January 1933. Later that year, Jones and Roberts founded the Augusta National Golf Club. Membership in the club was by invitation only and, under policies established by Roberts and Jones, the club would have no African American or women members; African Americans and women would not be invited to play in club tournaments; and all caddies at the club would be African American. Roberts later famously said, "As long as I am alive, golfers will be white and caddies will be black."[2]

After being turned down by the USGA in their attempt to have a US Open Championship held on their course in the early spring when the course was at its finest, Jones and Roberts set about scheduling a tournament of their own. They settled on an invitational tournament to be held annually in the early spring that they initially called the Augusta National Invitational. Their inaugural tournament was held on March 22–25, 1934. It was won by Horton Smith, who shot a 284 in the 72-hole, stroke-play event. Alister MacKenzie, who called the Augusta National his greatest creation, died in January 1934, two months prior to the inaugural event on the course.

Because of the quality and beauty of the Augusta National golf course and because it was sponsored by Bobby Jones, the tournament was an immediate success. From the beginning, it attracted the top golfers and was considered a major tournament by sportswriters and golfers. In 1938, the tournament was renamed "the Masters."

During World War II, Jones voluntarily enlisted in the US Army at age 39, where he served as an intelligence officer in the Army Air Corps. His superiors wanted him to raise money for the war effort by giving golfing exhibitions in the United States, but he insisted on serving in combat and was sent to the European theater. While in England, he made the acquaintance of General Dwight Eisenhower, whose affection for the game of golf was well known. In 1944, he participated in the Normandy invasion and spent two months with a front-line division interviewing German prisoners of war. He was discharged from the army after the war as a lieutenant colonel and returned to his Atlanta law practice.

Unfortunately, Bobby Jones's final years were disease-ridden and painful. In July 1956, after not feeling well for some time, he was diagnosed with syringomyelia, a chronic degenerative disease of the spinal cord causing sensory disturbances, muscle atrophy, and paralysis. He lived with the disease for 15 years until his death in December 1971 at age 69. His friend and benefactor Clifford Roberts committed suicide in 1979 by shooting himself in the head on the 13th green of his beloved Augusta National golf course.

During the Roaring Twenties, American golfers dominated tournament golf in both the United States and Britain. During the nine-year period ending in 1930, American golfers won the British Open eight times, the US Open seven times, the PGA Championship eight times, and the US Amateur all nine times. In addition, American teams won all six Walker Cup matches held during that period, mostly by lopsided scores. Only in the British Amateur did British golfers prevail, winning seven of the nine events.

Fueled by a stock market that many thought would never stop rising, American prosperity grew in record proportions during the Roaring Twenties. For the first time, millions of Americans had both disposable income and leisure time, a significant portion of which was devoted to golf. The number of Americans playing golf tripled during the decade, reaching five million in 1929. The number of golf clubs and golf courses also increased significantly. By 1929, Americans were playing golf on more than 4,500 golf courses. Late in the decade, golfers in Portland, Oregon, and Seattle, Washington, each had twenty courses to choose from; Miami, Florida, was adding a new golf course every year; and nearly a hundred small towns in Kansas had golf courses.

Some of our greatest golf courses were built during the Roaring Twenties. Pine Valley, George Crump's masterpiece in Clementon, New Jersey, opened in 1922; Cypress Point, Alister MacKenzie's creation on California's Monterey Peninsula, opened in 1928; Cherry Hills in Denver, Colorado, opened in 1922; Seminole in North Palm Beach, Florida, opened in 1929; Pinehurst No. 2, Donald Ross's masterpiece in Pinehurst, North Carolina, opened in 1925; the West Course at Winged Foot in Mamaroneck, New York, an A. W. Tillinghast creation, opened in 1923; the Lakeside Course at Olympic in San Francisco opened in 1924; and the Lower Course at Baltusrol in Springfield, New Jersey, another A. W. Tillinghast creation, opened in 1922. The incredible Pebble Beach Golf Links on the Monterey Peninsula in California opened in 1919, just a few months prior to the start of the Roaring Twenties.

Unfortunately, the phenomenal growth of golf in the United States came to a screeching halt on Tuesday, October 29, 1929, when the American stock market crashed, setting the stage for the Great Depression, which began in 1930 and lasted for a decade. While the Depression would put golf on the back burner for most Americans, the roots of golf in America were strong and in time the gift of the Scots would recover and grow as never before in its adopted land.

• 7 •

Golf during the Depression and War Years

$\mathcal{D}$uring the Great Depression, golf and other expensive pastimes took a back seat in most American households to the tasks of putting bread on the table and keeping the wolf away from the door. Soup kitchens and hobo jungles replaced country clubs as the hangouts of thousands of formerly wealthy Americans. Over a million golfers abandoned the game during the Depression, and hundreds of golf clubs closed because members could no longer afford the expense of membership. The golf courses of many failed golf clubs were acquired at bargain prices by municipalities and converted to public courses. The WPA aided public golf by building nearly 100 public golf courses during the 1930s.

With Bobby Jones no longer competing, the 1931 US Amateur was a wide-open affair and the field was stacked with promising young amateur golfers from all over the country. Of the 32 who qualified at the Beverly Country Club in Chicago, one of the oldest was 38-year-old Francis Ouimet. Five times during the past 10 years, he had made it to the semifinals of the match-play event, only to be closed out in matches that more often than not weren't even close. He had not won the event since 1914 and, with most of the qualifiers nearly a generation his junior, he knew he was running out of time to have a realistic chance of winning his favorite tournament.

In the first round he defeated 22-year-old John Shields, 4 and 3. In the second round, he defeated 20-year-old Frank Connolly, 5 and 4. In the quarterfinals, he handily defeated 21-year-old Paul Jackson and moved to the semifinals, his nemesis in years past, where his opponent was 19-year-old Billy Howell. After the 18-hole morning round of the 36-hole match, Howell was one-up, but 14 holes later they were all square. On the 33rd hole, Ouimet sank a 15-footer to go one-up on his young opponent. Two holes later Ouimet sank a 20-footer to close out the match 2 and 1.

The 36-hole final match pitted Ouimet against 27-year-old Jack West-land. Ouimet's putter was hot in the early going and he was four-up after nine holes. He was five-up after 18 holes and closed out the match 6 and 5 on the 31st hole. It was the same margin by which he had closed out Jerry Travers in the finals of the 1914 US Amateur at Ekwanok, 17 years earlier. The man whose historic victory in the 1913 US Open had done much to make golf a viable sport in the United States was a champion once again.

The year 1931, it seemed, featured the graybeards in tournament golf, as 35-year-old, Scottish American Tommy Armour won the British Open at Carnoustie. He came from five strokes behind in the final round to defeat Argentina's Jose Jurado by a single stroke, as Carnoustie's renowned finishing holes destroyed Jurado and Macdonald Smith, Armour's closest competitors. Born and raised in nearby Edinburgh, educated at Edinburgh University, and playing with only one good eye and one good shoulder, Armour was a gallery favorite throughout the tournament. He had served in the British army during World War I and a mustard gas explosion had caused him to lose the sight in both of his eyes. The explosion also embedded several pieces of shrapnel in his left shoulder that surgeons were unable to extract. During his convalescence, he regained sight in his right eye and was able to resume playing golf, a sport he had taken up as a lad and was quite good at.

After winning the French Amateur in 1920, Armour immigrated to the United States, where he tied for fifth in the 1920 US Amateur. He became a naturalized citizen of the United States and competed in local amateur tournaments until 1924, when he turned professional at age 28 and joined the PGA Tour. In 1925, he won his first professional tournament, the Florida West Coast Open. Two years later, he found his stroke and won five PGA Tour events, including the US Open at Oakmont Country Club. He ultimately won 25 PGA Tour events and three majors during his 11-year professional career. His majors, in addition to the US Open in 1927, included the PGA Championship in 1930 and the British Open in 1931. He also wrote a widely read instructional book on golf and endorsed a popular set of golf clubs.

In 1922, Gene Sarazen, as an unknown 20-year-old, had stunned the golfing world by winning both the US Open and the PGA Championship. However, he had not won a major since winning his second PGA Championship in 1923. Although he had won 22 PGA Tour events during the ensuing nine years, he had not won a major in nearly a decade and in the early 1930s many in the golfing world were beginning to think of him as a washed-up one-year-wonder.

In 1932, after warming up by winning the Coral Gables Open in Florida, he traveled to England to play in the British Open at Prince's. Using his newly invented sand iron for the first time in a major tournament, he tore the field apart, finishing five strokes ahead of runner-up Macdonald Smith and setting a British Open 72-hole record by shooting a 283. Returning to the United States, he went to Long Island to tune up for the US Open that would be held during the last week in June at Fresh Meadows Country Club in Queens, New York.

While practicing at Fresh Meadows, he decided that he should play conservatively in the tournament. Playing conservatively, he shot a 74 in the first round, a 76 in the second round, and a 38 on the front nine of the third round. Trailing the tournament leader by five strokes and seeing that he was getting nowhere playing conservatively, on the 10th hole he reverted to his normal aggressive style of play. Playing aggressively and taking more chances, he shot a 32 on the back nine and closed to within a stroke of the leader. Continuing his aggressive play in the final round, he shot a 66 to win the event by three strokes over runners-up Bobby Cruickshank and Phil Perkins and complete what sportswriters at the time called the greatest final 27 holes in US Open history. His impressive wins that year in the British and US Opens gave notice to the golfing world that the Squire was still a premier player. His status was further enhanced when he won the PGA Championship in 1933 and the Masters in 1935, where his incredible double-eagle on the 15th hole in final round paved the way to victory and the completion of a career Grand Slam.

In 1933, Johnny Goodman became the last amateur to win the US Open when he defeated Ralph Guldahl by a stroke to win the event at the North Shore Golf Club in Glenview, Illinois. The victory was especially satisfying to Goodman because in 1932 he had not been selected to play on the ten-man US Walker Cup team even though he was clearly one of the top amateur golfers in the country. His golfing credentials were impeccable. In the 1930 US Open, Bobby Jones, who won the event, was the only amateur with a better score than his and in 1932 he was the low amateur in the US Open and the runner-up in the US Amateur. However, he did not belong to a prestigious golf club and his supporters wondered openly whether his lack of social standing had caused the Walker Cup selectors to leave him off the team.

Johnny Goodman was born in December 1909 in the packinghouse district of South Omaha, Nebraska, the son of Lithuanian immigrants. His mother died while giving birth to her 13th child when Johnny was eleven years old and he was essentially orphaned at age 14 when his father abandoned the family. His first exposure to golf had come at age 12 when, while wandering along some railroad tracks with friends, he passed the Omaha Field Club, where, for the first time in his life, he saw people playing a game he later learned was golf. When told that he might be able to make some money by carrying bags for golfers, he went back to the Field Club and applied for a job. He was hired by the club and worked as a caddie for the next four years. He learned to play the game while working at the club, became quite good at it, and three years later won the Omaha Caddie's Championship.

On the night he graduated from high school in 1928, he and a couple of friends set out in an old car for the Broadmoor Golf Club in Colorado Springs, Colorado, where the Trans-Mississippi Amateur Golf Championship was to be played. He signed up for the tournament, scraped together enough money to pay the entry fee, and unbelievably won the event. When word of his victory reached South Omaha, the city declared a holiday and held a parade in his honor.

A year later, a friend at an Omaha packinghouse arranged for him to travel to California as a drover in a cattle car so he could play in the 1929 US Amateur at Pebble Beach. Although he did not win the event (he lost to Lawson Little in the second round), he raised a lot of eyebrows by defeating Bobby Jones in the first round. It was Jones's only loss in the US Amateur during the four-year period beginning in 1927 and ending in 1930.

Goodman's victory in the 1933 US Open convinced the Walker Cup selectors to include him on the team. He was selected to the Walker Cup team again in 1934, 1936, and 1938 and won the US Amateur in 1937. He remained an amateur throughout his career in tournament golf and supported himself and his family by selling insurance.

Lawson Little was a bullnecked slugger out of Stanford who looked more like a linebacker than a golfer. Born in Newport, Rhode Island, in 1910, he spent most of his younger years in the San Francisco area, where his father was a senior naval officer. When he graduated from Stanford in 1934 he was known as one of the best match-play golfers in the world. He enhanced that reputation by winning both the US Amateur and the British Amateur in 1934 and then winning both events again in 1935. To this day, he remains the only player ever to win both amateur championships in the same year more than once. His 14 and 13 victory in the finals of the 1934 British Amateur is still the record for a final-round margin of victory in the event. For some reason he was not as good in stroke play and, after turning professional in 1936, he won only eight PGA Tour events during his twenty-year career. His only win in a professional major came in 1940, when he won the US Open in a playoff with Gene Sarazen.

During the Depression years of the 1930s, the purses of professional golf tournaments decreased significantly. The purse of the US Open dropped to $6,000 during the Depression years and the winner's share was $1,000. The purse and winner's share of the Masters and the PGA Championship were about the same and the winner's share of the British Open was 100 pounds.

In 1936, the leading money-winner on the PGA Tour was Horton Smith with $7,885 in official winnings. Gene Sarazen won $5,480 that year. Like everybody else, professional golfers were struggling to get by during the Depression.

The interest of American sports fans in professional golf fell off during the middle and late 1930s. One reason for the decline was what might be called a lack of star power during those years. There were no superstars that sports fans could follow every week and develop an interest in. Walter Hagen and Gene Sarazen, the superstars of the 1920s and early 1930s, were past their prime and no longer won regularly. Hagen had not won a major since the 1929 British Open and had won only three PGA Tour events since 1932. Sarazen's last victory in a major came in the 1935 Masters and he had won only three PGA Tour events since then. Players like Horton Smith, Craig Wood, and Harry Cooper, who had replaced Hagen and Sarazen as the leading professional golfers, were not of the same caliber and did not capture the interest of American sports fans.

More so than in most sports, professional golf needs superstars to survive. Sports fans follow sporting events primarily because of their interest in one or more of the participants in the events. In team sports, the participant of interest is normally the home team. In professional golf, however, there are no home teams and sports fans follow golfing events because of their interest in one or more of the players. In most cases, the player of interest is the player they have heard the most about and appears to be a cut above the other players—let's call him a superstar. Without a superstar, interest in professional golf tends to fall off, while interest in the game improves significantly when a superstar appears. Interest in the game improves even more if there is more than one superstar because of the rivalry between the players.

To become a superstar in professional golf, a player must win regularly on the PGA Tour and must be in contention just about every week. He or she must also do well in the majors and have a playing style that sports fans find exciting. In most cases, this means that the player must play aggressively and not cautiously wait for an opponent to make a mistake. A player's chances of superstardom are enhanced if he or she has a good power game and is long off the tee, as American sports fans like to see golf balls hit a long way.

Fortunately for professional golf, three men born within seven months of each other joined the PGA Tour in the late 1930s and, in time, would become the superstars that professional golf needed to sustain it during the Depression and war years and lead it to a postwar revival. These men were Byron Nelson, Ben Hogan, and Sam Snead.

The son of a Texas grain merchant, John Byron Nelson Jr. was born in February 1912 in Waxahachie, Texas. When he was 11, his parents moved to Fort Worth, where, at age 12, he became a caddy at the Glen Garden Golf and Country Club in Fort Worth. One of his fellow caddies at Glen Garden was a quiet, taciturn boy named Ben Hogan. Caddies were not permitted to play during business hours at Glen Garden, so young Nelson practiced after the club closed for the day, often putting a white handkerchief over the hole so he could see it in the fading daylight.

In 1927, the club sponsored a caddies' tournament in which Nelson got the best of his friend Hogan by a single stroke in a battle of 15-year-old caddies. In February 1928, Nelson turned 16 and lost his job as a caddy—the club had a rule that caddies had to be younger than 16 years of age. However, the club gave him a junior membership and allowed him to continue to use its facilities. His game continued to improve and he started playing in local amateur tournaments, where he acquitted himself quite well. In 1930, at age 18, he won his first significant tournament—the Southwest Amateur.

In 1932, at age 20, he turned professional and played in as many local tournaments as he could afford. Discouraged by his lack of success, he quit professional golf in 1933 and went to work for an oil man in Texarkana. Knowing that Nelson's heart was in golf, the oil man found him a job as a club pro at the Texarkana Country Club. In 1934, Nelson started playing tournament golf again and late in the year finished second to Craig Wood in the Galveston Open.

In 1935, he became an assistant club pro at Ridgewood Country Club in Ridgewood, New Jersey. Later that year, he won his first PGA Tour event, the New Jersey State Open. In 1936, he won the Metropolitan Open and in 1937 he established himself as a force in professional golf by coming from four strokes behind with seven holes to play to overtake Ralph Guldahl and win the Masters by two strokes.

After a disappointing season in 1938, in 1939 he won four PGA Tour events, was the runner-up to Henry Picard in the PGA Championship, and put his name on the golf map for good by winning the US Open at the Philadelphia Country Club. In 1939, he won the Vardon Trophy, which had been established by the PGA of America in 1937. It was named after the great Harry Vardon, who died in 1937, and is awarded annually to the player on the PGA Tour with the lowest scoring average for the season.

Fifty-three years later, in 1980, the PGA Tour established another award called the Byron Nelson Award. It is awarded annually to the player on the PGA Tour with the lowest adjusted scoring average. The Byron Nelson Award has a slightly lower minimum round requirement than the Vardon Trophy, but in most years the same player wins both awards.

In 1940, Byron Nelson won three PGA Tour events, including the PGA Championship, where he defeated Sam Snead one-up in the finals. In 1941, he again won three PGA Tour events and was the runner-up in both the Masters and the PGA Championship. In 1942, he won three PGA Tour events and defeated his boyhood rival Ben Hogan in a playoff to win the Masters for the second time. The 30-year-old former caddy from Waxahachie had become the biggest name in professional golf.

William Ben Hogan was born on August 13, 1912, in Stephenville, Texas, the son of a blacksmith. In 1921, his family moved to Fort Worth. A year later, his father committed suicide with a gun in the family home. After the loss of their father, the three Hogan boys took jobs to help their mother, a seamstress, support her family. At age nine, Ben sold newspapers after school at a Fort Worth train station. At age 11, he took a job caddying at the Glen Garden Golf and Country Club in Fort Worth, where he met Byron Nelson. In the spring of 1928, when the club gave the popular Nelson a junior membership, it did not give one to Hogan. Consequently, when Hogan turned 16 in August and lost his caddying job because of his age, he had to find work elsewhere and play golf on a local public course.

In January 1930, he dropped out of high school during his senior year to pursue a career in professional golf. Small at five-foot, five-inches and 145 pounds, he struggled with a hook during his early years as a professional golfer. The first professional tournament he entered was the Texas Open in San Antonio in 1930, where he played poorly and won only a few dollars. To make a living during his early years in professional golf, he worked as a club pro at several small golf clubs in Texas. His goal, however, was to play on the PGA Tour, and he didn't keep any of the club pro jobs for long.

In 1932, while working as a low-paid club pro in Cleburne, Texas, he became reacquainted with Valerie Fox, a woman he had first met in high school in Fort Worth. After a three-year courtship, they were married in 1935. Throughout their courtship and during the early years of their marriage, Hogan continued his quest to make a living as a tournament pro. He went broke several times during this period, but with Valerie's support he continued his quest to become a successful tournament pro.

By 1938, after eight years in professional golf, he had improved his game to the point where he could join the PGA Tour. However, his financial struggles continued as he did not win his first PGA Tour event until his break-out year of 1940, when he won four PGA Tour events and was the tour's leading money-winner. He finished third in the US Open that year, behind Lawson Little and Gene Sarazen, and won his first Vardon Trophy.

In 1941, he won five PGA Tour events, tied for third in the US Open, won his second Vardon Trophy, and was again the leading money-winner on the tour. In 1942, he won six PGA Tour events, including the Hale America National Open Golf Tournament in Chicago, which was the USGA's replacement for the US Open during the war years. Held as a fund-raiser for war relief organizations, the Hale America raised $25,000, which the USGA donated to the USO and Navy Relief. Hogan received a $1,000 war bond for winning the event. He finished second to Byron Nelson in the Masters that year and was the leading money-winner on the tour for the third year in a row.

In March 1943, he was inducted into the army, where he served stateside in the Army Air Corps until his discharge in June 1945. After his discharge, he returned to the PGA Tour, where he won five events during what was left of the 1945 season. Since joining the PGA Tour in 1938, he had won 20 events, two Vardon Trophies, and had been the tour's leading money-winner three times. However, he had not won a major in 14 attempts and was thought by most to be a cut below Byron Nelson. At 33 years of age, he was afraid he might be running out of time to catch Nelson.

Samuel Jackson Snead was born on May 27, 1912, on a small farm near Hot Springs, Virginia. To get out of milking cows and plowing on his father's farm, he started caddying at the Homestead Golf Club in Hot Springs during his early teens. In high school, he played baseball, basketball, and football well enough to be offered athletic scholarships by a couple of colleges. He didn't start playing golf regularly until he was injured playing football and was told that playing golf might help his recovery. After graduating from high school in 1930, he took a job as a handyman at the Homestead Golf Club, where he refined his game and developed his incredible natural skills.

In 1934, he was hired as an assistant club pro by the Greenbrier Golf Club in White Sulphur Springs, West Virginia. Two years later, at age 24, he won his first significant tournament, the West Virginia Open, during which he shot a low round of 61. Later that year, he impressed the members of the Greenbrier Golf Club by outplaying Lawson Little, Johnny Goodman, and Billy Burke in an exhibition four-ball match at Greenbrier.

In 1937, Greenbrier sponsored him on a swing through the PGA Tour. Greenbrier's investment in the local player turned out to be a good one as the five-foot-eleven-inch, 185-pound natural athlete with one of the best golf swings anyone had ever seen won five events on the tour and was the runner-up to Ralph Guldahl in the US Open. One of the longest hitters on the tour, he won $8,800 in prize money in 1937 and was the tour's fourth-leading money-winner.

In 1938, his second year on the PGA Tour, he did even better, winning eight events and over $17,000 in prize money. He also won his first Vardon Trophy and got to the finals of the PGA Championship, where his putter deserted him and he lost 8 and 7 to Paul Runyon, a player he was outdriving by fifty yards a hole.

In 1939, he won three PGA Tour events and had the US Open in the palms of his hands. Playing on the Spring Mill course of the Philadelphia Country Club, he needed only a par on the par-five 72nd hole to win the event. Unfortunately, he wasn't aware of where he stood in the tournament and when a spectator told him he needed a birdie to win the event, he foolishly tried to cut a dogleg and hit his ball into some heavy rough. He then tried to hit a two-wood out of the rough and wound up with a terrible lie in a fairway bunker about 100 yards from the green. It took him two strokes to get out of the bunker and another to get to the green, where he three-putted and took a triple-bogie eight on the hole. He finished the event two strokes behind Byron Nelson, who won it.

Snead won three PGA Tour events in 1940 and six in 1941. In 1942, he won twice, including his first major—the PGA Championship at Seaview Country Club in Atlantic City, New Jersey, where he defeated Jim Turnesa, an army private on leave from nearby Fort Dix, 2 and 1 in the finals of the match-play event. Bothered by being jeered as a slacker during the tournament by a contingent of Turnesa's army buddies from Fort Dix, he enlisted in the navy a few days later. He served until September 1944, when he received an early discharge because of a back injury. The injury apparently wasn't too severe because he won two PGA Tour events shortly after being discharged.

Another player making waves on the PGA tour during the late 1930s was a big, broad-shouldered Texan named Ralph Guldahl. Born in Dallas, Texas, in November 1911, Guldahl joined the PGA Tour right out of high school and won his first event a year later at age 19. In the 1933 US Open, he missed a four-foot putt on the final hole and lost to Johnny Goodman by a stroke.

After disappointing seasons in 1934 and 1935, he quit the PGA Tour and worked as an automobile salesman for a few months. He rejoined the tour in 1936 and won the first of his three consecutive Western Opens. In 1937, he established himself as a player of note by winning the US Open at Oakland Hills Country Club in Birmingham, Michigan, with a record low 72-hole score of 281. In 1938, he became the last player to win the US Open wearing a necktie, and only the fourth player to win back-to-back US Opens, when he defeated Dick Metz by six strokes to win the US Open at Cherry Hills Country Club in Denver, Colorado. In 1939, he won his third major in three years by winning the Masters, where he defeated runner-up Sam Snead by a stroke.

The last of Guldahl's 16 wins on the tour came in the 1940 Milwaukee Open. Then, for reasons no one could understand, his game went south. Almost overnight he went from being one of the best players in the world to one who had a hard time breaking 80. Sam Snead and other friends on the tour tried to help him, he took movies of his swing, he practiced tirelessly, but nothing helped. He hadn't intentionally changed his swing and he hadn't changed his living habits (he didn't drink or smoke). He had just unaccountably lost his game. He quit the PGA Tour for good in 1941 and became a club pro. In 1961, he was hired as the club pro by the Braemar Country Club in Tarzana, California, where he worked as a golf instructor until his death in 1987. One of the members he instructed at Braemar was an eccentric billionaire named Howard Hughes.

In 1942, the PGA of America reduced the number of events on its tour to 24 because of the war. The USGA discontinued both the US Open and the US Amateur in 1942 and resumed them in 1946. The Masters was discontinued in 1943 and resumed in 1946, the PGA Championship was not held in 1943, and both the British Open and the British Amateur were discontinued in 1940 and resumed in 1946.

About 10 percent of the golf courses in the United States were closed at some point during the war years due to labor and equipment shortages. In the clubs and courses that remained open during the war years, shortages of labor, equipment, and supplies made it impossible for greenskeepers and golf-course superintendents to keep the fairways in prewar condition. Most courses compensated for the deterioration of their fairways by adopting a wartime version of "winter rules," whereby golfers could improve their lies in the fairway all year long.

Because the steel used in making golf clubs and the rubber used in making golf balls were needed for the war effort, in 1942 the US government banned the manufacture of golf clubs and golf balls for the duration of the war. Of particular concern to wartime golfers was the shortage of golf balls. Many clubs drained lakes and ponds to recover golf balls that had been hit into them. A golf club in Atlanta reported rescuing 16,000 golf balls from a lake it had drained. Although the recovered balls didn't play like new ones, wartime golfers were glad to get them because new golf balls were nowhere to be found.

Unlike Ben Hogan, Sam Snead, and most of tour regulars, Byron Nelson did not serve in the military during World War II. A blood disorder rendered him ineligible for military service. In 1943, professional golf took a back seat to the war effort as only three PGA Tour events and none of the majors were held. However, in 1944, with the war going our way, the PGA Tour was expanded to 22 events.

After failing to win a single event in 1943, Byron Nelson got back on track in 1944, winning seven tournaments and a record $35,000. In the PGA Championship, which was resumed in 1944, he missed three two-foot putts and lost one-up in the finals to little-known Bob Hamilton, a streaky, 28-year-old pro from Evansville, Indiana, who was playing in his first major. Hamilton won four PGA Tour events during his professional career and set a record in 1975 by shooting his age at age 59 in a tournament at the Hamilton Golf Club in Evansville.

In 1945 the PGA Tour was expanded to forty events and Byron Nelson picked up where he left off in 1944. The 1945 professional golf season actually began in December 1944 and Nelson started the season by winning the San Francisco Open in late December. After finishing second by a stroke to Sam Snead in the Los Angeles Open in January 1945, he won PGA Tour events in Phoenix, Corpus Christi, and New Orleans. After losing the Gulfport Open to Sam Snead in a playoff, he teamed with his friend Harold McSpaden to win the Miami International Four Ball. When the tour swung through the Carolinas in March, he won at Charlotte, Greensboro, and Durham. He wound up the winter tour by winning the Atlanta Open in April for his fifth consecutive victory and his eighth win of the season.

After taking a few weeks off, he traveled north to Montreal in June and won the Montreal Open, after which he traveled south to Philadelphia, where he won the Philadelphia Inquirer Open with a final round 63. The following week he won the Chicago Victory Open at Calumet Country Club in Chicago. The next PGA Tour event was the PGA Championship at Morraine Country Club in Dayton, Ohio, a match-play event wherein he played a total of 204 holes in 37 strokes under par. In the finals, he defeated former baseball player Sam Byrd, 4 and 3. Trivia experts will recognize Sam Byrd as the player who replaced an aging Babe Ruth defensively in the late innings for the New York Yankees.

Next up for Nelson was the Tam O'Shanter Open in Bloomfield, Michigan, a popular event on the tour because of its record $60,000 purse. The winner's share was $13,600, which was almost four times the winner's share of the major championships that year. With a record gallery of 105,000 looking on, Nelson shot an amazing 19-under-par 269 and won the event by eleven strokes over an aging Gene Sarazen and a recently discharged Ben Hogan, who tied for second place. During the first week in August, he went to Toronto for the Canadian Open, which he won by four strokes for his eleventh straight victory. His winning streak ended the following week at the Memphis Open, where amateur Freddy Haas, a 30-year-old insurance salesman, shot an 18-under-par 270 to win the event. It was the first time an amateur had won a PGA Tour event in nine years. Nelson shot a 276

Byron Nelson. His 11 consecutive wins and 19 tour wins in 1945 may never be equaled.
Library of Congress

and finished in fourth place. The following week he recovered and won the Supreme Open in Knoxville, Tennessee, by ten strokes.

Nelson later posted wins in the Esmeralda Open in Spokane and the Seattle Open, where he shot an incredible 29-under-par 259 to break the PGA Tour record for a 72-hole event by two strokes. The previous PGA Tour record of 261 had been set just two weeks earlier by Ben Hogan in Portland, Oregon. In fairness, it should be reported that Hogan's 261 was shot on a par-72 course, while Nelson's 259 was shot on a par-70 layout. Nelson's final win of the season came in the Fort Worth Open, which was held at the Glen Garden Golf and Country Club, where he and Hogan had caddied as teenagers.

In what has been called the greatest season ever by a professional golfer, Byron Nelson won 19 of the 35 PGA Tour events he played in and at one point won eleven in a row. He also finished second seven times, shot a PGA record low 18-hole score of 62 and a PGA record low 72-hole score of 259, and posted a PGA record low-scoring average of 68.33, a record that would last for fifty-five years. His official PGA winnings were $52,511, an amount that easily broke the previous record of $35,000, which he had set in 1944. For the second straight year, he was voted the Athlete of the Year by the sportswriters of the Associated Press, beating out Army football player and Heisman Trophy winner Doc Blanchard and Detroit Tiger pitcher Hal Newhouser for the honor.

Nelson's records of 19 PGA Tour wins in a season and eleven wins in a row have never been broken and probably never will be. The previous record for consecutive PGA Tour wins was four. Some critics have belittled his accomplishments, claiming that his competition was weak because most of the touring pros were in the military and did not play regularly on the PGA Tour. They also claim that his record low-scoring average was due in part to the wartime version of "winter rules" that had been adopted by many of the courses he played on. In Nelson's defense, it should be noted that the war ended on August 15 of that year and many of the tour regulars returned for at least a portion of the tour. Ben Hogan, for example, played in 18 PGA events that year and won five of them. Sam Snead, who was discharged from the US Navy in 1944, played in 26 PGA Tour events and won six of them. Snead had planned on playing a full schedule in 1945 until he broke his wrist playing softball in Hot Springs in June and had to sit out a good portion of the summer. Realistically, any advantage that Nelson may have gained by the imposition of the wartime version of "winter rules" was offset by the substandard condition of the fairways, greens, and bunkers on many of the courses he played on. In any event, his record performance created a lot of interest in professional golf, which once again had a superstar.

By late 1945, the shortages of labor, equipment, and supplies were about over and the popularity of both professional and recreational golf was at a ten-year high. According to industry sources, an estimated 70,000,000 rounds of golf were played by Americans in 1945, compared to the prewar total of 63,000,000 rounds played in 1941. By 1945, golf balls made with synthetic rubber had gotten enough play to prove their viability and the golf ball shortage had become a thing of the past. Many of the golf courses that had closed during the war reopened in 1945. However, a significant number of courses disappeared as land developers acquired them in anticipation of a postwar housing boom.

· 8 ·

The Revival of Golf after World War II

*1*946 was a good year for golf in the United States. Most of the clubs and courses that had closed during the war years reopened that year. Equally important, the production of golf balls and golf clubs was resumed and, spurred by a booming postwar economy, sales of both were brisk. With plenty of labor, equipment, and supplies now available, course maintenance returned to prewar standards and the wartime version of "winter rules" was dropped and golfers started "playing it as it lies" again. The number of recreational golfers surged in 1945 as returning servicemen flocked to the courses. A surprising number of servicemen had taken up golf during the war years through programs whereby golf clubs and balls were collected and given to servicemen by service organizations, enabling them to play on military golf courses or nearby civilian courses. Most public golf courses had let servicemen play for free during the war years.

With the war over, the PGA Tour returned to a full schedule of events in 1946. All of the majors were played and American players prevailed in all of them. Herman Keiser, back on the PGA Tour after spending thirty months at sea in the navy, won the Masters by a stroke over Ben Hogan, who missed forcing a playoff by three-putting the final green. Back from a three-year hitch in the army where he had waded ashore on Omaha Beach on D-day and earned two Purple Hearts in the Battle of the Bulge, Lloyd Mangrum won the US Open at Canterbury Golf Club in Cleveland in a playoff with Vic Ghezzi and Byron Nelson. Ben Hogan missed being included in the playoff when his five-footer on the final hole wouldn't drop. In the PGA Championship, played in match play at the Portland Golf Club in Oregon, Ben Hogan won his first major, defeating Porky Oliver 6 and 4 in the finals.

The event of the year in professional golf was the first British Open since 1939. Appropriately, it was played on Great Britain's greatest venue—the Old Course at St. Andrews. With Ben Hogan wrapped up in American tournaments and Byron Nelson taking some time off, only Sam Snead among the popular postwar American triumvirate made the trip to Scotland in early July to play in the British Open. This was the Slammer's first look at the cradle of golf and, like many other first-timers, at first sight he couldn't understand how such a flat, ordinary-looking course could have attained such a reputation. The aspect of the course that he found most appealing was the size and character of its greens. Putting was the weakest part of his game and, looking at the St. Andrews greens, he figured there was no way anybody was going to win the tournament with a putter on those huge, fast monsters.

Snead shot an opening round 71 and followed it up with another 71 in the second round. At the halfway mark, his 142 put him two strokes behind Henry Cotton, Britain's premier postwar player. On the 36-hole final day of the event, the dreaded St. Andrews wind appeared with gusts so hard that it blew balls resting on down-sloping greens clear off the green. Snead's 74 in the morning round was good enough to give him a share of the lead after 54 holes, tying him with Dai Rees from Wales, Bobby Locke from South Africa,

The historic home of the Royal and Ancient Golf Club of St. Andrews next to the 18th green on the Old Course.
© iStock / DEREKMcDOUGALL

and American Johnny Bulla. Henry Cotton couldn't handle the wind and shot himself out of contention early in the round.

Snead shot a 40 on the front nine of the final round. He handled the wind well but was hurt by a pair of short putts that wouldn't drop and a two-footer for a birdie that rimmed out. However, the wind got the best of Rees, Locke, and Bulla and they failed to take advantage of Snead's putting mishaps. Snead was playing a few holes behind the others and when he reached the tee box on the 17th hole, the infamous Road Hole, the others had finished and Snead knew he had only to play the last two holes in eleven strokes to win the event. Memories of his eight on the final hole of the 1939 US Open in Philadelphia must have entered his mind as he teed off on the 461-yard Road Hole. If such thoughts did enter his mind, they didn't bother him as his wind-aided drive missed the fairway bunkers and his four-iron to the green avoided the infamous Road Bunker and rolled onto the green, stopping close enough to the hole to enable him to get down in two. On the final hole, the Tom Morris Hole, his drive carried the famous Stone Bridge over Swilken Burn and landed in the fairway less than 100 yards from the green. His pitch to the green was true and his two-putt par put the finishing touches on his four-stroke victory over Johnny Bulla and Bobby Locke. He had conquered the Old Course at its fiercest and in so doing had won his first major since 1942.

In the United States, Byron Nelson, Ben Hogan, and Sam Snead were the players that fans flocking to the tournaments wanted to see. Hogan, Snead, and Nelson dominated the PGA Tour in 1946, winning 25 of the 45 events played that year. Hogan won 13 times, including the PGA Championship, while Snead and Nelson won six apiece. Hogan's 13 tour victories that year are still the second-most wins in a single season, exceeded only by Nelson's 19 wins in 1945.

In August, Byron Nelson shocked the golfing world by announcing his retirement from the PGA Tour. His great run in 1945 had taken a lot out of him. He had played in 35 PGA Tour events that year and another twenty during the first seven months of the 1946 season. He told friends that his nerves were frayed and his back ached. At 34, he decided he had had enough of the pressurized world of the PGA Tour and retired to his 1,500-acre ranch in Roanoke, Texas. His competitive golf would thereafter be limited to celebrity tournaments and special events like the Masters, where, as a previous winner, he was assured an invitation to play. He later became a highly respected golf commentator during the early years of televised golf and lent his name to a golf tournament—the Byron Nelson Championship in Houston.

With Nelson's retirement, professional golf lost its reigning superstar and it would now be up to Ben Hogan and Sam Snead to carry on their

Sam Snead. His 82 PGA Tour wins are the most ever.
Library of Congress

rivalry and keep professional golf on the American sports pages. With Byron Nelson retired and Sam Snead having an off year, only Ben Hogan, from the triumvirate that had dominated professional golf in 1946, played like a superstar in 1947. And even Hogan was not up to his 1946 standards, winning only seven PGA Tour events in 1947, down from his 13 wins of the previous year. Snead unaccountably went into a season-long slump in 1947 and did not win a single PGA Tour event that year.

In 1947, Sam Snead's place at the top of the leaderboard was taken over by Jimmy Demaret. A 37-year-old tour veteran from Houston, Demaret won six PGA Tour events that year, including his second Masters, which he won by two strokes over Frank Stranahan and Byron Nelson, who came out of retirement for the event. Demaret also won the Vardon Trophy and was the tour's leading money-winner. It was a career year for the jovial, uninhibited Texan, who occasionally moonlighted as a nightclub entertainer.

Sam Snead's inexplicable slump continued into the 1948 season, where his only tour victory came in the Texas Open. The 1948 season was all about Ben Hogan, who dominated the PGA Tour, winning ten events, including two majors. At one point, he won six events in a row. His first win of the season came in the Los Angeles Open at the Riviera Country Club in Pacific Palisades, California, near Los Angeles. In May, he won his second PGA Championship in three years, defeating Mike Turnesa 7 and 6 in the finals at Norwood Hills Country Club in St. Louis, Missouri. His victory earned him $3,500.

In June, he traveled back to the Riviera Country Club to play in the first US Open ever held on the West Coast. Riviera was now being called "Hogan's Alley" by sportswriters because of his impressive victories there in the last two Los Angeles Opens. A sizzling 67 in the first round at Riviera gave Hogan the first-round lead, but after the second round he was a stroke behind Sam Snead, who emerged from his slump long enough to set a 36-hole record for the event by posting a 138. In the third round, Snead's putter went cold and Hogan's 68 gave him a comfortable lead going into the final round. Hogan's final-round 69 earned him his first US Open title. Snead, whose putting woes continued in the final round, wound up in fifth place. Hogan's 276 put him two strokes ahead of runner-up Jimmy Demaret and broke Ralph Guldahl's US Open scoring record by five strokes. It was an amazing performance by the man who was now unquestionably the best golfer in the world. He closed out the 1948 season with wins in the Western, Reno, Denver, and Glendale Opens.

Hogan's first tournament of the 1949 season was the Los Angeles Open at the Riviera Country Club, which for the first time in three years he failed to win. (Lloyd Mangrum won it.) However, he recovered and won the Bing Crosby Pro-Am and the Long Beach Open. He played well in the Phoenix Open but lost to Jimmy Demaret in a playoff. In need of a rest, after the tournament he and his wife, Valerie, set out by automobile for their home in Fort Worth, Texas.

On the morning of February 2, 1949, while traveling from Phoenix to Fort Worth, Hogan was driving on a fog-shrouded highway near the small town of Van Horn in West Texas when his automobile was hit head-on by a Greyhound bus traveling in the opposite direction. An instant before the crash, Hogan flung himself across the seat in front of Valerie, who was sitting in the passenger seat, in an effort to protect her. The crash demolished the car and left Hogan with a fractured collarbone, a fractured pelvis, several broken ribs, and a badly fractured left ankle. Valerie was not seriously injured in the accident and in seeking to protect her, Hogan escaped an almost certain death, as the crash pushed the steering column through the driver's seat and would surely have crushed him had he not lunged toward Valerie.

Hogan was taken to a hospital in El Paso, Texas, where his injuries were treated. During his convalescence, he developed phlebitis in his legs and the doctors performed a procedure whereby they tied off some of the veins in his legs. The procedure probably saved his life, but it reduced the blood flow to his legs to the extent that there was a real possibility that he would never be able to walk normally again. He was in the hospital for 58 days before the doctors felt he was strong enough to leave and return to his home in Fort Worth. He weighed but 98 pounds when he left the hospital.

Determined to somehow, someday resume his career in professional golf, he embarked on a program of rehabilitation and exercise as soon as he returned home. Hoping to strengthen his weakened legs and build up his stamina, he started walking, inside his house at first and then out of doors. He did not pick up a golf club until late August and did not play a round of golf until November, when, with the help of a motorized golf cart, he played a faltering nine holes. A couple of weeks later, his legs wrapped in elastic bandages to facilitate blood circulation, he played his first 18-hole round since February. Exhausted by the undertaking and depressed by the realization that he might never fully recover, he went home and went to bed as soon as he finished the round.

With Hogan on the sidelines, Sam Snead got back on track in 1949. He won ten PGA Tour events that year, including two majors—the Masters and the PGA Championship. He also won the Vardon Trophy and was the tour's leading money-winner. He continued his good play in 1950, when he won eleven PGA Tour events and again won the Vardon Trophy, this time with a record low-scoring average of 69.23. It was a record that would last until it was broken by Tiger Woods fifty years later. (Byron Nelson's 68.33 scoring average in 1945 didn't count as a Vardon Trophy record because the trophy wasn't awarded during the war years.) Snead's eleven PGA Tour wins in 1950 are still the third-most ever, exceeded only by Nelson's 19 wins in 1945 and Hogan's 13 wins in 1946. Slammin' Sammy had recovered nicely from his two-year slump.

In early January 1950, Hogan felt strong enough to give tournament golf a try, so he sent in his application to play in the Los Angeles Open, which was scheduled for mid-January at the Riviera Country Club. When word got out that Hogan had filed to enter the Los Angeles Open, it was big news. "There's a possibility I'll play," he told a reporter, "but right now I can't say. I honestly don't know myself. I'll just have to wait and see how I'm feeling and how my game is working. One thing I can tell you for sure, though, I'm not going out there and shoot in the eighties."[1]

Hogan showed up for the event and his 73 in the first round raised some eyebrows. His 69 in the second round let everybody know that he was back on his game. His pair of 69s in the last two rounds would have won the event outright except that Sam Snead birdied the last two holes of the event

Ben Hogan. The champion who became a greater champion.
Library of Congress

to tie him for the lead. Ironically, Snead, not known for his putting, made a tough ten-footer on the 71st hole and a 20-footer on the final hole to catch his longtime rival. Snead won the 18-hole playoff the next day by four strokes over an obviously exhausted Hogan, but it was Hogan's performance in the tournament that everybody talked about.

After his good showing in the Los Angeles Open, Hogan signed on for the Bing Crosby Pro-Am the following week. Unfortunately, he tired quickly and played poorly at the Crosby. Thinking he was trying to do too much too soon, he took some time off after the Crosby and went back to Fort Worth to build up his strength and stamina. The next tour event he entered was the Masters in early April. He played the tough Augusta National course well and stayed in contention for three rounds before fading in the final round and finishing tied for fourth place with a 288. Jimmy Demaret's 283 beat runner-up Jim Ferrier by two strokes and made him the first three-time winner of the event.

Two months later, Hogan showed up at the Merion Cricket Club in Ardmore, Pennsylvania, for the US Open. He walked slowly and limped noticeably during the practice rounds, but it didn't seem to affect his shot-making and he was pleased with his play. He opened the tournament with rounds of 72 and 69 and was only a stroke off the lead at the halfway mark. Ahead, however, was Open Saturday, the 36-hole final day of the event. Hogan knew that playing 36 holes in a single day would test his strength and stamina to the limit. He shot a 71 in the 18-hole morning round and trailed leader Lloyd Mangrum by two strokes after 54 holes.

George Fazio, playing ahead of Hogan, shot a 70 in the afternoon round and was the early leader in the clubhouse. A weary Hogan knew on the tee box of the 12th hole that he had to play the last seven holes in two-over-par to overtake Fazio. He made the task more difficult by bogeying the 12th hole when his approach shot bounced over the green and he couldn't get down in two. He carded routine pars on 13 and 14 and missed a two-and-a-half-foot putt on 15 for another bogey. He parred the difficult 16th hole, but hit his tee shot into a green-side bunker on the par-three 17th hole. He blasted his sand shot to within five feet of the pin, but couldn't get the putt to drop. He now had to par the difficult 458-yard, par four 18th hole to catch Fazio. His drive on 18 was straight and sure and his one-iron to the green was a shot for the ages, landing on the left side of the green and rolling to a stop about 40 feet from the pin. Limping slowly up the 18th fairway, an obviously exhausted Hogan made his way to the ball, lined up his putt, and hit it about a yard past the hole. His three-footer coming back was firm and true and on Sunday morning there would be a three-way, 18-hole playoff for the US Open

Championship between Ben Hogan, George Fazio, and Lloyd Mangrum, who had caught Fazio late in the round.

Satisfied with his game, Hogan slept well that night and in the playoff the next day his strength and stamina held up well. He led Mangrum by a stroke and Fazio by three as they walked to the tee box on the par-four 16th hole, Merion's famous 445-yard Quarry Hole. Hogan hit two superb shots and was eight feet from the pin in two. Mangrum pulled his drive into the rough and was unable to reach the green in two. His pitch put him 12 feet from the pin. As he was about to putt, he noticed a bug on his ball. He bent over, picked up the ball, flicked the bug away, and replaced the ball, only to be hit with a two-stroke penalty by the USGA official. The rule at the time called for a two-stroke penalty if a player lifted and cleaned his ball on the green unless it had been stipulated beforehand that he could do so. Because no such stipulation had been made in this case, the official had no choice but to impose the penalty.

The tense situation grew worse when Mangrum sunk his 12-footer and Hogan missed his eight-footer. But for the penalty, the match would be tied. The tensions eased, however, when Hogan sank a 50-footer for a birdie on 17 and Mangrum bogeyed 18. Hogan defeated Mangrum by four strokes and Fazio by six to capture his second US Open title in three years. Golf's greatest player was not only back after his horrible accident, he was back on top.

Still recovering from the injuries suffered in the automobile accident, Hogan entered only five PGA Tour events in 1951. However, he won three of them, including two majors—his first Masters and his third US Open in four years. Snead won only two PGA Tour events in 1951, one of which was his third PGA Championship. Lloyd Mangrum won four PGA Tour events and the Vardon Trophy that year and was the tour's leading money-winner. It was a career year for the 37-year-old tour veteran from Trenton, Texas, whom sportswriters called the forgotten man of postwar golf.

In 1947 the USGA revised and simplified its Rules of Golf, reducing the number of rules from 61 to 21. The R&A refused to adopt the new rules and in 1951 a conference between representatives of the two rule-making bodies was held for the purpose of improving the integrity of the game by adopting a uniform set of rules that would govern the game of golf everywhere in the world. The matters to be dealt with at the conference included the abolishment of the stymie, the approval of the center-shafted putter, the penalties to be imposed for lost balls and balls driven out of bounds, and the size of the ball.

Though it was unpopular with most golfers from the beginning, the stymie had been permitted by the rules of golf since 1775, when the Gentlemen Golfers of Leith amended Article Six of their rules to provide that a ball blocking the path to the hole of an opponent's ball had to be lifted only if it was within six inches of the opponent's ball. In 1938, the USGA adopted a rule requiring that a ball creating a stymie had to be lifted upon request if the ball creating the stymie was within six inches of either the hole or the opponent's ball. The R&A abolished the stymie in 1946 by adopting a rule providing that a ball blocking the path of an opponent's ball to the hole had to be lifted upon request in all cases. At the conference it was decided that the 1946 R&A rule would be adopted universally and that the stymie would be abolished effective January 1, 1952. The abolition of the stymie did not go unopposed, however. Bobby Jones was so opposed to its abolition that in his book *Golf Is My Game,* he devoted an entire chapter to arguing for the restoration of the stymie.

The R&A had banned the center-shafted putter in 1910 on the grounds that it was a mallet and not a golf club, but the USGA had never banned it. At the conference it was decided that the center-shafted putter was a golf club and could be used universally.

In 1899, the R&A had adopted a rule providing that if a ball was driven out of bounds, another ball must be dropped at the place where the ball was last struck without the assessment of a penalty stroke (i.e., the penalty was loss of distance only). In 1920, the R&A had revised its rule to provide a penalty of one stroke in addition to loss of distance for balls driven out of bounds, with a proviso that the one-stroke penalty could be abolished by local rule. In 1946, the USGA adopted rules imposing a penalty of one stroke plus loss of distance for lost balls and loss of distance only for balls driven out of bounds. In 1950, the R&A adopted an experimental rule providing a penalty of loss of distance only for both lost balls and balls driven out of bounds. At the 1951 conference, it was decided that identical one stroke plus loss of distance penalties would be imposed for both lost balls and balls driven out of bounds. In 1960, the USGA reduced the penalty for both lost balls and balls driven out of bounds to loss of distance only. The revision lasted only a year, however, and in 1961 the stroke and distance penalty for both lost balls and balls driven out of bounds was restored by the USGA. The penalties have remained unchanged since then.

The R&A and the USGA could not agree on the size of the ball at the 1951 conference, so the R&A continued to use its 1.62-inch-diameter ball and the USGA stuck to its slightly larger 1.68-inch-diameter ball. Both balls were of the same weight. In 1990, the R&A abandoned its "small ball" and the 1.68-inch-diameter ball is now used universally.

Sam Snead got the best of his rival Ben Hogan in 1952. Slammin' Sammy won five tour events that year, including his third Masters, while Hogan's only tour victory came in the Colonial National Invitational in his hometown of Fort Worth. Hogan was in contention in the Masters for three rounds, but shot a 79 in the final round and finished tied for seventh place. In the US Open, played in June at the Northwood Club in Dallas, Texas, Hogan opened with a pair of 69s and had a two-stroke lead coming into the 36-hole final day. Playing in 96-degree heat, he faded to a pair of 74s on the final day and finished in third place, behind winner Julius Boros and runner-up Porky Oliver. Playing 36 holes in 96-degree heat took a lot out of his surgically repaired, 40-year-old body and he elected to sit out the rest of the season. His poor final-round showings in the Masters and the US Open, coupled with his limited playing schedule that year, convinced many that he was not the same player he had been before the accident.

In 1953, Hogan skipped both the California and the southern PGA Tour events and when he showed up in Augusta, Georgia, in April to warm up for the Masters he had not played a round of competitive golf since the US Open the previous June. He had used the layoff to strengthen his legs and stamina and to allow his damaged body to heal. The layoff did not appear to have affected his concentration and shot-making, as he posted rounds of 70, 69, 66, and 69 on Alister MacKenzie's masterpiece and won the event by five strokes. His 274 knocked five strokes off the record low score for the event. Hogan called his performance at Augusta the best he had ever played for seventy-two holes.

Feeling good about his game after his great performance at the Masters, Hogan traveled to Mexico City where he won the Pan American Open. He then went back to Fort Worth, where he won the Colonial National Invitational for the second year in a row. His next event was the 1953 US Open at Oakmont Country Club near Pittsburgh. At Oakmont he continued his good ball-striking and handled the lightning-fast greens with aplomb. His 149 at the halfway mark gave him a two-stroke lead over Sam Snead. On the 36-hole final day, he shot a 73 in the morning round and led Snead by a stroke after 54 holes. Playing together, Hogan and Snead shot identical 38s on the front nine of the final round. On the back nine, however, Hogan's magnificent 33 coupled with Snead's balky putter gave the Hawk a six-stroke victory over the Slammer. It was Hogan's fourth US Open Championship in six years and his third in the past four years. He joined Willie Anderson and Bobby Jones as the only four-time winners of the event. It was Snead's fourth second-place finish in the event and he remained the best American golfer who had never won the US Open.

In 1953, the PGA Championship and the British Open were scheduled for the same week. Because their playing dates overlapped, it was impossible for a player to play in both events. During the summer Hogan decided to skip the PGA Championship and play in the British Open at historic Carnoustie, where golf had been played since early in the 16th century. He arrived in Carnoustie ten days early to acclimate himself to the small British golf ball, Scottish weather, and "that other kind of golf," as he called links golf.[2]

He devoted most of his practice time to his fairway woods, figuring that Carnoustie's length would require him to use them for his approach shots on most of the long par-4s. Each night after dinner he walked the course to acquaint himself with the terrain and gauge the distances to various hazards. During his practice rounds he played three balls on each hole—one in the middle of the fairway and one on each side—in order to determine the best way to attack each hole. By the time the tournament started, he felt he knew enough about the course to play it intelligently.

Playing in a chilling wind and occasional light rain and hail, he shot a 73 in the first round, a score that put him three strokes behind American amateur Frank Stranahan, the first-round leader. The wind died overnight, but the occasional light rain showers continued. The rain didn't seem to bother Hogan, however, as he shot a 71 in the second round and trailed Scotsman Eric Brown and Welshman Dai Rees by two strokes at the halfway mark.

The weather for the 36-hole final day was a typical Scottish mixture of cold wind, gray skies, scattered rain showers, and occasional sunshine. Having picked up a touch of the flu, Hogan took a penicillin shot before setting out for the golf course. A record gallery of over 20,000 showed up for the final day of the event, many of whom had come to see the "Wee Ice Mon," as the Scots called Hogan, make his bid for Scottish immortality by winning at Carnoustie.

Hogan's 70 in the morning round tied him with Roberto De Vicenzo of Argentina for the 54-hole lead. In the afternoon round, a delicate chip-in birdie on the fifth hole and a follow-up birdie on the sixth hole enabled him to shoot a 34 on the front nine and pull well ahead of the rest of the field. A birdie on the final hole gave him another 34 on the back nine and a four-stroke victory over Tony Cerda, Frank Stranahan, Peter Thomson, and Dai Rees, all of whom tied for second. Hogan's final-round 68 was the low round of the tournament.

Hogan's win at Carnoustie was much admired by the Scots. His victory was also immensely popular in the United States and he was treated to a ticker-tape parade in New York City when he returned a few days later. His victory in the British Open had completed a career Grand Slam and he joined Gene Sarazen as the only players with victories in all four of the modern majors during their careers. His historic 1953 season, with victories in the Masters, the US Open, and the British Open, is deemed by many to have been the greatest single season by a player in the long history of the game.

Ben Hogan at his ticker-tape parade in New York City in 1953.
Library of Congress

His accomplishments were especially remarkable considering the injuries he had suffered in his automobile accident. Writer Herbert Warren Wind called Hogan "The champion who came back a greater champion."

Hogan essentially retired from the PGA Tour after his win at Carnoustie. His only tour victory after that came in 1959 when he won his hometown Colonial National Invitational for the fifth time. Beginning in 1954, he devoted most of his time and energy to the Ben Hogan Golf Company, a golf-club manufacturing business he had founded in Fort Worth. However, he continued to play in the Masters and the US Open and would later distinguish himself several times in those events.

One of the greatest ever to play the game, Ben Hogan is the only player ever to have won the Masters, the US Open, and the British Open in the same calendar year. His nine career major championships are the fourth-most ever, and he is one of only five players to have achieved a career Grand Slam by winning each of the four modern majors at least once during his career. He won the Vardon Trophy three times and is still widely thought of as one

An awesome foursome. Byron Nelson, President Dwight D. Eisenhower, Ben Hogan, and Clifford Roberts at the Augusta National Golf Club.
Library of Congress

of the two or three best ball-strikers ever to play the game, which is amazing considering his size—five-feet, five-inches and 145 pounds. His book, *Five Lessons: The Modern Fundamentals of Golf*, written with Herbert Warren Wind, is one of the most widely read instructional books on golf ever written.

Sam Snead played regularly on the PGA Tour until the middle 1960s. His last tour victory came in 1965, when, at age 52 years, 10 months, and 12 days, he won the Greater Greensboro Open for the eighth time and became the oldest player ever to win an event on the regular PGA Tour. After retiring from the regular PGA Tour, he played on the Senior PGA Tour for another 18 years. His last win on the Senior Tour came in 1982 at age 70. His 82 wins on the regular PGA Tour and his 165 professional wins are both records that may never be broken. He won seven majors and four Vardon Trophies during his 45-year career in professional golf, but he never won the US Open.

In the mid-1950s, professional golf was faced with a problem it had not experienced since the late 1930s—it did not have a superstar. Ben Hogan and

Sam Snead were both in their mid-forties and no longer played regularly on the PGA Tour. Hogan's last win in a major came in 1953 when he won the British Open and Snead's last win in a major came in 1954 when he won his third Masters.

To retain its popularity with American sports fans, professional golf needed replacements for Hogan and Snead. Fortunately, several young professionals who had joined the PGA Tour in the 1950s showed promise of being able to fill that role. Included in this group were smooth-swinging Gene Littler from San Diego, the winner of the 1953 US Amateur; Billy Casper, a plump, quiet, methodical shot-maker also from San Diego; Ken Venturi from San Francisco, who had taken lessons from Byron Nelson; and steady Dow Finsterwald from Athens, Ohio, whose short game was close to magical. Two other promising newcomers were burly Mike Souchak, a former Duke football player from Berwick, Pennsylvania, who could hit the ball out of sight, and Arnold Palmer, the winner of the 1954 US Amateur. Only time and the fortunes of golf would determine which, if any, of these players would become the superstars professional golf needed to compete with football and the other team sports in the televised world of the 1960s.

· 9 ·

Let Us Play

The African American Experience in Golf

$\mathcal{D}$uring its early years in the United States, golf was not only a rich man's game, it was a white man's game. The early golf clubs had no African American members to speak of and few African Americans played golf. During the 1920s, however, African Americans started playing golf, and the first African American–owned golf clubs were established, mostly by African American businessmen and professionals seeking a place to play the game they had grown to enjoy.

The first documented African American–owned golf club in the United States was the Shady Rest Golf and Country Club in Scotch Plains, New Jersey. The club was purchased by African American owners in 1921 and featured horseback riding, croquet, a tennis court, and a nine-hole golf course. It later became a social hub for Duke Ellington, Count Basie, Sarah Vaughn, and other African American celebrities. One of Shady Rest's first club pros was John Shippen Jr., the African American who had played in the 1896 US Open at Shinnecock Hills as a 16-year-old.

Several other African American–owned clubs that featured golf were established during the Roaring Twenties. The Booker T. Washington Country Club was established in 1924 in Buckingham, Pennsylvania. The Citizens Golf Club was established by African American owners in Washington, D.C., in 1925. The Mapledale Country Club in Stow, Massachusetts, was purchased by African American owners in 1926, and in 1928 the Parkridge Country Club in Corona, California, was purchased by a group of African American businessmen.

Dewey Brown was a light-skinned African American who, at age nine in the early 1900s, began working and caddying at golf clubs in New Jersey. During the course of his employment he learned to play golf and, in time, became an accomplished player. He was also an accomplished golf-club craftsman and in 1922 he crafted a set of golf clubs for President Warren G. Harding. In 1928, at age 30, he joined the PGA of America. The PGA of America wasn't aware of it at the time, but it had accepted its first African American member.

In 1934, while he was working as an assistant club pro at the Shawnee Country Club in Shawnee-on-Delaware, Pennsylvania, PGA officials became aware of Dewey Brown's race and terminated his membership in the organization. At about the same time, the PGA of America amended its bylaws and adopted a provision limiting membership in the organization to "professional golfers of the Caucasian race."

After the termination of his PGA membership, Dewey Brown continued his career in golf, working mostly as a greenskeeper and golf-course superintendent. In 1947, he purchased the Cedar River Golf Club, a nine-hole facility in Indian Lake, New York, where he remained until he retired in 1972.

Like Major League Baseball and most other professional sports in the United States at the time, professional golf was a whites-only sport during the 1920s and 1930s. African Americans were not invited to play in PGA events and were excluded from the PGA Tour. In the late 1930s, however, the exclusion of African Americans from professional sports in America started to raise some eyebrows. The character and popularity of professional boxer Joe Louis fanned the flames of integration, especially after he became a national hero in June 1938 by virtue of his first-round knockout of Nazi Germany's Max Schmeling in Yankee Stadium before a crowd of 70,000 mostly white Americans.

In 1925, Dr. Albert Harris and Dr. George Adams, two Washington, D.C., physicians, founded the United States Colored Golfers Association, which a year later changed its name to the United Golfers Association (the UGA). In 1925, the association sponsored an event it called the National Colored Golf Championship. Held at the Shady Rest Golf and Country Club in Scotch Plains, New Jersey, it was the first national tournament held for African American golfers. In 1926, the UGA sponsored an event it called the Negro National Open Golf Championship, which was played at the Mapledale Country Club in Stow, Massachusetts. Even though the winner received only $25 in prize money, the tournament attracted the best African American golfers in the country and became an annual event.

The UGA also scheduled a series of golf tournaments for African American professional golfers that were known collectively as the UGA Circuit. The tournaments were held on inexpensive public courses and the purses were paltry, but until the 1960s they were the only tournaments open to African American professional golfers. Several African American golfers who later played on the PGA Tour started their professional careers playing on the UGA Circuit.

Joe Louis was an avid golfer, and in August 1941, he sponsored and hosted the first Joe Louis Open at the Rackham Golf Course, a municipal course in Huntington Woods, Michigan. The tournament was open to professional and amateur African American golfers and offered purses of up to $2,000, which was big money for African American professional golfers in those days. The second Joe Louis Open was held in 1945 (it was not held during the war years) and the final one in 1951.

Ted Rhodes was born in 1913 in Nashville, Tennessee. He began caddying at an early age at country clubs in the Nashville area and by his late teens had become an accomplished golfer. He joined the Civilian Conservation Corps in the late 1930s and served in the US Navy during World War II. After his discharge from the navy, he gave golfing lessons to Joe Louis and entertainer Billy Eckstine. He later became one of Louis's personal golf instructors and Louis sponsored him on the UGA circuit. He won the Negro National Open Championship three times and the Joe Louis Open four times. In 1948, at the Riviera Country Club near Los Angeles, he became the second African American (after John Shippen Jr. in 1896) to play in the US Open, an event sponsored by the USGA. In the first round he shot a 70 and trailed Ben Hogan, the tournament leader and eventual winner, by only three strokes. He faded in the later rounds, however, and wound up tied for 51st place.

Earlier that year, Rhodes had played under a sponsor's exemption in the Los Angeles Open, a PGA Tour event, and had finished in 21st place. Also playing in the event was his friend Bill Spiller, another African American UGA professional, who finished in 34th place. At the time, the PGA of America had a rule it called "the top sixty rule" whereby any player who finished in the top sixty of a PGA Tour event automatically qualified to play in the next event. The next scheduled PGA Tour event was the Richmond Open, and Rhodes and Spiller showed up and paid their entry fees. However, after playing a practice round they were informed by PGA officials that they could not play in the event because they were not PGA members and were not eligible for PGA membership because of their race. The PGA of America apparently decided that the Caucasians-only rule took precedence over the top sixty rule.

In 1952, Joe Louis received a sponsor's exemption to play as an amateur in the San Diego Open, a PGA Tour event. The PGA of America at first refused to let him play in the event because he was not a Caucasian but later relented and permitted him to play when news of the exclusion of the popular Louis drew widespread criticism. Bill Spiller also entered the event under a sponsor's exemption, but after making the cut he was informed that he could not continue playing in the tournament because he was not a Caucasian. Shortly after the event, the PGA of America changed its policy and permitted nonmembers with sponsor's exemptions to play in PGA Tour events, regardless of their race. However, the organization retained its "Caucasians-only" membership requirement.

The most important early African American professional golfer was Charlie Sifford. Born in Charlotte, North Carolina, in June 1933, he learned to play golf as a teenager while working as a caddy at a local, whites-only golf club. When he was seventeen, he moved to Philadelphia, where he played golf on public courses and became quite good at the game. In 1948, at age 26, he turned professional, and, with financial support from entertainer Billy Eckstine, he quit his job and joined the UGA Circuit. Four years later, in 1952, he won the first of his six Negro National Open Championships. In 1957, he entered and won the Long Beach Open, an event that was cosponsored by the PGA of America but was not an official PGA Tour event. He was not permitted to play in official tour events because of his race.

In 1959, he sent a letter written in longhand to Stanley Mosk, the attorney general of the state of California, explaining that because of his race he was barred by the PGA of America from playing in the PGA Championship that was scheduled to be held at the Wilshire Country Club in Los Angeles in 1962. Mosk advised the PGA of America that it was illegal under California law to bar a competitor from participating in a sporting event because of his race and threatened legal action against the PGA of America if Sifford was barred from playing in the 1962 PGA Championship in Los Angeles because of his race.

The PGA of America responded to Mosk's threat by moving its 1962 Championship from Los Angeles to the Aronimink Golf Club in Newton Square, Pennsylvania. Mosk informed attorneys general in other states of the PGA's actions and policies and asked for their support in overcoming the injustices being imposed on African American professional golfers by the PGA of America. Faced with threatened legal actions in several states, in November 1961, the membership of the PGA of America passed a resolution removing the Caucasians-only membership requirement from its bylaws. In December 1961, Charlie Sifford, at age 39, became the first African American to receive a PGA player's card entitling him to play in PGA Tour events.

In early 1962, Sifford became the first African American to play in a PGA Tour event in the South when he played in the Greater Greensboro

Open. Prior to the start of the tournament, he received a death threat warning him that if he showed up he would be shot. He showed up and was paired with South African Gary Player in the first round. In his autobiography, Player described the harassment that Sifford endured at Greensboro: "They screamed 'Go home nigger,' they kicked his ball into the rough. . . . 'How can anybody play golf with this going on?' Sifford said in the scorer's tent. Yet he went out again the next day. He refused to be beaten, even though at times he was a very bitter man."[1] Sifford held up well and finished the event tied for fourth place.

Because he did not begin playing on the PGA Tour until he was 39 years old, Sifford's stay on the tour was not lengthy, but he played long enough to win two events. In 1967, he won the Greater Hartford Open and in 1969, at age 47, he won the Los Angeles Open. In 1975, he won the Senior PGA Championship, then the only tournament held for professional golfers over 50. Always a quality player but never a superstar, he played in 12 US Open Championships and six PGA Championships during his career and his best finish was a tie for 21st place in the 1972 US Open. He never attempted to play in the British Open and was never invited to play in the Masters.

Other African American professional golfers who were among the first to join the PGA Tour were Lee Elder, Calvin Peete, Pete Brown, Jim Dent, and Jim Thorpe. Lee Elder was born in Dallas, Texas, in July 1934 and moved to California at age 12 to live with his sister following the death of his parents. He started playing golf at age 16 while working as a caddie at Pebble Beach Golf Links. A few years later, he was invited to play a round of golf with boxer Joe Louis, who was impressed with his game and arranged to have Ted Rhodes give him a series of lessons. In 1959, Elder was drafted into the army, where he won a couple of military tournaments. After his discharge from the army in 1961, he turned professional and joined the UGA circuit. In 1968, at age 33, he joined the PGA Tour. In 1971, accompanied by Gary Player, he traveled to Johannesburg, South Africa, to play in the South African PGA Championship, where he became the first African American to play in a professional golfing event in South Africa.

In 1975, he became the first African American to play in the Masters, where he failed to make the cut. He was invited to play because he had won a qualifying event—the 1974 Monsanto Open in Pensacola, Florida. It was ironic that he had qualified by winning the Monsanto Open because when he had played in that event in 1968 he had to change his clothes in the parking lot because the members of the host club would not permit him to use their clubhouse. During his PGA career, he won four events on the regular PGA

Tour and eight events on the Senior PGA Tour. In 1979, he became the first African American to play in the Ryder Cup.

Calvin Peete was born in Detroit, Michigan, in July 1943. As a child, he had suffered a badly broken left arm that was left permanently bent because it was not set properly. He began playing golf at age 23 on a public course in Genesee Valley Park near Rochester, New York. He became quite good at the game and in 1975, at age 32, he quit his job as an agricultural supply salesman to try his hand at professional golf. He qualified for and joined the PGA Tour the same year. His first PGA Tour victory came on July 15, 1979, when he won the Greater Milwaukee Open.

In 1980, he became the second African American to play in the Masters and the first to make the cut. He finished in a tie for 19th place. The most successful of the early African American professional golfers, he won 12 PGA Tour events between 1979 and 1986. In 1984, he had the lowest-scoring average on the PGA Tour and won both the Vardon Trophy and the Byron Nelson Award. He also led the PGA Tour in driving accuracy for ten con- secutive seasons beginning in 1981. He played in 25 majors and made the cut 23 times, with four top-10 finishes. His best finish in a major was a tie for third place in the 1982 PGA Championship.

In 1983 and 1985, he was selected to play on the US Ryder Cup Team. However, Ryder Cup Team members were required to have a high school graduation diploma and he didn't have one. To qualify for the team, he took classes and earned his GED (General Educational Development) certificate.

Pete Brown was born in Port Gibson, Mississippi, in February 1935. He learned to play golf while working as a caddie at a local municipal golf course. In 1954, at age 19, he turned professional and joined the UGA Circuit. He won the Negro National Open Championship in 1961 and 1962 and joined the PGA Tour in 1963. In 1964, he became the first African American to win a PGA Tour event when he won the Waco Turner Open. He won one other PGA Tour event and later played on the Senior PGA Tour for several years.

Jim Dent was born in Augusta, Georgia, in May 1939 and learned to play golf while working as a caddie at the Augusta National Golf Club. He turned professional and joined the PGA Tour in 1965. He won the Florida PGA Championship three years in a row beginning in 1976 but never won a PGA Tour event. He is notable because of his success on the Senior PGA Tour, where he won twelve events between 1989 and 1998.

Born in Roxboro, North Carolina, in February 1949, Jimmy Lee Thorpe was taught to play golf by his father, who was a fairways superinten- dent at a local golf course. A talented running back in football, Thorpe at- tended Morgan State University on a football scholarship. He began playing golf professionally after leaving Morgan State and in 1972 joined the PGA Tour, where he won three events during the mid-1980s. In 1982, he became the third African American to play in the Masters but failed to make the cut. During his career in professional golf, he played in 27 majors and had three top-10 finishes. His best showing in a major was a fourth-place finish in the 1984 US Open. He later won thirteen events and one major on the Senior PGA Tour.

Although he was not as successful on the PGA tour as Lee Elder and Calvin Peete, it was Charlie Sifford who broke the color line in professional golf. While Elder, Peete, and the other early African American pros certainly didn't have it easy, it was Charlie Sifford who endured the death threats and verbal and physical abuse that went with being the first African American on the PGA Tour. He is considered by many to be the Jackie Robinson of professional golf. In 2006, he received an honorary doctor of laws degree from St. Andrews University in Scotland. In 2014, he was awarded the Presidential Medal of Freedom, the highest civilian honor for an American, by President Barack Obama.

Late in his life, Sifford wrote a widely read autobiography entitled *Just Let Me Play: The Story of Charlie Sifford, the First Black PGA Golfer*. In 2009, in speaking about his book during an interview with a writer for *Sports Illustrated* magazine, he said, "I just wanted to show that a black man could play this game and be a gentleman. I did that."

The professionals weren't the only African Americans being denied the right to play golf during the first half of the 20th century. African American recreational golfers also found it difficult to find courses to play on, especially in the South. Although there were a few African American–owned golf clubs, most African American golfers couldn't afford the expense of club membership and played on public courses.

In the North, most public golf courses were not segregated and for the most part African Americans were permitted to play on them without restriction. However, segregation existed in some northern states; in 1932, the city of Gary, Indiana, built two golf courses, one was a "whites-only" 18-hole course and the other was a nine-hole course for African Americans. Some privately owned daily-fee courses in the North had policies or practices limiting the playing rights of African Americans.

In the South, recreational golf was a Jim Crow sport from the beginning and golf courses were segregated. During the early years of golf in the South, virtually all public golf courses, whether publicly or privately owned, were open to white golfers only. A few cities established separate golf courses for African Americans, but they were usually small and poorly maintained.

In an attempt to keep public golf courses segregated and yet give African Americans a place to play the game, in the 1920s cities in the South began permitting African Americans to play on city-owned golf courses at specified times. In 1923, the City of St. Louis, Missouri, opened its public golf courses "to the exclusive use and enjoyment of colored persons" on Mondays from 6:00 a.m. until noon. During the rest of the week, the courses were reserved for the exclusive use of white golfers. A few years later, the City of Miami, Florida, adopted a policy of permitting African Americans to play on the city-owned Miami Springs Golf Course on Mondays. In 1949, the City of Norfolk, Virginia, granted African Americans the exclusive use of the city-owned Memorial Park Golf Course on the second weekend of each month and on Wednesdays and Fridays of the other weeks. Other southern cities that followed this practice included Portsmouth, Virginia; Huntsville, Alabama; and Nashville, Tennessee.

Dr. Hamilton Holmes was an African American physician who conducted a family practice in Atlanta, Georgia. His son, Oliver, was a respected minister in the same city and his brother, Alfred, was a union steward at the Lockheed aircraft plant in nearby Marietta, Georgia. They shared a passion for golf and on July 23, 1951, the three Holmes men, joined by George Bell, an African American family friend, attempted to play at the Bobby Jones Golf Course, a public course owned by the City of Atlanta. Located in the affluent northwest section of the city, it was known as a "whites-only" course and was off limits to African Americans. When the Holmes foursome attempted to register in the pro shop, they were told they could not play there. "The head pro told us straight out that we couldn't play there," Bell later testified. "He said they didn't allow no niggers at Bobby Jones."[2] They were escorted off the premises and advised not to return.

A few weeks later, the three Holmes men and Bell filed a legal action against the City of Atlanta in the Federal District Court in Atlanta seeking to desegregate Atlanta's municipal golf courses. The City of Atlanta opposed the action and prevailed in the trial court. The case, entitled *Holmes v. Atlanta*, drew the attention of the Atlanta chapter of the NAACP, which offered to assist Holmes and Bell with the appeal of the case to the Circuit Court of Appeals in New Orleans, Louisiana. The offer of assistance was accepted and the NAACP directed its legal staff, which included a talented attorney named Thurgood Marshall, to assist in the appeal.

The appeal to the Circuit Court of Appeals in New Orleans was unsuccessful and the ruling in favor of the city was affirmed. Another appeal was filed, this time with the US Supreme Court in Washington, D.C. The Supreme Court accepted the appeal and on November 11, 1955, issued a ruling reversing the rulings of the lower courts and directed the Federal District

Court in Atlanta to order the desegregation of all municipal golf courses in the city of Atlanta.

As in Atlanta, the desegregation of public golf courses in the South was accomplished largely through or because of legal actions filed by African American golfers in the federal courts. Even before the Supreme Court's ruling in *Holmes v. Atlanta*, federal district courts in several southern states had ordered the desegregation of municipal golf courses in several southern cities. In 1950, a federal district court in Maryland ordered the City of Baltimore to permit African Americans to play on its municipal golf courses. In 1951, a federal district court in Kentucky ordered the City of Louisville to open all city-owned golf courses to African American golfers. Seeing the writing on the wall, in 1954, the City of Houston, Texas, granted African Americans unrestricted access to all of its municipal golf courses. In 1955, a federal district court in Texas granted African Americans unrestricted access to all city-owned golf courses in Fort Worth. Thanks largely to the federal courts and the African American golfers who were willing to incur the expense and burden of filing and maintaining the legal actions, by 1960 segregated publicly owned golf courses in the United States had become a thing of the past.

In 1952, the USGA held its US Amateur Public Links Championship at the Miami Country Club in Miami, Florida. The club informed the USGA that African Americans were not permitted to play on their course and would therefore not be permitted to compete in the Public Links Championship. The USGA's policy at the time was to leave the decision on the exclusion of players from USGA-sponsored events in the hands of the club hosting the event. In this case, the USGA stuck to its policy and permitted the Miami Country Club to exclude African Americans from the 1952 Public Links Championship. The USGA drew intense criticism for permitting racial discrimination in a USGA-sponsored event. The organization later changed its policy and refused to hold USGA competitions at clubs that excluded African Americans and other minorities from membership. USGA-sponsored events are now held only at clubs with open membership policies.

Bill Wright was an African American amateur golfer from the state of Washington. On July 18, 1959, he won the 34th US Public Links Championship at the Wellshire Golf Course in Denver, Colorado, and became the first African American winner of a USGA-sponsored national golf championship.

Arnold Palmer, Television, and a New Era of Golf

In 1950, only one American household in ten had a television set. By 1960, nine American households in ten had at least one television set. More importantly, what Americans saw on television influenced their choices. Television, for example, played a significant role in the 1960 presidential election between John F. Kennedy and Richard M. Nixon. It is thought that one of the reasons Kennedy won the election was that he looked better on television than Nixon during their televised debates. What Americans saw on television also influenced the choices they made as to the sports they played and followed, and one of the big winners was golf. Television changed golf from a sport that most Americans had heard of and read about to one that they could watch, understand, and appreciate.

The first PGA Tour event to be televised was the Tam O'Shanter World Championship in Chicago, which was televised on August 23, 1953, by ABC using a single camera with a wide-angle lens stationed behind the 18th green. An estimated 646,000 television viewers watched the event and the experiment was deemed a success. The viewers of the event were treated to a good show as Lew Worsham holed a 100-yard approach shot on the final hole to win the event by a single stroke. Jimmy Demaret, who was doing the television commentary for ABC, got a little carried away while watching Worsham's shot; when the ball rolled into the hole, he shouted, "The son of a bitch went in!"

George S. May, the organizer of the Tam O'Shanter, paid ABC $32,000 to televise the event. The following year, ABC televised it for free and by 1960 the television networks were paying upwards of $150,000 to televise a few select tournaments. The networks learned early on that televised golf attracted advertisers with deep pockets, and it quickly became apparent that television was a game changer for professional golf. There was money to be made by everyone involved—the networks, the tournament sponsors, the PGA of America, and the players. The US Open was televised beginning in 1954, the Masters in 1956, and the PGA Championship in 1958.

When the 1960s arrived, professional golf still had no superstar. During the late 1950s, none of the half-dozen candidates for superstardom had established themselves as the player professional golf needed to sustain its popularity and boost its television ratings. Billy Casper won ten PGA Tour events during the last five years of the 1950s, including one major (the 1959 US Open), but his laid-back playing style and lack of charisma did not catch on with American sports fans and he did not become a superstar. Good as he was, he just wasn't the kind of player that sports fans turned on their television sets to watch. Gene Littler won 13 PGA Tour events during the same five-year period, but he failed to win a major in twelve attempts. Dow Finsterwald won the Vardon Trophy in 1957 and eight PGA Tour events during the last five years of the 1950s, including one major (the 1958 PGA Championship), but the absence of power in his game kept him from superstardom. Ken Venturi also won eight PGA Tour events during that period, but he failed to win a major in twelve attempts and did not become a superstar.

Burly Mike Souchak, a former Duke football player with an awesome power game, won 10 PGA Tour events during the last five years of the 1950s and in 1955 shot a 257 in the Texas Open, which at the time was the lowest score ever shot in a 72-hole PGA Tour event. Of all the players then on the tour, only six-foot-five-inch, 240-pound George Bayer could hit the ball further than Souchak. Although he appeared to have all the tools, he had failed to win a major in 14 attempts and had not become a superstar. Arnold Palmer, whose power game, charisma, and go-for-broke style of play was a favorite of galleries and television viewers alike, won 13 PGA Tour events during the last five years of the 1950s, including one major (the 1958 Masters), but he would have to win a few more majors to become the superstar that professional golf and the television networks were looking for.

Arnold Daniel Palmer was born on September 10, 1929, in Latrobe, Pennsylvania, a town of about 8,000 located 30 miles east of Pittsburgh. In 1921, Palmer's father was hired as the greenskeeper of a nine-hole golf course operated by the Latrobe Country Club. A few years later, he became the club pro in addition to being its greenskeeper. Young Arnold grew up on the golf course and throughout his youth assisted his father in maintaining the course.

His father taught Arnold how to play golf as soon as he was big enough to swing a golf club and from the beginning emphasized the importance of a hard swing. He wasn't as concerned with balance and mechanics as he was in just taking a good cut at the ball. Arnold would follow his father's advice throughout his long career in golf.

Young Arnold developed his golfing skills early. He played in his first national tournament, the USGA Junior National Championships in Los Angeles, at age 17. He played halfback on the Latrobe High School football team for a while, but gave it up because it interfered with golf. Academically, he was a good but indifferent student. During his high school years, he was the best golfer that anyone in Latrobe had ever seen and he knew exactly what he wanted to do when he grew up. He wanted to be a professional golfer—not a club pro, but a tournament pro who played on the PGA Tour. What he couldn't figure out was how to get to play enough golf to become good enough to play on the pro tour. The answer to his dilemma came when he met 17-year-old Buddy Worsham at a golf tournament in the summer of 1947. Worsham was the younger brother of Lew Worsham, the winner of the 1947 US Open.

Buddy Worsham had been recruited to play golf at Wake Forest University in Winston-Salem, North Carolina, a school that was upgrading its golf program from a club sport to the intercollegiate level and was looking for promising young golfers. Worsham recommended Palmer to the golf coach at Wake Forest, who found Palmer a scholarship, and in September 1947, Buddy and Arnold enrolled together at Wake Forest.

Palmer's days at Wake Forest were some of the happiest of his life. He and Buddy were close. They had parties, friends, and dates and got to play a lot of golf on good golf courses for a very good college golf team. Dow Finsterwald, who played on the Ohio University golf team during this period, later described his first encounter with Arnold Palmer: "The first time I met Arnie was in 1949, Ohio University against Wake Forest at Carolina Country Club. I had to play Palmer. Man, they had a good team. Buddy Worsham was darn good, too."[1] Palmer got the best of Finsterwald in their match and the Demon Deacons demolished the Bobcats.

Palmer led Wake Forest to the Southern Conference Championship in 1948 and was low medalist in the NCAA Golf Championships in 1949 and 1950. His good times came to an abrupt end in the autumn of 1950, however, when Buddy Worsham was killed in an automobile accident while returning to Winston-Salem from a dance at Duke University in Durham. Twenty-one-year-old Arnold was devastated by Buddy's death. Nothing was fun at Wake Forest after that, and a few weeks later he dropped out of school and enlisted in the US Coast Guard.

After finishing boot camp, he was assigned to a Coast Guard unit in Cleveland, Ohio, which, fortunately for Palmer, was a hotbed of golf at the time. Soon after arriving in Cleveland, he met up with some golf-oriented businessmen who liked his game and gave him a complimentary membership in a local golf club. Despite making only $140 a month as a Yeoman Third Class in the Coast Guard, he got to play a lot of golf on good golf courses during his three-year tour of duty, all of which was spent in Cleveland. When he was discharged in January 1954, he returned briefly to Wake Forest and then left and returned to Cleveland, where he worked briefly as a paint salesman for one of his golfing buddies.

In 1953, while still in the Coast Guard, he had qualified for the US Open, but he played poorly and missed the 36-hole cut. In 1954, after leaving the Coast Guard, he won several local amateur golf tournaments in the Cleveland area and again qualified for the US Open, where he again played poorly and missed the cut. His big break came later that year when his employer paid for his trip to Detroit to play in the US Amateur at the Country Club of Detroit. This time he played well and won the match-play event, defeating several of the best amateur golfers in the country in the process. A few weeks later, at a golf tournament in Pennsylvania, he met Winnie Walzer and fell madly in love. It was love at first sight for both of them, and they were married a few months later.

Palmer's victory in the 1954 US Amateur put him on the golfing map, and in November of that year he turned professional and joined the PGA Tour. His first PGA Tour victory came in August 1955 when he won the Canadian Open and collected $2,400 in prize money. While he did not win again in 1955, he won two PGA Tour events in 1956, three events in 1957, and three events again in 1958, including his first major—an exciting one-stroke victory in the Masters that was set up by a dramatic eagle on the 13th hole in the final round. After the tournament, which was nationally televised by CBS, he was asked to remain in Augusta to play a round of golf on Monday with another well-known golfer—President Dwight D. Eisenhower, who, like a growing number of American sports fans, liked Arnold Palmer a lot.

In November 1958, Palmer met Mark McCormack, a young lawyer from Cleveland who owned a company that assisted professional golfers in obtaining bookings for golf exhibitions. After meeting with McCormack, Palmer agreed to let National Sports Management, McCormack's company, book his golfing exhibitions in 1959. All went well and at the end of the year, Palmer, who had no taste for business matters and was beginning to get endorsement requests from product manufacturers, asked McCormack to handle all of his business affairs. Palmer and McCormack shook hands on an agreement that would later result in Palmer becoming the first professional athlete to earn a million dollars a year in endorsements. Starting with Wilson Sporting Goods and L&M Cigarettes, his endorsements eventually included

Arnold Palmer. More than any other player, he made professional golf what it is today.
Library of Congress

a host of products ranging from motor oil and automobiles to clothing and soft drinks. The public liked his good looks, vitality, and sincerity, and his endorsements would keep him among the highest-paid athletes in the world well into his eighties.

Palmer followed up his 1958 successes with three more PGA Tour victories in 1959 and a near miss at the Masters, where he hit his ball into Rae's Creek on the 12th hole in the final round and took a triple bogey that cost him the tournament. Art Wall birdied five of the last six holes to win the event.

Palmer started fast in 1960, claiming his first win in January at the Palm Springs Desert Golf Classic in Southern California, where he won the PGA Tour's first-ever five-round tournament with a final-round 65. "That round was the beginning," he later commented. "It put me in orbit. It became the source, I think, that fed me through the rest of the year."[2] He followed up his win in the Desert Classic with victories in the Texas Open in February and the Baton Rouge and Pensacola Opens in March. When he arrived in Augusta for the Masters in April, he was at the top of his game.

Also showing up in Augusta for the Masters were rising stars Billy Casper, the current US Open Champion; Dow Finsterwald, the winner of the Los Angeles Open in January; Mike Souchak, the winner of the San Diego Open in January; and Ken Venturi, the winner of the Bing Crosby National Pro-Am in January. They were joined by veterans Sam Snead, looking for his fourth Masters title; Byron Nelson, seeking his third Masters title; and Ben Hogan, also seeking his third Masters title. Other entrants included Jack Nicklaus, a plump, crew-cut, 19-year-old amateur from Ohio State University who had won the US Amateur in 1959, and Gary Player, a 24-year-old professional from Johannesburg, South Africa, who had won the British Open in 1959. The 1960 Masters had the makings of a memorable tournament. It would be nationally televised by CBS.

When they teed it up on Thursday morning and the putts started counting, Ken Venturi went out in a course-record 31 and looked for all the world like a young Ben Hogan. He experienced putting difficulties on the back nine, however, and ballooned to a 42, giving him a one-over-par 73 for the day, a score that was matched by Ben Hogan. Powerful Mike Souchak shot an impressive 34 on the front nine, but followed it up with a 38 on the back nine to post an even-par 72 for the day, a score that tied him with Gary Player and put him five strokes behind Arnold Palmer, the first-round leader who shot an impressive 67 and was accompanied throughout the round by a large, enthusiastic gallery. Dow Finsterwald's impeccable short game produced a

71 and young Jack Nicklaus hit a lot of greens and missed a lot of putts for a first-round 75.

In Friday's second round, Ben Hogan's 68 set the pace, followed by Ken Venturi's 69 and Dow Finsterwald's 70. Normally an excellent putter, Arnold Palmer putted poorly and posted a 73 for the round, but his huge gallery stayed with him and continued to make a lot of noise. When the day ended, Palmer's four-under-par 140 led the way, followed closely by Ben Hogan, Dow Finsterwald, Claude Harmon, and Walter Burkemo, all of whom were tied for second at 141. Another stroke back at 142 were Billy Casper and Ken Venturi. Jack Nicklaus shot a second-round 71 and at 146 was in the middle of the pack, where he was joined by a fading Mike Souchak. Gene Littler's horrid 82 in the second round caused him to miss the cut, as did Byron Nelson. Sam Snead never got it going, but he made the cut and would be around for the weekend.

In the third round on Saturday, Arnold Palmer missed most of the greens and made most of his putts, while Ben Hogan hit most of the greens and missed most of his putts. They each posted an even-par 72. Billy Casper and Ken Venturi shot 73s and Dow Finsterwald shot a 74. When all the scores were posted, Palmer had a one-stroke lead over Hogan, Casper, Venturi, Finsterwald, and Julius Boros. Going into the final round there were six players within one stroke of the lead and television viewers throughout the land would be glued to their sets on Sunday to watch the event unfold. At the Augusta National, it was no secret that the gallery's favorite was Arnold Palmer. This tournament was the birthplace of Arnie's Army.

In the final round, Arnold Palmer and Billy Casper were paired, as were Dow Finsterwald and Ken Venturi. Ben Hogan was paired with Julius Boros. When play started, Hogan's putting woes caused him to drop out of contention on the front nine. Julius Boros and Billy Casper ran into a string of bogies early in the round and also dropped out of contention. For some reason, the tournament leaders did not go off in consecutive groups and Finsterwald and Venturi started nearly an hour ahead of Palmer and Casper. By the time Palmer teed off on the first hole, he trailed Venturi, who had birdied two of the first four holes, by a stroke. Palmer made his situation worse by hitting his drive on the first hole into the ninth fairway. But in typical Palmer fashion, he bent his long approach shot around a stand of pine trees and left it twelve feet from the pin. When he sank the 12-footer, he was tied with Venturi for the lead.

Venturi and Finsterwald played the front nine flawlessly, carding a 33 and a 34 respectively. Their steady play continued on the back nine and, after 17 holes, they were tied for the lead at five under par, one stroke ahead of

Palmer. Venturi was on the green in two on the par-four 18th hole, while Finsterwald's approach shot found a green-side bunker. When Venturi two-putted and Finsterwald needed three to get down from the bunker, Venturi went to the clubhouse with a one-stroke lead over Finsterwald and Palmer, who was on the tee box of the 15th hole, the hole where Gene Sarazen had made his famous double eagle in 1935. Palmer pulled his drive to the left and, unlike the Squire, was unable to reach the green in two and had to settle for a disappointing par. On the par-four 16th hole, Palmer's four-iron approach shot came up 30 feet short of the pin and he again had to settle for a par. He now had but two holes left in which to catch Venturi.

On the 400-yard, par-four 17th hole, his approach shot came up 35 feet short of the pin. After twice standing over his ball and walking away, he finally stroked it and seconds later watched it disappear into the hole for the birdie he needed to catch Venturi. A grinning Palmer ran to the hole, removed the ball, and punched the air with his fist. Arnie's Army responded with a cheer that could be heard in Atlanta, and headed for the 18th hole.

On the 18th hole, the hole that had done Finsterwald in, Palmer ripped his drive down the right side of the fairway, barely missing the pine trees that line that side of the fairway. His six-iron to the green hit the pin and spun to a stop six feet away. A few minutes later, he holed the six-footer to defeat Venturi by a stroke and claim his second Masters title in three years. The television ratings for the tournament were off the charts. Once again, Palmer was asked to spend another day in Augusta and play a Monday round of golf with President Eisenhower—which, of course, he did.

As for the others in the tournament, Ben Hogan's bid for his first major in seven years ended in failure as he three-putted his way to a 75 in the final round and wound up tied with Gary Player for sixth place. It was sad to see a great player like Hogan, who could still strike his woods and irons about as well as he ever had, fall to pieces on the greens, where he seemed to freeze over the ball, seemingly unable to decide how hard or in what line to strike the ball. Young Jack Nicklaus also shot a 75 in the final round and tied Billy Joe Patton for low amateur honors. He wound up tied for 13th overall, a stroke ahead of Mike Souchak, who tied for 16th. At 47 years old, Sam Snead beat them both and finished tied for 11th place.

The 1960 US Open was played in June at Cherry Hills Country Club in Denver, Colorado. Essentially the same players who had played in the Masters showed up for the nationally televised event. Although Arnold Palmer, after his spectacular finish at the Masters, was the center of attention and the pretournament favorite at Cherry Hills, there were other golfers of interest as well. Ben Hogan was striking the ball well, had worked on his putting, and very much wanted his record fifth US Open title. Sam Snead had won a couple of tournaments recently and there was hope that this would be the year he would break his US Open jinx. Mike Souchak was playing well and many liked his chances, and young Jack Nicklaus, though an amateur, had his admirers. If Ken Venturi, Dow Finsterwald, Billy Casper, Julius Boros, or Doug Sanders should catch fire for a couple of rounds, any of them could win the event.

The 7,004-yard, par-71 layout at Cherry Hills, coupled with the thin air of the Mile High City, where the ball travels up to 10 percent farther than at sea level, raised concerns that record low scores would be shot in the tournament. Ben Hogan, after shooting a pair of 67s in practice rounds, predicted that his US Open record low score of 276 set at Riviera in 1948 would fall. Golf-course architect Desmond Muirhead called Cherry Hills "a course that rewards adventurous shots, not merely the most accurate shots."

When the tournament opened on Thursday morning, Arnold Palmer started poorly. He pushed his drive on the first hole to the right and the ball rolled into a ditch that runs through the rough on the right side of the fairway. His mistake cost him a double bogey on the hole. He recovered nicely, however, and played the rest of the round at one-under-par and posted a one-over-par 72 for the day. Mike Souchak's three-under-par 68 was the best round of the day and made him the leader. Ben Hogan was doing well until the ninth hole when he snap-hooked his drive and hit a man in the stomach. The shot seemed to unnerve him and he wound up shooting a four-over-par 75. Jack Nicklaus shot an even-par 71 and was the low amateur.

Leading the way in Friday's second round were Mike Souchak and Ben Hogan with four-under-par 67s. Doug Sanders was next at 68, followed by Dow Finsterwald and Sam Snead at 69. Arnold Palmer shot an even-par 71. At the 36-hole mark, Souchak's seven-under-par 135 set a US Open 36-hole record, easily beating Sam Snead's 138 set at Riviera in 1948. Doug Sanders was next at 139, followed by Jerry Barber, Jack Fleck, and Dow Finsterwald at 140. Sam Snead, Billy Casper, and three others were next at 141, and Jack Nicklaus and Ben Hogan were at even-par 142. Arnold Palmer at one-over-par 143 trailed Souchak by eight strokes and was barely in contention. By the end of the second round, Arnie's Army had dwindled to a couple of dozen die-hards.

Next up was "Open Saturday," when two 18-hole rounds would be played, one in the morning and the other in the afternoon. In the morning round (the third round), 47-year-old Ben Hogan and 20-year-old Jack Nicklaus, who were paired, each posted a two-under-par 69, a score that was bettered in the third round only by the 68 shot by Julius Boros. Mike Souchak was paired with Doug Sanders, whom he didn't like. He was at even par until the 18th hole, where a double bogey bumped him to 73 for the round. Doug Sanders, who didn't like playing with Souchak any more than Souchak liked playing with him, shot himself out of contention with a 77. Dow Finsterwald and Jerry Barber stayed in the hunt with one-under-par 70s, as did Jack Fleck with an even-par 71. Sam Snead and Billy Casper shot 73s and became also-rans. Arnold Palmer, whose army had again dwindled to about 30 when the round ended, mixed five birdies with six bogeys for a one-over-par 72 in the morning round and was only an errant shot or a bad putt away from joining Snead and Casper as also-rans.

When the morning round ended, Mike Souchak was the 54-hole leader at 208, followed by Dow Finsterwald, Julius Boros, and Jerry Barber at 210 and Ben Hogan, Jack Nicklaus, and Jack Fleck at 211. Gary Player, Johnny Pott, and singer Don Cherry, an amateur, were next at 212. Arnold Palmer at 215 trailed Souchak by seven strokes going into the final round on Saturday afternoon. To catch Souchak, he would have to pass nine other players.

Among the contenders, Arnold Palmer was the first to tee off in the afternoon round. The first hole at Cherry Hills is a 346-yard, slightly downhill, par-four hole with a ditch in the rough on the right side of the fairway. Most players used a fairway wood off the tee to avoid the ditch and the heavy rough next to it. Palmer, however, had used a driver off the tee on each of the three previous rounds in vain attempts to drive the green.

One of the longest hitters on the tour, Palmer was convinced that he could drive the green and in the final round again pulled the driver out of his bag and teed the ball up low. Taking a hard swing, with his incredibly strong wrists and forearms providing most of the power, he crushed his drive and sent it flying low and fast through the thin Denver air headed straight toward the green. The ball landed 50 yards short of the green and rolled to a stop pin-high on the right fringe of the green, about 30 feet from the pin. To the large gallery around the first tee and to the millions watching the event on television, it looked like he had driven the green.

His eagle putt wouldn't fall, but his birdie putt found the bottom of the cup. Charged up by his play on the hole, his momentum carried over to the holes that followed. He chipped in from 35 feet on the second hole, hit his approach shot to within a foot of the cup on the third hole, and sank an 18-footer on the fourth hole, all for birdies. He had picked up four strokes in four holes to start the final round. Arnie's Army quickly reassembled and their loud cheers after each birdie gave notice to Souchak and the nine other players ahead of Palmer on the leaderboard that their man was making birdies in bunches.

After settling for a par on the par-five fifth hole, Palmer sank a 25-foot side-hiller for a birdie on the par-three sixth hole, after which he threw his visor to the crowd in celebration. He finished the front nine with a birdie on seven, a bogey on eight, and a par on nine, the combination of which gave him an incredible 30 on the front nine.

Souchak teed off in the final round about a half hour after Palmer and was under the impression that Palmer had driven the first green. In the first three rounds, he had used a fairway wood for his tee shot on the first hole and had fared well. In the final round, however, he opted for a driver and proceeded to hit his ball into the ditch in the right rough—the same ditch that had cost Palmer a double bogey in the first round. Souchak suffered a similar fate and when he walked off the first green there was only one stroke left of his seven-stroke lead. Even though he recovered and made a couple of birdies during the middle of the round, when he bogeyed the ninth hole his lead was gone.

Souchak's failures gave other players chances to win the event. Don Cherry was three under par and a stroke out of the lead on the par-five 17th hole, the green of which is surrounded by water. After a good drive, he elected to go for the green on his second shot rather than laying up short of the water and hitting a short pitch to the green with his third shot. He didn't quite get all of his four-iron and the ball splashed into the water a few feet short of the green. He took a double-bogey seven on the hole and was three strokes behind with one hole to go. He had gambled away his chances of winning the event.

Ben Hogan was tied for the lead with Palmer and Jack Fleck at four under par after sinking his longest putt of the day—a 20-footer for a birdie on fifteen. On sixteen, he had a chance to be alone at the top, but his 12-footer wouldn't drop and the three-way tie at the top continued. On the par-five 17th hole, he elected to lay up with his second shot, rather than go for the green, as Cherry, playing ahead of him, had done. His layup was executed perfectly, leaving him with a short pitch over the water to the green. His pitch to the green cleared the water and landed safely on the green, a few feet short of the pin. However, he had struck the ball so cleanly and crisply and had imparted so much spin on it that when it landed on the green, instead of stopping or rolling toward the hole it started rolling back toward the water.

An incredibly disappointed Hogan stood there and watched his ball roll off the front of the green into the water. He took off his shoes and played the half-submerged ball out of the water hazard, but was unable to get down in two and took a bogey six on the hole. The bogey cost him a share of the lead and, he figured, any chance of winning the fifth US Open Championship he so coveted. Disappointed and discouraged, he triple-bogeyed the final hole and walked to the clubhouse to watch the rest of the tournament on television. Years later, when asked if his finish in Denver was a disappointment, he replied, "It sure was. I wanted that one so much. It was awful. I felt terrible after that 17th hole, not only because I had knocked myself out of a chance to win, but because I had played it stupidly. I cut that third shot too fine."[3]

Jack Fleck was tied for the lead at four under par on the 13th hole when the treacherous Cherry Hills greens got the best of him. He three-putted from seven feet on 13, three-putted 16, missed a three-foot birdie putt on 17, and missed a four-foot par putt on the final hole. He missed five makeable putts on the last six holes, three of which were less than four feet in length, and it cost him the U.S. Open.

After carding a birdie on the 12th hole, Jack Nicklaus was leading the tournament by a stroke at five-under-par when the tough Cherry Hills greens got to him. On 13, he three-putted from 12 feet to lose the lead. Shaken, he three-putted from 40 feet on 14 and then missed a five-foot birdie putt on 16, a 12-foot birdie putt on 17, and a 12-foot par putt on the final hole. All told, he missed six makeable putts on the last six holes, and it cost him his first major.

When he walked off the 13th green, Julius Boros was tied for the lead with Arnold Palmer and Jack Fleck at four under par. He then made a bogey from a bunker on 14, parred 15 and 16, and missed a three-foot birdie putt on 17. His bogey from a bunker on 18 ended his chances of winning his second US Open.

After his incredible 30 on the front nine gave him a share of the lead, Arnold Palmer ate a sandwich and headed for the back nine. Instead of wilting on the back nine as the others had done, he recorded eight pars and a birdie. His par on the final hole was set up by an eighty-yard pitch to within three feet of the cup. His 35 on the back nine gave him a final-round 65, which at the time was the lowest final-round score ever shot by a winner of the US Open.

Palmer finished the tournament with a four-under-par 280 and posted a two-stroke victory over runner-up Jack Nicklaus, whose 282 was the lowest score ever posted by an amateur in the US Open. 47-year-old Ben Hogan hit 34 of 36 greens in regulation on the final day, an amazing feat on a US Open course. However, because of his putting woes, his misfortune on the 71st hole, and throwing in the towel on the final hole, he wound up tied with Don Cherry for ninth place. The fears of record low scoring in the event turned out to be unfounded as Hogan's record low of 276 was not threatened and only eight players broke par.

Arnold Palmer's legendary final round at Cherry Hills, coupled with his incredible win at the Masters in April, established him as the favorite golfer of millions of sports fans who had watched the events on television. His performances had made him the face of professional gold and a household name among American sports fans. The search for a successor to Ben Hogan and Sam Snead was over. Palmer was the right man for the times. Unlike Hogan, who seldom smiled or showed emotion, rarely spoke to his playing partner, and considered galleries a nuisance, Palmer was outgoing and gregarious, wore his emotions on his sleeve, and loved galleries.

For Ben Hogan, the 1960 US Open was an incredible disappointment and a last hurrah. For 19-year-old Jack Nicklaus, his performance at Cherry Hills was a warning shot. Mike Souchak, who had shown so much promise, never fully recovered from his collapse at Cherry Hills. Though he rebounded and won his next tour event, the Buick Open in July, he never won another major and won only four more PGA Tour events during the rest of his career.

Prior to 1960, most American professionals did not play in the British Open. Ben Hogan had played in it once—in 1953, when he won it. Byron Nelson had played in it twice (in 1937 and 1955), and Sam Snead twice (in 1937 and in 1946, when he won it). Even though it was by tradition a major championship, the long plane ride, the expense of the trip, its paltry prize money, and the necessity of qualifying kept most American professionals away. The fact that it was inconveniently scheduled between the US Open and the PGA Championship and the necessity of missing American tournaments to play over there also kept the American pros away.

In 1960, even Gary Player, the defending champion, had to qualify for the British Open, and it was not until 1966 that the winners of the US Open and the PGA Championship were exempted from qualifying. In 1959, the purse (the total prize money) of the British Open was $13,400 and the winner's share was $1,000. The purse of a typical American tournament at that time was around $20,000. In 1960, the purse of the US Open was $60,720, the purse of the Masters was $87, 050, and the purse of the PGA Championship was $63,130. The winner's shares were $14,400, $17,500, and $11,000, respectively. Although the purse of the British Open was increased to $19,600 in 1960, it was still paltry compared to the American majors.

Despite all of the financial reasons for not playing in the British Open in 1960, Arnold Palmer decided to travel to Scotland and attempt to qualify for the event, which was being held in early July on the Old Course at St. Andrews. His reasons for going were pride and tradition. He wanted to match Ben Hogan's much-acclaimed triple-crown triumph in 1953, when he won the Masters, the US Open, and the British Open in the same year. Palmer figured he could even exceed Hogan's accomplishment if he could win the PGA Championship later in July and lay claim to the first modern Grand Slam. (The term *Grand Slam* was coined by Palmer that year and was picked up by several sportswriters.) In addition, 1960 was the 100th anniversary of the British Open, making the event a special occasion and Palmer wanted to be a part of it.

With Winnie in tow, he arrived in St. Andrews two weeks early to acclimate himself to links golf, the nuances of the Old Course, the small British ball, and Scottish weather. The pretournament favorites, in addition to Palmer, were Gary Player, the defending champion, and Peter Thomson, an intellectual, well-read Australian who, after finishing second to Ben Hogan in 1953, had won the event four times in the next six years.

After qualifying with rounds of 67 on the New Course and 75 on the Old Course, Palmer was raring to go on Wednesday, the traditional starting day of the British Open. (St. Andrews has seven golf courses—the Old Course, the New Course, which was built in the 1890s to alleviate overcrowding on the Old Course, the Eden Course, the Jubilee Course, the Strathtyrum Course, the Balgove Course, and the Castle Course.)

The weather on Wednesday was cold with scattered light rain and fog. It was typical Scottish links weather except there was no wind. In the first round, powerful Roberto De Vicenzo of Argentina led the way with a 67, followed by Kel Nagle, a quiet, 39-year-old Australian, who shot a 69. Arnold Palmer and three others were next at 70, while Peter Thomson and Gary Player posted 72s. In Thursday's second round, De Vicenzo shot another 67 and remained two strokes ahead of Nagle, who also shot a 67. Palmer's 71 gave him a 141, which tied him with Thomson and put him one stroke ahead of Player. Palmer was seven strokes behind De Vicenzo, which, a couple of sportswriters pointed out, was one stroke closer to the lead than he had been after the second round at Cherry Hills.

The third and fourth rounds were to be played on Friday. In the third round, played on Friday morning, De Vicenzo took a double bogey on the 14th hole and lost the lead to Nagle, his playing partner, who birdied the hole. Palmer, playing just ahead of De Vicenzo and Nagle, also birdied fourteen and, at five under par, trailed Nagle by two strokes and De Vicenzo by one. However, three holes later he three-putted the difficult Road Hole green for the third straight time and fell another stroke back. His momentum gone, he took another three-putt bogey on eighteen and trailed Nagle by four strokes and De Vicenzo by two after 54 holes. Gary Player and Peter Thomson struggled in the third round and dropped out of contention. Shortly after the third round ended, the light drizzle that had started at mid-morning turned into a downpour and the final round was postponed until Saturday morning.

In the final round on Saturday morning, Palmer started like he had in the final round at Cherry Hills. On the par-four first hole, he drove the ball to within twenty yards of the green and got down in two for a birdie. On the par-four second hole, he hit his approach shot to within two feet of the hole to set up another birdie. As usual, Palmer attracted most of the gallery and each birdie was greeted with a loud cheer that could easily be heard by Nagle and De Vicenzo, who were playing just behind Palmer. Palmer ran out of birdies after the second hole, however, and when Nagle birdied seven and eight, his lead was back to four strokes. Palmer birdied 13 and Nagle three-putted 15, the combination of which gave Nagle a two-stroke lead when Palmer went to the tee box on the Road Hole, his nemesis so far in the tournament

This time, after a good drive his approach shot rolled off the back of the green and down an embankment. Disdaining a short pitch to the green, he pulled out his putter and rolled the ball up the embankment and onto the green, where it stopped about two feet from the cup. He sank the two-footer for a par and stayed within two strokes of Nagle with one hole to go. On the final hole, Palmer ripped his drive to within a hundred yards of the green and pitched his second shot to within four feet of the cup.

Nagle was looking at a difficult nine-footer for his par on the Road Hole green when the cheers of Arnie's Scottish Army informed him that Palmer had birdied the final hole. Nagle's lead was now but a single stroke. If he missed the putt, his lead would be gone. Undaunted, he sank the tough nine-footer and went to the final hole needing a par to avoid a playoff with the best player in the world. His drive on the final hole split the fairway and his nine-iron pitch to the green left him three feet from the hole. His deliberate two-putt par earned him the silver claret jug. His 278 beat Palmer by a stroke and tied the record low 72-hole score for the 100-year-old event. It took a record score to beat Arnold Palmer in 1960.

Bitterly disappointed by his loss at St. Andrews (thirty years later he still called it the biggest disappointment of his career), Palmer hustled back to the States to honor his commitments in other tournaments, the most important of which was the PGA Championship in late July at Firestone Country Club in Akron, Ohio. In anticipation of Palmer's appearance, advance sales for the event had set a record.

The PGA Championship had been converted from match play to stroke play in 1958. The change had been made at the request of the television networks. The networks hated match play because the tournament took forever to play and all too often the most popular players were eliminated in the early rounds, leaving the big-money weekend slots to be filled with no-name players that viewers would not watch. The PGA of America was informed that if it wanted to showcase its tournament on television, it would have to convert it to a stroke-play event, which, of course, it did.

The Firestone course had been redesigned and toughened for the event by noted golf-course architect Robert Trent Jones (not to be confused with Robert Tyre "Bobby" Jones Jr., the player). The course was now a difficult, 7,165-yard, par-70 layout. Arnold Palmer arrived in Akron five days early to check it out for himself. Also showing up early for the event were defending champion Bob Rosburg, veterans Sam Snead and Ben Hogan, and most of the tour regulars who had played in the Masters and the US Open earlier in the year. It was the first time Hogan had played in the PGA Championship since he won the event in 1948. For Snead, who had won the event three times and had been playing well recently, it would be his twentieth appearance. Gary Player and Jack Nicklaus did not play in the tournament.

When the tournament started on Thursday morning, a record gallery of 12,625 was there to greet the players. Pretournament favorite Arnold Palmer jumped out in front with an impressive first-round three-under-par 67. In second place was 48-year-old Sam Snead, who shot a 68 and was the only other player under par. Ken Venturi, Don January, and Doug Sanders were next at even-par 70. Jay Hebert (pronounced A-Bear), a 37-year-old former Marine from Louisiana, shot a 72, while Ben Hogan, whose putting woes continued, shot a disappointing 74, as did defending champion Bob Rosburg.

In the second round on Friday, Arnold Palmer, with 75 percent of another record gallery following him, never recovered from a double-bogey six on the third hole and shot a disappointing 74. His 36-hole total of 141 trailed new leader Jay Hebert by two strokes. Alone in second place was Don January at 140. Sam Snead shot a second-round 73, which tied him with Palmer and Doug Sanders at 141. Ken Venturi was next at 142. Ben Hogan shot a 73 and trailed Hebert by eight strokes.

In Saturday's third round, Palmer, Hebert, and Snead played together and took most of the gallery with them. Palmer was at even par for the round until he came to Firestone's signature hole—the 625-yard, par-five, 16th hole, where he tried unsuccessfully to hit a three-wood out of a fairway bunker and took a triple-bogey eight. His momentum gone, he bogeyed the last two holes and turned in a five-over-par 75 for the round. His 54-hole total of 216 put him six strokes behind 54-hole leader Doug Sanders, who shot a 69 and was alone at the top at even-par 210. Sam Snead, who continued to play well, shot an even-par 70 and was tied for second place at 211 with Jay Hebert and Jim Ferrier, a 45-year-old Australian who shot a 66, the low round in the tournament so far. Bothered by the 90-degree heat, Ben Hogan shot a disappointing 78 and did not make the 54-hole cut.

In Sunday's fourth round, Arnold Palmer bogeyed two of the first four holes and fell eight strokes behind the leader. Although he made a couple of birdies later in the round and shot an even-par 70 for the day, he never made a run at the leaders and finished the tournament tied for seventh place at 286. Late in the day, Sam Snead made a great birdie on the monster 16th hole and took a one-stroke lead over Jay Hebert and Jim Ferrier. It looked like Snead was going to win the tournament until he missed the green on seventeen and a poor chip led to a bogey. On eighteen, he again missed the green, but this time he chipped to within four feet of the cup. Needing to make the four-footer to tie his playing partner, Jim Ferrier, for the tournament lead, he missed it on the high side and finished tied for third place. Nevertheless, it was an amazing performance by the 48-year-old tour veteran who had joined the PGA Tour in 1936. Doug Sanders, playing on his 27th birthday, was tied for the lead with two holes to go but bogeyed the last two holes and finished tied with Sam Snead for third place. Jay Hebert, playing in the group behind Snead and Ferrier, sank a clutch eight-footer for a birdie on 17 and parred the final hole to win the event by a stroke over Ferrier.

The PGA Championship was another disappointment for Arnold Palmer, whose attempt to win a third major in 1960 again came up short. However, his year was a rousing success with eight PGA Tour wins, two majors, and a record $75,263 in official winnings. More importantly, he had established himself as the best player in the game and the favorite golfer of millions of American sports fans. He was now the king of professional golf and its reigning superstar.

The emergence of Arnold Palmer, the advent of televised golf, and the great tournaments played that year combined to make 1960 a breakthrough year in American golf, both professional and recreational. As in 1913, when Francis Ouimet's incredible victory over Harry Vardon in the US Open had popularized golf and resulted in millions of Americans taking up the game, beginning in 1960 the popularity of recreational golf in the United States soared as never before. The number of Americans playing golf doubled during the next decade and would continue to increase steadily for the next half-century.

• 11 •

The Phenomenal
Growth of Golf after 1960

The number of Americans playing golf increased phenomenally after 1960. The National Golf Foundation reports that there were 8.6 million golfers in the United States in 1960 and 40 years later, at the close of the 20th century, there were 29 million. The number of golf courses in the United States also increased significantly during the last 40 years of the 20th century. There were about 8,000 golf courses in the United States in 1960 and at the close of the 20th century there were more than 14,000.

In some parts of the country, the increase in the number of golf courses was even more pronounced. In Denver, Colorado, and its suburbs, for example, there were 16 golf courses in 1960. At the close of the 20th century, there were 80. The number of public golf courses in the greater Denver area increased from nine to 60 during that 40-year period, and the number of private golf clubs and country clubs increased from seven to 20. Throughout the country, city councils and county commissioners responded to the demands of their constituents and built or acquired municipal golf courses. Recreation districts built and maintained public golf courses, and land developers built golf courses to enhance the value of their building sites.

During the early years of the sport, caddies played an important role in the game of golf. Their existence was noted in the early rules of golf, and they appear in most of the accounts, photographs, and paintings of early golf matches. It seems as though every golfer in those days had a caddy to carry his or her clubs, even though the clubs were light and few in number and golf bags did not exist. Today, however, caddies, in the classic sense, are seen only in professional golf and a few top-level amateur tournaments. They are not used at all on public golf courses, and most private clubs use them only as

135

forecaddies, who walk or ride ahead of the golfers and locate their balls while the golfers ride separately in motorized golf carts. Caddies have essentially been replaced by motorized golf carts in American recreational golf. How, when, and why did this change occur?

The first motorized golf cart was built and used in 1932, but motorized carts were not widely used until the late 1950s. Even then they did not replace caddies at most private golf clubs. The demise of caddies as carriers of golf clubs and dispensers of advice began in 1960, when George S. May, the flamboyant owner of the Tam O'Shanter Golf Club in Chicago, fired all of his caddies and bought motorized golf carts to replace them. To accommodate his members, he reportedly mowed the roughs short to make it easier for them to find their own golf balls.

While traditionalists condemned May's action, club pros liked the idea because pro shops could collect fees from golfers who rode in motorized golf carts, whereas they normally collected nothing from golfers who hired a caddy because caddies did not customarily share their fees with the pro shop. Most recreational golfers soon came to prefer motorized golf carts over caddies because the carts carried them as well as their clubs.

By the late 1960s, the use of motorized golf carts had become the rule rather than the exception in American recreational golf. According to the National Golf Foundation, about 70 percent of all rounds of recreational golf played in the United States today are played in carts. The USGA's Green Section reports that the use of a cart is required in 16 percent of all golf facilities in the United States.

The widespread use of carts beginning in the 1950s contributed significantly to the growing popularity of golf. Carts enabled those who were unable or unwilling to endure the five-to-seven-mile walk in a typical round of golf to play and enjoy the game. The number of seniors playing golf increased significantly after the arrival of carts. Carts have enabled or prompted hundreds of thousands of older golfers to continue playing the game, often into their eighties and nineties. The National Golf Foundation reports that about 2 million of the 26 million recreational golfers in the United States today are over the age of 70, and of the 14 million "core" golfers (those who play at least eight rounds per year), 1.6 million are 70 or older. The average age of all recreational golfers is 54 years.

The advent of motorized golf carts brought about changes in the design and layout of golf courses. As many walkers have noticed, golf course designers no longer feel obligated to locate tee boxes within a short distance of the green of the preceding hole. Carts have also enabled golf course designers to include a hill or two in the layout of a golf course without making the course unpopular with recreational golfers. The advent of motorized golf carts closed an avenue to professional golf that for generations had been available to socially and financially disadvantaged young golfers. Before motorized golf carts came along, most of the great professional golfers in the United States had learned to play golf while working as caddies. Walter Hagen, Gene Sarazen, Byron Nelson, Ben Hogan, and Sam Snead all started out as caddies and learned to play the game while so employed. Of the great professional golfers who have emerged since the advent of carts in the 1950s, only one (Lee Trevino) started out as a caddie. The others were taught the game by instructors at golf clubs and perfected their game by playing junior and college golf, options that are not available to most disadvantaged young golfers.

The 1961 Masters was a two-man contest between Arnold Palmer and South African Gary Player. After two rounds, they were tied at the top at 137. In the third round, played on Saturday, Player's 69 gave him a four-stroke lead over Palmer, who carded a 73. In the final round on Sunday, they both shot 35s on the front nine, but the scores were washed out when heavy rains forced the cancellation of the round.

When the final round was replayed on Monday, Player made a couple of early birdies and upped his lead over Palmer to six strokes. The lead started disappearing, however, when Palmer heated up and started making birdies while Player, playing two holes ahead, bogeyed 10 and double-bogeyed 13. When Player missed a short putt on 15, giving Palmer a one-stroke lead, he was clearly on the ropes.

Palmer came to the tee box on the 14th hole nursing a one-stroke lead. He knew that Player was scrambling for pars and figured that if he could play the last five holes in even par, the tournament was his. After making routine pars on 14 and 15, he had to scramble a bit to par 16 and 17, but he did. On 18, after a good drive, he hit his second shot into a green-side bunker. He hit his bunker shot a bit thin and the ball skidded off the far side of the green and rolled down an embankment. Using his putter, he struck his fourth shot a bit too hard and the ball rolled 15 feet beyond the hole. When his 15-footer wouldn't drop, his double-bogey on the final hole gave Player a one-stroke victory.

Gary Player's victory over Arnold Palmer in the 1961 Masters, coupled with his British Open victory in 1959, established the 25-year-old South African as a player to be reckoned with on the PGA Tour. A year later, he became a legitimate challenger to Arnold Palmer as the best player in the game when he won his third major in three years with an exciting one-stroke victory over Bob Goalby in the 1962 PGA Championship.

Gary Player was born on November 1, 1935, in a small town near Johannesburg, South Africa. His father was a mine captain who worked in the gold mines in the Johannesburg area. His mother died of cancer when he was seven. Academically, he was an average student in school but excelled in cricket, rugby, swimming, and track. He was introduced to golf by his father when he was 15 and took an immediate liking to the game. He practiced tirelessly at a local public golf course and within a year and a half was shooting close to par.

When he finished his schooling, he took a job as an assistant club pro at the public course where he played. Two years later, in 1955, he was hired as an assistant club pro by a golf club in Johannesburg, where he met George Blumberg, a well-heeled manufacturer who thought the five-foot-six-inch, 150-pound bundle of energy had what it took to become one of the great golfers in the world. With financial assistance from Blumberg, Player went to England to improve his game by playing against the best British players. By 1956, he had improved his game enough to win the South African Open and post a fourth-place finish in the British Open.

In 1957, he married Vivienne Verwey, the daughter of the club pro at the public course where he had learned to play golf. Sponsored by Blumberg, he made his first visit to the United States that year and garnered a third-place finish in the Greater Greensboro Open on the PGA Tour. Encouraged by his success, he returned to the United States again in 1958, where he was invited to play in the Masters and qualified for the US Open. He failed to make the 36-hole cut at the Masters, but two months later, playing in devastating heat, he finished second to Tommy Bolt in the US Open at Southern Hills Country Club in Tulsa, Oklahoma. After the event, he credited the improvement in his game to the hours he had spent watching Ben Hogan practice. Later that summer, he traveled to England and posted a seventh-place finish in the British Open. A year later, he hit the jackpot and won the 1959 British Open at Muirfield Links in Gullane, Scotland.

The 1962 US Open was played in June at Oakmont Country Club near Pittsburgh, Pennsylvania. The event marked the arrival of yet another challenger to Arnold Palmer's reign as the king of golf. In the first two rounds at Oakmont, Arnold Palmer was paired with 21-year-old Jack Nicklaus, who had turned professional six months earlier and had yet to post a win in the 16 PGA Tour events he had played. Young Nicklaus had his work cut out for him at Oakmont because the course is less than an hour's drive from Latrobe and Arnie's Army was keyed up and out in full force for the event. In the first round, Palmer's 71 bettered Nicklaus's score by a stroke. In the second round,

Palmer shot a 68 and shared the tournament lead with Bob Rosburg at 139. Jack Nicklaus shot a 70 and trailed the leaders by three strokes.

Next up was "Open Saturday," when two 18-hole rounds would be played. In the morning round, the tournament leaders more or less held their ground until the 17th hole, a 292-yard, par-four hole whose small green is guarded by a ring of bunkers. Palmer bounced his tee shot between two of the bunkers and onto the green, where it stopped 12 feet from the pin. When he holed the 12-footer for an eagle, he was alone at the top by a stroke. However, he then three-putted the 18th green and the bogey dropped him back into a tie for the tournament lead with Bobby Nichols going into the final round on Saturday afternoon. Jack Nicklaus trailed the leaders by three strokes at that point.

In the final round, Palmer had a two-stroke lead over Nichols and Phil Rodgers after eight holes. Nicklaus, playing two holes ahead of Palmer, trailed him by three strokes. Palmer was thinking birdie after his drive on the 480-yard, uphill, par-five ninth hole. When he hit his second shot into some heavy rough next to the green, about 50 feet from the pin, his prospects for a birdie looked even better. However, the blade of his pitching wedge got caught up in the heavy grass and his chip shot failed to clear the rough. His follow-up chip shot came up short of the hole, leaving him with a seven-footer for his par, which he missed. Instead of picking up a stroke on the hole, he had lost a stroke. When Nicklaus sank an eight-footer for a birdie on 11, he was within a stroke of Palmer. Nichols and Rodgers, playing several holes ahead, had run into trouble and were no longer in contention. The event was now a two-man affair between Arnold Palmer, the best player in the world, and Jack Nicklaus, the rookie pro who had never won a PGA Tour event.

On the par-three 13th hole, Palmer hit his tee shot into a green-side bunker and was unable to get down in two. When Nicklaus got his par on 15, he and Palmer were dead even. Both players scrambled for pars the rest of the way, got them, and wound up tied at the top at 283. The US Open Championship, the greatest prize in American golf, would be decided in an 18-hole playoff on Sunday.

In the Sunday playoff, young Nicklaus quieted the huge, pro-Palmer gallery by jumping out to an early lead. After eight holes, he had a four-stroke lead over Palmer. Arnie's Army started coming to life on the ninth hole, however, when their man canned a 10-footer for a birdie. When he followed it up with another birdie on 11, cutting Nicklaus's lead to two strokes, his army was alive and well. With a big drive and a monstrous three-wood, Palmer got home in two on the 603-yard, par-five 12th hole and chalked up yet another birdie. Pumped up and trailing by only a stroke, he went to the par-three 13th hole, a hole he had bogeyed on Saturday afternoon. This time, he avoided the bunker and landed his tee shot in the middle of the green, about thirty-five feet from the pin. Normally a bold putter, he uncharacteristically left his first putt four feet short of the hole. His four-footer was off-target and he bogeyed the hole, while Nicklaus carded a two-putt par. Two strokes down and out of momentum, Palmer was unable to mount another charge and his missed tap-in putt on the last hole made Nicklaus a three-stroke winner. Young Jack Nicklaus had won his first tournament as a professional and it was a big one. Another challenger to Arnold Palmer's reign as the king of golf had arrived.

Jack William Nicklaus was born on January 21, 1940, in Columbus, Ohio, and grew up in Upper Arlington, an upper-middle-class suburb of Columbus. His father owned a chain of drugstores in the Columbus area and was a member of the prestigious Scioto Country Club in Columbus, whose golf course was a Donald Ross creation. Bobby Jones had won the US Open there in 1926. Taught by his father, who was a scratch golfer and a big Bobby Jones fan, and by Jack Grout, the head pro at Scioto, young Nicklaus started playing golf early and developed quickly. Big, strong, and talented for his age, he shot a 74 at Scioto when he was twelve, qualified for the US Amateur at age 15, and won the Ohio Open when he was 16.

Jack Nicklaus. The Golden Bear's 18 majors are the most ever.
Library of Congress

A good athlete, he played guard for the Upper Arlington Golden Bears High School basketball team, averaging 18 points a game as a senior, when he was named honorable mention All-State. His high school appears to have been the source of the "Golden Bear" nickname given to him by sportswriters later in his career. In September 1958, he enrolled as a prepharmacy major at Ohio State University, his father's alma mater, where he joined a fraternity and earned above-average grades in his classes. The only sport he played at Ohio State was golf, and he didn't play much of that until his junior year because of NCAA rules and his involvement in national amateur golf.

NCAA rules at that time prohibited freshmen from playing varsity sports, so he was unable to play for the Ohio State golf team as a freshman. During his sophomore year, he was able to play in only a few of the Buckeye's golf matches because he was selected for the US Walker Cup team and played in several important amateur tournaments, including the British Amateur, where he made it to the quarterfinals. In June of that year, he played in the 1960 US Open at Cherry Hills in Denver, where he finished second to Arnold Palmer and was the low amateur.

His performance at Cherry Hills impressed a lot of people. Especially impressive was his length off the tee. In a practice round at Cherry Hills, aided by a mild following wind, the five-foot-eleven-inch, 215-pound phenom needed only a drive and a seven iron to reach the green on the 550-yard, par-five 17th hole (the hole that ended the hopes of Ben Hogan and Don Cherry in the tournament).

Gene Littler said of young Nicklaus, "I first played with Jack in the 1959 Open at Winged Foot. He was Fat Jack then. Geez, he hit the ball so far."[1] Sportswriter Dan Jenkins wrote, "Nicklaus was awesome as an amateur, obviously the next great player. Golfers had been 'long' before Jack, but not as straight and long, and not even as long. His length, particularly with the long and mid irons, changed golf architecture."[2]

In late June, Nicklaus played for Ohio State in the 1960 NCAA Golf Championship and was eliminated in the second round. His credentials as a great amateur golfer took another hit a couple of weeks later when six three-putt greens led to his defeat in the fourth round of the US Amateur. Later that summer, he married Barbara Bash, an Ohio State co-ed from Columbus whom he had been dating since his freshman year.

The newly married amateur got back on track later in the year at the 1960 World Amateur Team Championship at Merion Golf Club near Philadelphia, where he shot rounds of 66, 67, 68, and 68. His 269 put him 13 strokes ahead of runner-up Deane Beman. *Sports Illustrated* called his performance at Merion the best performance by an amateur golfer since

Jack Nicklaus, Gary Player, and Arnold Palmer, the superstars of the 1960s, playing at Firestone Country Club in Akron, Ohio, in 1963.
Library of Congress

the Bobby Jones Grand Slam in 1930. The comparison to Jones must have pleased young Nicklaus, whose golfing idol had always been Bobby Jones.

In 1961, Nicklaus was again in position to win the US Open as an amateur, this time at Oakland Hills Country Club in Birmingham, Michigan. After eleven holes in the final round, he trailed Gene Littler by a single stroke. With his powerful long game, the 566-yard, par-5 12th hole looked like a reasonable birdie opportunity and his chances of catching Littler looked promising. Instead, it took him three to get on and three more to get down on the hole and he dropped a stroke to Littler. He never caught Littler and finished in a tie for fourth place. Littler defeated Doug Sanders and Bob Goalby by a stroke to win his first (and only) major. For the second year in a row, Nicklaus was the low amateur in the event.

A few weeks later, he won the 1961 US Amateur at Pebble Beach Golf Links in California. His play at Pebble Beach was as spectacular as his play at Merion in 1960 had been. Playing on one of the toughest golf courses in the world, he was 20 strokes under par in the 112 holes he played in the match-play event. Pebble Beach had never been played better. He won 9 and 8 in the semifinals and 8 and 6 in the finals. He was now clearly the best amateur golfer in the world. The only question was when he would turn pro and how good he would be as a professional.

During his junior year at Ohio State, Nicklaus won the 1961 Big Ten individual championship by 22 strokes and led Ohio State to the team championship. Later in the year, he won the NCAA Individual Golf Championship and became the first player ever to win that event and the US Amateur in the same year. A short time later, he consulted sports agent Mark McCormack, who told him he could make $100,000 a year in endorsements if he gave up his amateur status and turned professional. After much thought, he dropped out of Ohio State in November 1961 and joined the PGA tour.

During the decade of the 1960s, Arnold Palmer, Gary Player, and Jack Nicklaus replaced Ben Hogan, Sam Snead, and Byron Nelson as the superstars of professional golf, and its popularity soared as never before. Between them, they won 17 of the 40 majors played during the 1960s. The only other player to win more than one major during that decade was Julius Boros, who won two. During the seven-year period beginning in 1960, nobody but Palmer, Nicklaus, and Player won the Masters. Arnold Palmer won 43 PGA Tour events during the '60s, while Jack Nicklaus won 30 and Gary Player 10. Billy Casper won 33 PGA Tour events during the 1960s, but he won only one major in 30 attempts and remained a notch below Palmer, Nicklaus, and Player in the hierarchy of professional golf.

Arnold Palmer dominated professional golf during the first three years of the 1960s like no player before him. During that three-year period (1960–1962), he won five majors, two Vardon Trophies, and 22 PGA Tour events. However, his reign as the king of golf was a short one because after 1962 his only win in a major came in 1964, when he won his fourth Masters. When Gary Player won the US Open in 1965, he joined Gene Sarazen and

Ben Hogan as the only players to achieve a career Grand Slam with victories in each of the four modern majors at least once.

Jack Nicklaus won the 1967 US Open at Baltusrol Golf Club in Springfield, New Jersey, defeating runner-up Arnold Palmer by four strokes while shooting a 275, a score that broke Ben Hogan's US Open record set in 1948 by a stroke. Few noticed it at the time because no one had ever heard of the guy, but the fifth-place finisher in the event was a 27-year-old assistant club pro from Horizon Hills Country Club in El Paso, Texas, named Lee Trevino. Born on December 1, 1939, in Dallas, Texas, to a family of Mexican descent, Lee Trevino was raised in a home without electricity or running water by his mother and his grandfather, who worked as a gravedigger. Lee never knew his father, who abandoned the family when Lee was a toddler. He was introduced to golf by an uncle who gave him a few golf balls and an old golf club when he was ten.

When Trevino was 14, he quit school and took a job at the Dallas Athletic Club, where he earned $30 a week working as a caddy and a shoeshine boy. As an employee of the club, he was allowed to practice golf on three short holes behind the caddy shack. Unlike Jack Nicklaus, Arnold Palmer, and most of the other professional golfers he would later compete against, he never had a coach or an instructor. His game was entirely self-taught and natural.

In December 1956, at age 17, he enlisted in the US Marine Corps. When he finished basic training, he was assigned to the Third Marine Division in Okinawa, where he spent four years as a machine gun operator. While in the Marine Corps, he was able to play golf and won a couple of Armed Forces tournaments in Asia. After completing his enlistment in December 1960, he was hired as an assistant club pro at a golf club in El Paso, Texas. He played in local tournaments for five years before entering the Mexican Open in 1965, where he finished in second place. In 1966, he qualified for the US Open, made the cut, and finished tied for 54th place. He qualified for the event again in 1967 and finished in fifth place, eight strokes behind Jack Nicklaus. His showing in the 1967 US Open earned him PGA Tour privileges for the rest of the year. Although he didn't win any PGA Tour events that year, he played well enough to win $26,000 in prize money, which was big money for the twenty-six-year-old former shoeshine boy.

In 1968, the US Open became a four-day event for the first time. The USGA succumbed to the wishes of the television networks and abandoned tradition by lengthening the event to four days and doing away with "Open Saturday," when 36 holes had traditionally been played. Thirty-six holes on

Saturday and none on Sunday just didn't cut it with either the television networks or their viewers.

The 1968 US Open was played at Oak Hill Country Club in Rochester, New York, and evolved into be a three-man contest between Jack Nicklaus, Lee Trevino, and Bert Yancy, a 29-year-old pro from Florida who had overcome a bipolar disorder to play on the PGA Tour. In the opening round on Thursday, Yancy shot a 67 and led the tournament by two strokes over Trevino. Nicklaus, who hit good shots but missed five makeable putts, was five strokes back at 72. In the second round on Friday, Yancy and Trevino shot a pair of 68s and Yancy maintained his two-stroke lead. Nicklaus shot a 70 and trailed Yancy by seven strokes. Yancy matched Trevino's 69 in the third round and maintained his two-stroke advantage. Nicklaus shot another 70 and trailed Yancy by eight strokes going into the final round on Sunday.

Yancy must have used up all of his good shots in the first three rounds, because on Sunday he couldn't do anything right and lost nine strokes to Nicklaus in the first nine holes. At the turn, Nicklaus was a stroke ahead of Yancy but trailed Trevino by three strokes. Trevino increased his lead with birdies on eleven and twelve and the tournament looked to be his. Coming up the 13th fairway, Trevino, who hardly anybody in the USGA knew, walked up to Joe Dey, the executive director of the USGA who was serving as a rules observer for the event, slapped him on the back, and said with a big grin, "I'm just trying to build up as big a lead as I can so I won't choke."[3] Professional golf was fortunate to have a player of Trevino's wit, talent, and charisma on the tour.

Instead of choking, Trevino played the last five holes in even par and finished the event four strokes ahead of runner-up Nicklaus. Trevino shot a 69 in the final round and became the first player ever to shoot four rounds in the sixties in the US Open. His 275 tied the record low score for the event set the previous year by Nicklaus. The PGA Tour had the makings of yet another superstar.

Julius Boros won the 1968 PGA Championship at Pecan Valley Golf Club in San Antonio, Texas, defeating Arnold Palmer and Bob Charles by a stroke. In winning the event at age 48 years, four months, and 18 days, Boros became, and is still, the oldest player ever to win a major professional golf championship. On the final hole, Palmer, who had never won the event and trailed Boros by a stroke, hit a mammoth three-wood out of the rough to within eight feet of the hole but missed the tying eight-footer and failed to catch Boros. Even though Boros set an age record in winning the event, it is better known as the PGA Championship that Palmer lost.

In 1968, Jack Nicklaus went into a slump—the first of his career. Although he finished second in both the US and British Opens and won two PGA Tour events that year, he tied for fifth-place in the Masters and missed the cut in the PGA Championship and wasn't the dominating player he had been in previous years. In 1969, he won three PGA Tour events, but for the first time in his professional career was not in contention in any of the majors. He tied for 24th in the Masters and tied for 25th in the US Open, an event won by Orville Moody, a 35-year-old former army sergeant from Oklahoma who had never won a PGA Tour event and would never win another. However, 20 years later, in 1989, "the Sarge" won the US Senior Open and became only the fourth player to win both the US Open and the US Senior Open.

In the fall of 1969, while on a flight back to the United States from London after the Ryder Cup matches, Nicklaus decided to lose some weight, hoping it would help his game. With the aid of his wife, Barbara, he went on a diet when he returned home and stuck with it until his weight dropped from 210 pounds to 190. Earlier in the year, he had let his crew cut grow out, an appearance change that made him look more mature. He now looked like a 30-year-old man who played golf for a living. "Fat Jack" had become "the Golden Bear."

His appearance change didn't seem to affect his golf game right away, however, and during the early months of 1970 his slump continued. He won the Byron Nelson Golf Classic in May in a playoff with Arnold Palmer, and then tied for forty-fourth in the US Open in June, breaking 75 only once during the event. Another opportunity to pull out of his slump came in July when he traveled to Scotland to play in the British Open on the Old Course at St. Andrews.

When the air is calm, the Old Course is a drive and pitch course for modern professional golfers using today's clubs and balls. The air was calm during the first round of the 1970 British Open and the scores showed it. Forty-three of the 134 participants broke par. They were led by Neil Coles, an English pro, who shot a 65. Englishman Tony Jacklin, the defending champion, shot a 67 and Lee Trevino and Jack Nicklaus shot 68s. On the second day, the winds returned and the scores went up. Trevino, who had learned to play golf on the wind-swept plains of West Texas, handled the wind well and shot a 68, the low score of the round, and claimed the 36-hole lead at 136. Nicklaus shot a 69 and, along with Jacklin, trailed Trevino by a stroke. In the third round, the winds continued and Trevino matched par with a 72. His 208 gave him a two-stroke lead over Nicklaus and Jacklin, who carded 73s. Doug Sanders shot an impressive 71 and joined Nicklaus and Jacklin at 210.

In the fourth round, Trevino, normally one of the best putters on the tour, unaccountably lost his putting stroke on the front nine and went on a three-putt binge that knocked him out of contention. After that it was nip and tuck between Jacklin and Nicklaus, who were playing together, and Sanders, who was playing in the group behind them. After 15 holes, Jacklin and Sanders were tied for the lead, a stroke ahead of Nicklaus. Jacklin fell a stroke behind Sanders and into a tie with Nicklaus when he three-putted 16 and took a bogey. Nicklaus and Jacklin both parred 17, the Road Hole, and moved to 18, the Tom Morris Hole.

Playing the Road Hole immediately after Nicklaus and Jacklin, Sanders hit his second shot into the Road Hole bunker. Looking at a sure bogey, he stayed in the hunt with a magnificent sand shot and a great putt to remain a stroke ahead of both Nicklaus and Jacklin. On 18, Nicklaus and Jacklin were both on the green in two, with Nicklaus's ball considerably closer to the hole than Jacklin's. Jacklin needed three to get down and fell two strokes behind Sanders. Nicklaus, who needed to get down in one to catch Sanders, couldn't get his birdie putt to drop and his tap-in par sent him to the clubhouse a stroke ahead of Jacklin, but a stroke behind Sanders, who still had to play the Tom Morris hole.

Sanders came to the Tom Morris Hole needing only a par to win his first major. A great drive left him within pitching distance of the green. However, the wind blew his pitch 35 feet past the pin and his first putt came up three feet short of the hole. Needing to sink the three-footer to win the tournament and avoid a playoff, he pushed it to the right and missed it. The 110th British Open would be decided on Sunday in an 18-hole playoff between Nicklaus and Sanders.

In the Sunday playoff, the St. Andrews winds were blowing and Nicklaus failed to get a birdie on the first 13 holes. However, he parred them all and built up a four-stroke lead over Sanders, who was having trouble with the wind. On 14, Sanders got the first birdie of the day by either player. On 15, he picked up another stroke with his second birdie and on 16 he picked up still another stroke when Nicklaus needed three to get down from the fringe. They both recorded two-putt pars on the Road Hole and the match moved to the 354-yard Tom Morris Hole with Nicklaus leading by a stroke.

With the wind to his back, Sanders hit his drive to within a short pitch of the green on 18. Nicklaus's drive bounced onto the green and rolled off the back, coming to rest on some dried grass a few yards behind the green. Sanders pitched his second shot to within inches of the hole. Knowing he needed to get down in two to match Sanders's sure birdie, Nicklaus lobbed a delicate pitch onto the green and watched it roll to a stop eight feet short of the hole. Needing to drop the eight-footer to win the event, he stood over the ball seemingly forever and then stroked it lightly and waited. When the ball caught the left edge of the cup and dropped into the hole, he threw his putter into the air in celebration. He had won the British Open and was sure his slump was over. It was—during the next three years, he would win four majors and 16 PGA Tour events.

Since its founding in 1916, there had been a conflict within the PGA of America between the club pros and the touring professionals over the allocation of the organization's revenues. The club pros, who constituted the bulk of the membership, wanted most of the organization's revenues to be used to promote golf at the local level. The touring pros, whose tournaments produced most of the organization's revenue, wanted the bulk of the organization's revenues to be used to increase the purses of the tournaments on the PGA Tour. The organization's revenues increased substantially during the 1960s because of television revenues, and the conflict between the club pros and the touring pros intensified

At the conclusion of the 1968 PGA Championship at Pecan Valley Country Club in San Antonio, Texas, several touring pros voiced dissatisfaction with the number of club pros in the event. A short time later, the touring pros formed an organization of their own and started scheduling a tour independently of the PGA of America. Later that year, after intense negotiations, the club pros and the touring pros agreed on a compromise whereby a new division within the PGA of America called the Tournament Players Division was created. The Tournament Players Division was given its own commissioner and ten-person policy board composed of four tournament players, three PGA officials, and three businessmen. It was also allowed to schedule and manage the events on the PGA Tour.

The best golfers in the world during the decade of the 1970s were Jack Nicklaus, Lee Trevino, and Gary Player. Together, they won 16 of the 40 majors played during that decade, with Nicklaus winning eight and Player and Trevino four apiece. Only four other players on the tour won more than one major during the 1970s—Tom Watson won three and Dave Stockton, Johnny Miller, and Hale Irwin won two apiece. One of the majors that Johnny Miller won was the 1973 US Open at Oakmont Country Club, where he was in 12th place going into the final round, six strokes behind Arnold Palmer and three other co-leaders. In the final round, he shot an incredible eight-under-par 63 and passed 11 players, including Palmer, Player, and Trevino, and won the event by one stroke. His final-round 63 is still the lowest final-round score ever shot by the winner of a major championship.

In 1974, Miller won eight PGA Tour events and was the tour's leading money-winner. In 1975, he won four PGA Tour events, and in 1976 he won three, including the British Open, which he won by six strokes over Jack Nicklaus and Seve Ballesteros. On the verge of superstardom, he did not win another event until 1980 and never won another major. His four-year run from 1973 to 1976 was a good one, but it wasn't enough and he came up short of superstardom.

When Gary Player won the British Open in 1974, he became the only player in the twentieth century to win the British Open in three different decades, having previously won the event in 1959 and 1968. Four years later, at age 42, he won his final major with birdies on seven of the last 10 holes to win the 1978 Masters by a stroke over Hubert Green. No fan of the apartheid government in his home country, in 1971 he risked his enormous popularity in South Africa by accompanying African American golfer Lee Elder and African American tennis player Arthur Ashe to South Africa to play their respective sports in South African tournaments.

During the summer of 1971, Lee Trevino had an incredible run, winning the US Open, the Canadian Open, and the British Open in a span of 20 days. In 1970 and 1971, Trevino was invited to play in the Masters but declined the invitations. In 1972, he accepted the invitation and played in the Masters but kept his shoes and clubs in the trunk of his car rather than use the locker room facilities in the Augusta National clubhouse. When asked about this by sportswriters, he commented that had he not qualified as a player they wouldn't have let him on the grounds except through the kitchen.

In the mid-1970s, another young challenger started making waves on the PGA Tour. Tom Watson, a 25-year-old, third-year pro from Kansas City by way of Stanford University, won the 1975 British Open at Carnoustie, defeating Australian Jack Newton in a playoff. After an off-year in 1976, when he failed to win a single PGA Tour event, Watson started his run at Nicklaus in 1977. After winning the Bing Crosby National Pro-Am and the San Diego Open early in the year, in April he went to Augusta, Georgia, to play in the Masters. After three rounds, he was alone at the top with a three-stroke lead over runner-up Jack Nicklaus. In the fourth round, Nicklaus made his move and posted birdies on six of the first 13 holes to pull within a stroke of the young challenger. Watson hung on, however, and his birdie on 17 put him a stroke ahead of Nicklaus, whose bogey on 18 made Watson a two-stroke winner.

Neither Watson nor Nicklaus contended in the US Open in June, but in July they met again for another head-to-head encounter in the British Open at Turnberry Golf Links in Ayrshire, Scotland. Known as one of the greatest links players in the world, Watson was thought by many to have an advantage over Nicklaus on the links at Turnberry. After three identical rounds of 68, 70, and 65, the two Americans were tied at the top, three strokes ahead of the field. Paired in the final round, Nicklaus built up a three-stroke lead over Watson during the first 12 holes. However, with a birdie on 13 and a Nicklaus bogey on 14, Watson pulled to within a stroke and when he canned a 60-footer for a birdie on 15, they were dead even. On 17, Watson managed still another birdie, which Nicklaus was unable to match when his four-foot birdie putt wouldn't drop. With a hole to go, Watson had a one-stroke lead over Nicklaus.

On 18, they both hit good drives, but Nicklaus's approach shot left him 30 feet from the hole while Watson's approach shot left him a scant two feet from the hole. Nicklaus put the heat on his young opponent, however, by sinking his 30-footer. Known to have trouble with short putts, Watson steadied himself and calmly sank the two-footer to win his second British Open in three years. His final-round 65 gave him a 268 for the event, a score that broke the 72-hole record score at the British Open, first set by Arnold Palmer in 1962, by an incredible eight strokes. Professional golf had another superstar on its hands.

With his win at Turnberry, Watson had defeated Nicklaus in head-to-head encounters twice in four months in major championships and there were many who thought that he had replaced Nicklaus as the number-one player in the world. However, the Golden Bear wasn't ready to step down just yet. In 1978, he returned to Scotland and won the British Open on the Old Course at St. Andrews, the ultimate links course, handily defeating Watson, who finished tied for 14th. When he won both the US Open and the PGA Championship in 1980, Nicklaus's status as the number-one player in the world was firmly established. But not for long, because Watson then made one of the greatest runs in the history of professional golf, winning five majors in four years. He won the British Open in 1980, 1982, and 1983, the Masters in 1981, and the US Open in 1982.

In the 1982 US Open at Pebble Beach, Watson and Nicklaus engaged in one of the most memorable US Open Championships ever played. Playing three groups ahead of Watson in the final round, Nicklaus, who very much wanted his record fifth US Open title, caught Watson, the tournament leader, with five consecutive birdies on the back nine and retired to the clubhouse tied for the lead. When Watson reached the 210-yard, par-three 17th hole, he remained tied with Nicklaus. Nicklaus's chances of winning the event looked promising when Watson hit his tee shot into a patch of rough a few feet to the right of the green, leaving him with a difficult, downhill pitch onto a down-sloping green. In typical US Open fashion, the thick, heavy rough had been allowed to grow long for the event. With the championship at stake and a national television audience looking on, Watson, using a sand wedge, pitched the ball cleanly out of the tangled grass of the rough onto the edge of the green, where it started rolling downhill toward the hole, showing no signs of slowing down. For a second, it looked like the ball would roll well past the hole. However, the ball hit the flag stick squarely and dropped into the hole for a birdie, giving him a one-stroke lead with a hole to go. With the pressure off, he birdied 18 as well and won the event by two strokes.

By winning five majors and 15 PGA Tour events in four years, together with the three majors and three Vardon Trophies he had won in the late 1970s, by 1983 Tom Watson had established himself as the best player in the world. His stay at the top was brief, however, because after winning his fifth British Open in 1983 (only Harry Vardon, with six, has won more), he won only four more tour events during the rest of his career and never won another major.

Stars from the past reappeared periodically during the 1970s and '80s. In 1979, 67-year-old Sam Snead, playing in his final year on the PGA tour, became the first player to shoot his age when he shot a 67 in the second round of the Quad Cities Open. Two days later, in the fourth round, he broke his own record by shooting a 66. Unfortunately for Sam, his two historic rounds were not enough to win the event. On August 19, 1984, 44-year-old Lee Trevino, who had not won a major in 10 years, took his sixth and final major by winning the PGA Championship at Shoal Creek Country Club in Birmingham, Alabama. He finished four strokes ahead of runners-up Lanny Wadkins and 48-year-old Gary Player.

Jack Nicklaus's finest hour came in April 1986 when he played in his 28th Masters. Going into the final round, he trailed third-round leader Greg Norman by four strokes. After playing the first eight holes in even par, he caught Norman with birdies on 9, 10, and 11. Norman, meanwhile, double-bogeyed 10 and lost the tournament lead to Seve Ballesteros, Nicklaus's playing partner. Nicklaus passed Norman with a birdie on 13, but still trailed Ballesteros by four strokes. He started his run at Ballesteros with a sensational eagle on the par-five 15th hole. Ballesteros bogeyed the hole and Nicklaus pulled to within a stroke of the tournament leader. Nicklaus followed up his eagle on 15 by sticking his tee shot on the par-three 16th hole three feet from the pin to set up a birdie that tied him with Ballesteros, who parred the hole. Nicklaus left his approach shot on 17 10 feet from the pin and a few minutes later drained the straight-in 10-footer to pull two strokes ahead of Ballesteros, who bogeyed the hole. Both Nicklaus and Ballesteros parred the final hole and Nicklaus retired to the clubhouse two strokes ahead of Ballesteros and one stroke ahead of Tom Kite, but tied with Greg Norman, who had recovered and come on strong with consecutive birdies on 14, 15, 16, and 17. Both Kite and Norman had one hole left to play.

Needing a birdie on 18 to catch Nicklaus, Kite stuck his approach shot 10 feet from the pin. Minutes later, however, he missed the side-hill 10-footer on the high side. With four consecutive birdies under his belt and needing one more to win his first major, or a par to force a playoff, Norman hit his drive on 18 in the middle of the fairway. However, he then pushed his approach shot into the gallery to the right of the green and followed it up with a pitch that left him 15 feet from the hole. When the Australian's 15-footer wouldn't drop, Nicklaus claimed his sixth and final Masters title. It was also his 18th and final career major. He had played the last 10 holes in seven under par and had shot a final-round 65, including an amazing 30 on the pressure-packed final nine holes. By winning the event at age 46, he became, and is still, the oldest player ever to win the Masters. He won his first Masters in 1963 and the 23-year span between his first and last Masters titles is a record that may never be broken.

When Arnold Palmer drove the green on the first hole at Cherry Hills in the 1960 US Open, he did it using a rubber-wound golf ball and a driver composed of a steel shaft and a persimmon clubhead. At the time, solid-core golf balls, graphite shafts, metal woods, titanium clubheads, and oversized drivers were yet to be invented.

The demand for golf equipment created by the phenomenal growth of recreational golf in the 1960s and 1970s spurred manufacturers to innovate and introduce improvements in golf equipment. Traditional manufacturers like Spalding, Wilson, and MacGregor were challenged by new companies like TaylorMade, Callaway, and Karsten Manufacturing, the makers of Ping golf products.

When the 1960s arrived, the balata-covered, rubber-wound Haskell golf ball had been the ball of choice of both professional and recreational golfers for half a century. In the mid-1960s, E. I. DuPont de Nemours and Company developed a synthetic resin called Surlyn, which was used as a covering on golf balls. Surlyn covers were more durable than balata covers and did not cut as easily. Not surprisingly, Surlyn soon replaced balata as the covering on most golf balls. At about the same time, synthetic materials began replacing rubber as the core of golf balls and golf balls became classified as two-piece, three-piece, and four-piece balls, depending on the number of layers of their components.

In the late 1960s, Spalding introduced the first solid-core golf ball. A two-piece ball, it was composed of a solid resin core that eliminated the need for rubber windings or other layered components and a cover made of either Surlyn or urethane. Golfers got more distance from solid-core balls than from wound balls and most recreational golfers switched to them. However, many professional and low-handicap recreational golfers continued to use wound balls because they were easier to control around the greens, had a softer feel, and were easier to spin.

A detriment of the early solid-core golf balls was that they occasionally split into fragments. This happened often enough so that in 1976 the USGA adopted a rule providing that "if a ball breaks into pieces as the result of a stroke, the stroke shall be replayed without penalty." USGA Rule 20-5, adopted in 1984, requires the replacement ball to be dropped unless the stroke breaking the ball occurred in a teeing area, in which case the replacement ball may be teed.

During the 1960s and '70s, the USGA adopted rules dealing with the makeup and manufacture of golf balls. These rules, which are set forth in appendix III of the USGA's Rules of Golf, provide that golf balls must not be substantially different from the traditional and customary form and make of golf balls. The rules also impose standards for the weight, initial velocity, distance, and carry of golf balls. Manufacturers must comply with these standards in order for their balls to qualify for use in events sanctioned by the USGA.

In 1961, Karsten Manufacturing introduced perimeter weighted irons, an innovation that increased the size of the "sweet spot" of an iron by distributing more weight to the perimeter of the clubhead. The concept caught on and oversized, perimeter-weighted irons became popular with both recreational and professional golfers.

In 1969, Frank Thomas, a design engineer with Shakespeare Sporting Goods, working in conjunction with Union Carbide, invented the graphite shaft. The early graphite shafts were expensive and golf clubs made with them did not sell well. Subsequent changes in the manufacture and composition of graphite shafts substantially reduced their cost, and by the mid-1990s graphite shafts were being used in both woods and irons with much success. Graphite shafts are made of a carbon fiber composite and are substantially lighter and more flexible than steel shafts. Because graphite-shafted clubs are lighter and easier to swing than steel-shafted clubs, they produce higher club-head speeds and more distance than their steel-shafted counterparts, but with slightly less accuracy. Most recreational golfers prefer graphite shafts in both woods and irons because of the greater distance they get from them. However, many professional and low-handicap recreational golfers prefer steel shafts, especially in irons, because of their greater accuracy.

Another significant change in golf clubs during the 1980s was the introduction of metal woods. The first metal woods were made by Pinseeker Golf in 1976. Made with hollow stainless-steel heads, they did not catch on right away. In 1979, TaylorMade introduced a set of stainless-steel metal woods that achieved some market success, but metal woods did not sell in big numbers until the advent of titanium clubheads in the 1980s. Gary Adams, the founder of TaylorMade Golf, is credited with being the father of the metal wood. With design help from others, he developed the TaylorMade Burner and Tour Preferred metal woods, and millions of them were sold beginning in the late 1980s.

Callaway Golf was another early manufacturer of metal woods. In 1991, Calloway introduced the "Big Bertha," the first oversized metal driver. Made with a large, hollow, stainless steel clubhead, the Big Bertha gave golfers more distance than traditional wooden drivers and was an immediate market success. In subsequent years, Callaway came out with the "Bigger Bertha" and the "Great Big Bertha" and other manufacturers began producing oversized drivers of their own. When titanium replaced stainless steel in the heads of metal woods in the 1990s, the distance produced by oversized drivers increased again and golf clubs with persimmon heads became collector's items.

By the late 1990s, metal woods and oversized drivers had taken over the market, and the USGA began imposing limits on both the size of the clubhead and the amount of "springlike effect" that the faces of these clubs could produce. Terms like *coefficient of restitution* and *moment of inertia* were devised to measure the springlike effect of clubfaces of metal woods. Over stiff opposition from club manufacturers, who wanted no restrictions, the USGA eventually determined that the size of a clubhead could not exceed 460 cubic centimeters and that the maximum coefficient of restitution would be 0.830.

A significant happening in professional golf during the early 1980s was the establishment of the Senior Tour. The first PGA event for senior golfers was the Senior PGA Championship, which was established by the PGA of America in 1937 for professional golfers over the age of 50. For 43 years, it was the only championship for senior golfers. Sam Snead dominated the event during the 1960s and '70s, winning it six times in ten years beginning in 1964. The feasibility of creating a separate PGA Tour for senior golfers was established in 1978 by the success of a golfing event created for television called the Legends of Golf, which featured televised matches between pairs of well-known older golfers. Sam Snead and Gardner Dickinson won the initial event, which was televised nationally by NBC and drew a sizeable audience.

The Senior PGA Tour was established by the PGA of America in 1980 when four tournaments for professional golfers over the age of 50 were held. One of these tournaments was the US Senior Open, which was initiated that year by the USGA. The tour for senior golfers was originally called the Senior

PGA Tour, but in 2002 it was renamed the Champions Tour. In 2016, its name was changed to the PGA Tour Champions.

The popularity of the Senior PGA Tour was given a big boost when Arnold Palmer joined the tour and won one of the initial events. The other first-year senior tournaments were won by Charlie Sifford, Don January, and Roberto DeVicenzo, who won the first US Senior Open. Arnold Palmer won the US Senior Open in 1981 in a playoff with Billy Casper and Bob Stone and became the first player to win the USGA's three signature events—the US Amateur, the US Open, and the US Senior Open. Ten years later, Jack Nicklaus joined him in that honor when he won his first US Senior Open.

There are now five major tournaments on the Champions Tour— the US Senior Open, the Senior PGA Championship, the Senior Players Championship, the Senior Open Championship (aka the Senior British Open), and the Tradition. These events constitute what are called the five senior majors.

Players like Arnold Palmer, Jack Nicklaus, Gary Player, Lee Trevino, and Tom Watson, who were superstars during their careers on the regular PGA Tour, were also highly successful on the Champions Tour, and their presence contributed much to making the Champions Tour popular and successful. However, the most successful player on the Champions Tour has been Hale Irwin, whose 45 senior wins are the most ever. He has also won seven senior majors (only Jack Nicklaus with eight has won more) and is the leading career money-winner on the Champions Tour with more than 26 million dollars in official winnings through the close of the 2017 season. The former football player (he was an all-conference defensive back for the University of Colorado in the late 1960s) had a remarkable career in golf. While in college, he won the NCAA Individual Golf Championship in 1967. He joined the regular PGA Tour in 1968 and won 20 PGA Tour events, including three US Open Championships, during his career on the regular PGA Tour. Only Willie Anderson, Bobby Jones, Ben Hogan, and Jack Nicklaus, with four, have won more US Open Championships than Hale Irwin. His US Open Championships came in 1974, 1979, and 1990, when, at age 45, he became, and is still, the oldest player ever to win the US Open.

In the late 1980s, professional golf in the United States was faced with a problem it had not had to deal with for 30 years—it did not have a superstar. Of the great triumvirate of Arnold Palmer, Gary Player, and Jack Nicklaus, later joined by Lee Trevino and Tom Watson, only Jack Nicklaus was still playing on the regular PGA tour and his victory in the 1986 Masters was his last win in a major. Arnold Palmer and Gary Player had retired from the regular tour and Lee Trevino's victory in the 1984 PGA Championship was his last win in a major. Tom Watson's last win in a major came in the 1983

British Open. By the late 1980s, the superstars who had arrived during the 1960s and '70s were superstars no more, and the PGA Tour needed replacements in order to retain the immense popularity it had attained during the quarter-century following the arrival of Arnold Palmer in 1960.

During the 14-year period between 1986, when Jack Nicklaus won his final major, and the end of the 20th century, the only American player who won more than two majors was Payne Stewart, who won three. The best golfer in the world during that period was Nick Faldo, an Englishman, who won six majors. A conservative, methodical player who disliked galleries and whose victories always seemed to be the result of his opponent's mistakes, Faldo did not catch on with American sports fans and did not become a superstar in the United States, even though he was immensely popular in Europe. Payne Stewart was denied superstardom by his untimely and tragic death in an airplane crash in October 1999 while travelling in a Learjet from his home in Orlando, Florida, to a season-ending tournament in Houston, Texas.

Both Seve Ballesteros, a dashing Spaniard with an exciting playing style, and Greg Norman, the long-hitting Great White Shark from Australia, displayed superstar potential in the early 1980s. However, Ballesteros, after winning four majors in five years beginning in 1979, cooled off after 1984 and won only two PGA Tour events and one major after that. Greg Norman won the British Open in 1986 and 1993 and was the runner-up in seven majors between 1984 and 1995. However, he essentially disappeared from the PGA Tour after his meltdown in the 1996 Masters, where he carried a six-stroke lead into the final round, only to collapse and lose to Nick Faldo by five strokes in front of a national television audience. After the meltdown, he won only two more PGA Tour events.

Fortunately for professional golf, several talented young players joined the tour during the 1990s, each of whom appeared to have superstar potential. Included in this group were John Daly, Phil Mickelson, Vijay Singh, Ernie Els, Jim Furyk, David Duval, Tiger Woods, and Sergio Garcia. The situation was similar to that faced by professional golf in the late 1950s, when replacements for the aging triumvirate of Ben Hogan, Sam Snead, and Byron Nelson were needed and players like Billy Casper, Dow Finsterwald, Ken Venturi, Mike Souchak, Gary Player, and Arnold Palmer joined the tour.

John Daly was born in April 1966, in Carmichael, California. When he was four, his family moved to Dardanelle, Arkansas, and later to Jefferson City, Missouri, where he attended high school. In high school, he lettered in football and golf, which he had started playing on local public courses when he was five. In golf, he won the Missouri State High School Championship and was famous locally for his distance off the tee. In football, he was a kicker and set several state high school kicking records. After high school, he attended the University of Arkansas on a golf scholarship and played briefly on the Razorback's golf team before dropping out of school during his sophomore year. In 1986, he qualified as an amateur for the US Open, but shot a first-round 86 and missed the 36-hole cut.

He turned professional in 1987 and won the Missouri Open that year. After playing locally for four years, he joined the PGA Tour in 1991. As a tour rookie, he qualified as an alternate for the PGA Championship at Crooked Stick Golf Club in Carmel, Indiana, and unbelievably won the event. He was the first alternate qualifier ever to win the PGA Championship and was named the PGA Rookie of the Year. He won two more tour events during the next four years and in 1995 he came out of nowhere to win the British Open on the Old Course at St. Andrews, defeating Constantino Rocca of Italy in a playoff.

By the end of the twentieth century, Daly had won four tour events, two of which were majors. Standing five-foot, eleven-inches tall and weighing 250 pounds, he was prodigiously long off the tee and in 1997 became the first PGA Tour player to average over 300 yards off the tee over the course of a full season. His all-out swing and length off the tee, his non-country-club appearance and demeanor, and his tumultuous personal life (he had already been married and divorced three times) attracted a cult following, and he drew sizeable galleries just about every time he played. With a playing style that attracted galleries and an ability to win majors, he clearly had superstar potential. Only the passage of time would tell whether he could harness his immense natural talent and become a consistent winner on the PGA Tour, a requirement for superstardom in the United States.

Born in San Diego, California, in June 1970, Phil Mickelson spent his youth in San Diego and Scottsdale, Arizona. Naturally right-handed, he learned to swing a golf club left-handed as a boy by watching his right-handed father swing a golf club and mirroring the swing. He started playing golf before he started school and at age 10 won the Junior World Golf Championship. He graduated from high school in San Diego and attended Arizona State University on a golf scholarship. While at Arizona State, he was a first-team NCAA All-American for four straight years, won NCAA Individual Championships in 1989, 1990, and 1992, and led the Sun Devils to an NCAA Team Championship in 1990. He also won the US Amateur Championship that year and became the first player with a left-handed swing to do so. In 1990 and 1991, he was the low-scoring amateur in the US Open and in 1991 he was the low amateur in the Masters. In 1991, he became the sixth (and last) amateur to win a PGA Tour event when he won the Northern Telecom Open in Tucson, Arizona.

In 1992, he graduated from Arizona State, turned professional, and joined the PGA Tour. His first professional win on the PGA Tour came in February 1993, when he won the Buick Invitational. By the end of the 20th century, he had won twelve events and had accumulated more than $8 million in official winnings, but he had not won a major. His best finish in a major came in 1999 when he finished second to Payne Stewart in the US Open. Already a consistent winner on the PGA Tour, he had obvious superstar potential, but he would have to win a few majors to become one.

Vijay Singh was born in February 1963 in the town of Loutoka on the island of Fiji in the South Pacific. As a boy, he played cricket, soccer, and the island's most popular sport, rugby. He was taught to play golf by his father, who was an airplane technician who doubled as a golf instructor at a local golf club. The best amateur golfer on the island as a teenager, Singh turned professional at age 19. Two years later, in 1984, he won the Malaysian PGA Championship. In 1988, he traveled to Africa and became the first man of color to win the Nigerian Open. In 1989, he joined the European Tour, where he won four events in four years.

In 1993, at age 30, he came to the United States and joined the PGA Tour. In June of that year, he won his first PGA Tour event, the Buick Classic, defeating Mark Wiebe in a playoff. Later in the year, he finished fourth in the PGA Championship and was named the PGA Rookie of the Year. After going winless in 1994 because of back and neck injuries, he won seven events over the next four years, including his first major—the 1998 PGA Championship. By the end of the twentieth century, he had won eight PGA Tour events and one major, together with seven events on the European Tour, where he also played. He would have to continue to win regularly on the PGA Tour and win a few more majors to become a superstar in the United States, but he clearly had the talent and work ethic to do so. However, at age 37, his age was working against him.

Ernie Els was born in Johannesburg, South Africa, in October 1969. He was introduced to golf when he was eight years old by his father, who was a trucking company executive and a member of the Kempton Park Country Club near Johannesburg. A scratch golfer when he was 14, young Els was also a skilled junior tennis player and won the Eastern Transvaal Junior Tennis Championship at age 13. At age 14, he dropped tennis to concentrate on golf and in 1984 he won the World Junior Golf Championship, defeating Phil Mickelson in the finals. In 1986, a few months after his 17th birthday, he became the youngest winner of the South African Amateur Championship, breaking Gary Player's age record in doing so.

He turned professional in 1989 and started playing on the South African Tour, where he won six events in 1992. In 1994, he joined both the European

Tour and the PGA Tour in the United States, where he was named the PGA Rookie of the Year. His first victory on the PGA Tour came during his rookie year when he won the US Open at Oakmont Country Club, defeating Colin Montgomery and Loren Roberts in an 18-hole playoff despite going bogey, triple-bogey on the first two holes. In 1997, he again won the US Open, this time at Congressional Country Club in Bethesda, Maryland, where he became the first foreign two-time winner of the event since Alex Smith in 1910.

Known as "the Big Easy" because of his six-foot-four-inch, 210-pound frame and the unforced smoothness of his golf swing, Els won five PGA Tour events in addition to his two US Open titles prior to end of the twentieth century. He had also won five events on the European Tour during the 1990s. The immensely talented South African clearly had the talent to become a superstar in the United States. Working against him was the time he spent on the European Tour, which most American sports fans do not follow.

Jim Furyk was born in May 1970 in West Chester, Pennsylvania. He spent his early years in suburban Pittsburgh, where his father worked as an assistant club pro at several golf clubs. He was introduced to the game at an early age by his father and played junior golf as a teenager. In high school, he played basketball and won a state high school golf championship. After graduating from high school, he attended the University of Arizona on a golf scholarship, where he was a two-time All-American and led the Wildcats to an NCAA Golf Championship in 1992. Later that year, he left college, turned professional, and joined the Nike Tour. In 1994, he qualified for and joined the PGA Tour. His unorthodox swing features a loop at the top of his backswing and he has been described as looking as though he was trying to swing a golf club in a telephone booth.

His first professional victory came in 1995, when he won the Las Vegas Invitational, an event he won again in 1998 and 1999. By the end of the 20th century, he had won four PGA Tour events and had had five top-10 finishes in majors. Already a contender in the majors, he would have to win a few majors and win more consistently on the PGA Tour to become a superstar.

David Duval was born in Jacksonville, Florida, in November 1971. He was taught to play golf at an early age by his father, who was the club pro at Timuquana Country Club in Jacksonville, Florida. An outstanding golfer at an early age, in 1989, at age 17, he won the US Junior Amateur Championship. In 1990, he enrolled at Georgia Tech on a golf scholarship, where he was an NCAA All-American for four straight years and was the 1993 National College Player of the Year. While at Georgia Tech, he entered the BellSouth Classic, a PGA Tour event, as an amateur and led the field after the third round. After the close of the 1993 college golf season, he left

Georgia Tech, turned professional, and joined the Nike Tour, where he played for two years.

In 1995, he qualified for and joined the PGA Tour, where he posted seven second-place finishes but no wins during his first two years. His first PGA Tour victories came in October 1997, when he won three consecutive events, including the Tour Championship, which he won by one stroke over Jim Furyk. During the next two years, he won eight tour events, including the 1999 Players Championship, and became the number-one ranked player in the world. In 1998, he had the lowest-scoring average on the tour and won both the Vardon Trophy and the Byron Nelson Award. He was also the tour's leading money-winner with over 2.5 million dollars in official winnings. He was the second leading money-winner in 1997 and 1999 and won over eight-million dollars during last three years of the 20th century.

In 1999, he shot a 59 in the final round and made an eagle on the final hole to win the Bob Hope Desert Classic by one stroke. It was only the third time a player had broken 60 in a PGA Tour event and the first time such a score had been shot in a final round. However, his best showing in a major during this period was a second-place finish in the 1998 Masters. A gifted player with an appealing playing style and already a consistent winner on the tour, he needed only to win a few majors to become the superstar that professional golf was looking for.

Eldrick "Tiger" Woods was born in Cypress, California, on December 30, 1975. He was nicknamed Tiger by his father, a Vietnam War veteran, after a Vietnamese friend of his who went by that name. His father, Earl Woods, was an African American US Army officer and his mother, Kultida Punsawad Woods, was of mixed Thai, Chinese, and Dutch ancestry. Introduced to golf by his father at a very young age, Tiger was a phenomenal golfer as a youth, winning the Junior World Golf Championship six times before his 15th birthday. He won the US Junior Amateur Championship a record three times and, at age 15, was the youngest winner ever. At age 18, he became the youngest-ever winner of the US Amateur, an event he won a record three times in a row beginning in 1994.

In the fall of 1994, he enrolled at Stanford University on a golf scholarship and in 1995 was an NCAA First-Team All-American and the PAC-Ten Player of the Year. In 1996, after winning the NCAA Individual Golf Championship and his third consecutive US Amateur title, he dropped out of Stanford, turned professional, joined the PGA Tour, and signed endorsement contracts with Nike and Titleist that were reportedly the most lucrative in the history of the game. He won two of the 11 tour events he entered that year and was named the PGA Rookie of the Year. In 1997, he won four events and was the tour's leading money-winner with slightly more than two million dollars in official winnings. In April 1997, he became the first African American to win a major championship when he won the Masters by an incredible 12 strokes over runner-up Tom Kite. His 270 broke the tournament record of 271 that was first set by Jack Nicklaus in 1965, and at age 21, he was the youngest-ever winner of the event. He was the fourth African American to play in the event, the others being Lee Elder, Calvin Peete, and Jim Thorpe.

After an off-year in 1998 when he won only one event and did not contend in any of the majors, in 1999 he won seven events and the PGA Championship. He also won the Vardon Trophy and the Byron Nelson Award and was the leading money-winner on the tour with over 6.5 million dollars in official winnings. His eight tour wins that year were the most since Johnny Miller's eight wins in 1974. With the most appealing playing style since Arnold Palmer and already a consistent winner on the tour with a couple of majors under his belt, Tiger Woods appeared to have the potential to become not only a superstar but one of the greatest players in the long history of the game.

The final player with superstar potential to join the PGA Tour in the 1990s was Sergio Garcia. Born Sergio Garcia Fernandez in Borriol, Castellon, Spain, in January 1980, he was taught to play golf at an early age by his father, who was the club pro at a golf club in Madrid, Spain. An incredible golfer at an early age, he won the club championship at his father's golf club at age 12. In 1995, at age 15, he became the youngest-ever winner of the European Amateur Championship. A year later, he made the cut in a European Tour event as an amateur at age 16. In 1998, at age 18, he won the British Amateur and reached the semifinals of the US Amateur.

In 1999, he turned professional at age 19 and joined both the European Tour and the PGA Tour in the United States, where he finished second to Tiger Woods in the PGA Championship. He also won two events on the European Tour that year. An incredible iron player, the 19-year-old Spaniard clearly had the talent to become a superstar in the United States as well as in Europe, where he was already very popular. To become a superstar in the United States, he would have to win a few majors and win consistently on the PGA Tour, both of which he appeared to be capable of doing.

As the 20th century drew to a close, the PGA Tour still did not have a superstar, but any or all of the eight young players described above appeared to be capable of filling that role. At the close of the 1999 golf season, five of those players were ranked among the top ten players in the world. Tiger Woods was ranked number one, followed by David Duval at number two, Ernie Els at number five, Vijay Singh at number seven, and Phil Mickelson at number nine. Only time and the fortunes of golf would determine which of these talented players would become the superstars that professional golf needed to stay on the American sports pages in the 21st century.

• *12* •

Golf in the 21st Century

$\mathcal{D}$uring the last few decades of the 20th century, golfers began using long-handled putters. In using such a putter, a player typically anchors either the top of the handle or the forearm of the hand holding the top of the handle against their body and swings the club by pushing the handle from below with the other hand. In 2016, the USGA and the R&A, acting jointly, adopted a rule dealing with long-handled putters. The rule provides that a player may not anchor any part of a club to their body, either by anchoring the club directly to their body or by anchoring their forearm to their body. The rule-makers felt that anchoring a club to a player's body was not a fundamental part of the game and that doing so gave a player an unfair advantage over a player who did not do so. The penalty for violating the rule is loss of hole in match play and two strokes in stroke play.

In 1986 the International Federation of PGA Tours adopted a system for rating the performance of professional golfers called "Official World Golf Ranking." Devised initially by sports agent Mark McCormack, the system was adopted on the initiative of the Championship Committee of the Royal and Ancient Golf Club of St. Andrews, which was seeking a method of ranking players from various tours around the world. Under this system, points are awarded to players for finishes in sanctioned events and players are ranked worldwide according to the number of points they accumulate divided by the number of sanctioned events they have played in. The number of points awarded to a player in a sanctioned event is determined by the quality of the event and by a player's finish in the event. For example, if 100 points are awarded to the winner of an event, the runner-up gets 60 percent of the winner's share, or 60 points, while the third-place finisher gets 40 percent of the winner's share, the fourth-place finisher gets 30 percent, and the percentage is prorated on down to the sixtieth-place finisher, who gets 1.5 percent of the winner's share.

The quality of a sanctioned event is determined by the rankings of the players in the event. The higher the quality of the event, the more points are awarded for winning it. One hundred points are awarded to the winner of each of the four professional majors. The other sanctioned events are assigned point totals ranging from 24 to 80, depending on the quality of the event. Rankings are published weekly under this system and a list of the top ten players in the world is issued at the end of each golf season.

The widespread interest shown by the public in the four professional majors, coupled with the revenue generated by the high television ratings of those events, has prompted the creation of other high-profile golfing events. The first such event was the Tournament Players Championship (the TPC), which was conceived, organized, and added to the PGA Tour by Tour Commissioner Deane Beman in 1974. The first TPC was held at the Atlanta Country Club in Marietta, Georgia, in the summer of 1974. It carried a purse of $250,000 and attracted most of the top professionals. Jack Nicklaus won the inaugural event by two strokes over J. C. Snead (Sam's nephew) and collected the $50,000 winner's share.

The TPC was held at other venues in 1975 and 1976, and in 1977 was moved to the Oceanside Course of the Sawgrass Country Club in Ponte Vedra Beach, Florida. In 1982, the event was moved to the newly created Players Stadium Course at Sawgrass, where it has since remained. At Sawgrass, the TPC was played in late March until 2007, when it was moved to the weekend that includes the second Saturday in May, a date that puts it midway between the Masters and the US Open. The TPC is now called the Players Championship.

The aspect of the Players Championship that is most attractive to the players is its purse, which is the largest of any single golfing event in the world. After starting at $250,000 in 1974, the purse has increased steadily and in 2017 was an incredible $10,500,000, the winner's share of which was $1,890,000. Because of the size of its purse and the magnificence of its venue at Sawgrass, the Players Championship is viewed by some as an unofficial fifth major. Official World Golf Ranking awards 80 points to the winner of the Players Championship.

Another attempt to create high-profile professional golfing events was the creation of the World Golf Championships in 1999. The World Golf Championships (the WGC) are a series of four professional golf tournaments organized by the International Federation of PGA Tours with the intent of creating high-profile tournaments that will challenge the traditional majors in popularity and attract the best professional golfers from tours throughout the world. The names and locations of the WGC tournaments change periodically and, so far, have been held in 10 countries on five continents.

The WGC tournaments are official money events on the PGA Tour, the European Tour, and the Japan Golf Tour and are officially sanctioned events in the Asian Tour, the PGA Tour of Australasia, and the Sunshine Tour in South Africa. The prize money offered by the WGC tournaments is comparable to that offered by the traditional majors, and they attract most of the top professional golfers in the world. Official World Golf Ranking typically awards 75 points to the winner of a WGC tournament, but the number varies depending on the quality of the event. The status of the WGC tournaments is about the same as the Players Championship, which is a cut above a typical PGA Tour event but a notch below the traditional majors.

Still another attempt to create high-profile professional golfing events was the creation of the FedEx Cup competitions by the PGA Tour in 2007. The FedEx Cup is a championship trophy donated by Federal Express, a principal sponsor of the competition. It is awarded to the winner of a points-based playoff competition that is composed of four tournaments whose names and locations change periodically. The four FedEx Cup tournaments are the Northern Trust, the Dell Technologies Championship, the BMW Championship, and the Tour Championship, in that order.

To qualify for the FedEx Cup competition, a player must be a member of the PGA Tour and must earn enough points during the regular tour season to be one of the top 125 point leaders at the close of the season. For purposes of the FedEx Cup competition, the regular season begins in October of the previous year and ends in August of the current year. Points are awarded to the winners and finishers of PGA Tour events during the regular season in much the same manner as in the World Golf Championships. The number of points awarded to the winners of events during the regular season varies from 250 to 600, depending on the quality of the field in the event. Nonwinning finishers are awarded proportionately fewer points than the winners, depending on where they finish. At the close of the regular season, the 125 players with the highest point totals are invited to participate in a four-event playoff.

The first playoff event is the Northern Trust, which was formerly called the Barclays. It is held in late August and is played on a venue in the New York City area. Two thousand points are awarded to the winner of the event, with proportionately fewer points awarded to nonwinning finishers. All points awarded to finishers in the first playoff event are added to the points a player had accumulated during the regular season. After the first playoff event, the field is cut to the top 100 point leaders, who are invited to participate in the second playoff event.

The second playoff event is the Dell Technologies Championship, which is played in early September on a venue in the Boston, Massachusetts, area. Again, 2,000 points are awarded to the winner, with proportionately fewer points awarded to the nonwinning finishers, and the points won in the event are added to the points a player had previously accumulated. The field is then cut to the top seventy points leaders, who are invited to play in the third playoff event, the BMW Championship, which is played in mid-September on a venue in the Chicago area. Again, 2,000 points are awarded to the winner, with proportionately fewer points awarded to the nonwinning finishers, and the points won in the event are added to the points a player had accumulated in the previous FedEx Cup events.

After the third event, the field is cut to the top 30 points leaders and the points are reset so that the leader has 2,000 points, the second-place player has 1,800 points, and so on down to the 30th-place player, who is given 168 points. The purpose of resetting the points is to ensure that each of the 30 finalists will have a chance of winning the FedEx Cup by winning the final event, while giving those who have accumulated the most points the best chance of winning. Each of the top five players can win the cup by winning the final event. The final event is the Tour Championship, which is held in late September at a venue in the Atlanta, Georgia, area. The player with the highest points total after the completion of the Tour Championship wins the FedEx Cup and the 10 million-dollar winner's share of the 35-million-dollar purse. The winner of the first FedEx Cup in 2007 was Tiger Woods.

The first major of the twenty-first century was the Masters in April 2000, and all of the eight promising young players who had joined the PGA Tour in the 1990s played in the event. Vijay Singh withstood late challenges from Ernie Els and David Duval and won the event by three strokes. Ernie Els finished second, one stroke ahead of David Duval. Tiger Woods finished fifth, Phil Mickelson tied for seventh, Jim Furyk tied for 14th, Sergio Garcia tied for 40th, and John Daly did not make the cut.

The rest of the 2000 season belonged to Tiger Woods, who heated up after the Masters and won the next six PGA Tour events. It was the longest winning streak on the tour since Ben Hogan's six consecutive wins in 1948. The second major of the 2000 season was the US Open, which was held at Pebble Beach Golf Links in California. Playing on one of the toughest courses in the world, Tiger Woods shot a 12-under-par 272 to win the event and broke or tied nine US Open records in so doing. He finished an amazing 15 strokes ahead of runners-up Ernie Els and Miguel Angel Jimenez. His

Pebble Beach golf links, where Tom Watson and Jack Nicklaus battled in the 1982 U.S. Open and Tiger Woods broke or tied nine U.S. Open records in 2000.
© iStock / isogood

12-under-par score broke the US Open record of eight-under-par set by Ben Hogan in 1948 and later tied by Jack Nicklaus and Hale Irwin. His 15-stroke margin of victory broke the tournament record of 13 set by Alex Smith in 1906. Woods's share of the purse was a record $800,000 and *Sports Illustrated* magazine called his performance at Pebble Beach the greatest in the history of golf. As for the other promising young players—David Duval and Vijay Singh tied for eighth place, Phil Mickelson tied for 16th, Sergio Garcia tied for 46th, Jim Furyk finished 60th, and John Daly withdrew from the event.

The third major of the 2000 season was the British Open, which was held on the Old Course at St. Andrews. Tiger Woods took a commanding lead in the event with a first-round 67 and a second-round 66. After that it wasn't much of a contest as Woods continued his phenomenal play by shooting a 67 in the third round and a 69 in the final round to finish with a 19-under-par 269, eight strokes ahead of runners-up Ernie Els and Thomas Bjørn. With his victory, Woods joined Gene Sarazen, Ben Hogan, Jack Nicklaus, and Gary Player as the only players to achieve a career Grand Slam with victories in each of the four modern majors. At age 24, Woods was by far the youngest player to achieve that honor.

Like all professional golfers that year, the seven other promising young players who had joined the tour in the 1990s were finding it hard to keep up with Tiger Woods. In the British Open, David Duval, Phil Mickelson, and

Vijay Singh tied for eleventh place, Sergio Garcia tied for 36th, Jim Furyk tied for 41st, and John Daly, who had won the event on the same course in 1995, didn't make the cut. Only Vijay Singh, with a victory in the Masters, and Ernie Els, with three second-place finishes in majors, were able to stay within sight of the streaking Tiger Woods, who was having a year for the ages.

The final major of the 2000 season was the PGA Championship, which was held at Valhalla Golf Club in Louisville, Kentucky. Tiger Woods again started fast, posting a first-round 66 and a second-round 67. This time, however, he didn't run away from the rest of the field and his third-round 70 put him one stroke ahead of journeyman pro Bob May going into the final round on Sunday. After nine holes in the final round, Woods and May were tied for the lead. May, who was having the tournament of his life, took a one-stroke lead with a birdie on 11. On the 16th green, May, still leading by a stroke, had a golden opportunity to put Woods away as Woods was faced with a difficult 12-footer for par while May had a four-footer for birdie. Woods, putting first, sank his 12-footer while May couldn't get his four-footer to drop.

Given a new lease on life, Woods caught May with a birdie on 17. Woods then birdied the 542-yard, par-five 18th hole, but May matched him by sinking a clutch 15-footer, and the event moved to a three-hole, total score playoff. Woods won the playoff by a single stroke and became only the second player, after Ben Hogan in 1953, to win three majors in the same calendar year. It was the first time the PGA Championship had been successfully defended since 1937.

During his incredible 2000 season, Tiger Woods won three majors and nine of the 20 PGA Tour events he played in. He also won the Vardon Trophy and the Byron Nelson Award with a record low-scoring average of 67.79. His official winnings that season were a PGA Tour record $9,188,321, and for the third straight year he was ranked number one on Official World Golf Ranking's year-end list of the top ten players in the world.

After his spectacular 2000 season, Tiger Woods was well on his way to becoming the superstar professional golf needed. The same could not be said for the seven other promising young players. They would have to start giving Woods some competition to have any chance of attaining superstardom. Even Woods would have to follow up on his incredible 2000 season with another good season to retain his status.

Tiger Woods started fast in 2001. In March, he won the Bay Hill Invitational by a stroke over Phil Mickelson, and the Players Championship by a stroke over Vijay Singh. Next up was the Masters, where he continued his good play, averaging 305 yards off the tee, hitting 59 of 72 greens in regulation, and making 23 birdies. As well as he played, however, he couldn't shake

David Duval, who was also having a great tournament. With two holes to go in the final round on Sunday, Woods led Duval by a stroke. On 17, Woods, playing in the group behind Duval, missed the green and was faced with a testy up and down. At about the same time, Duval had a four-footer for a birdie on the 18th green. Woods made a great chip and got down in two on 17, while Duval missed his four-footer on 18, the combination of which gave Woods a one stroke lead going to the final hole. Seemingly oblivious to pressure, Woods birdied the final hole and won the tournament by two strokes over Duval, whose 274 was the lowest score ever posted by a nonwinner at the Masters.

By winning the 2001 Masters, Woods became the first player to win four consecutive majors and hold all four major professional golf titles at the same time. However, because the titles were not all won in the same calendar year he was not deemed to have won a Grand Slam. The sportswriters called it a "Tiger Slam."

Tiger Woods's historic run in the majors ended two months later at Southern Hills Country Club in Tulsa, Oklahoma, the site of the 2001 US Open. Woods started slowly, never found his "A-Game," and finished in 12th place. South African Retief Goosen won the event in a playoff with Stewart Cink. The next major was the 2001 British Open at Royal Lytham

Tiger Woods on the Bosphorus Bridge in Istanbul, Turkey, in 2013. His 79 tour wins and 14 majors made him a legend around the world.
© iStock / Czgur

in England, which David Duval won by three strokes over Niclas Fasth of Sweden to claim his first major. Tiger Woods again played poorly and finished in a tie for 25th place.

The 2001 PGA Championship, the final major of the year, was played at the Atlanta Athletic Club in Duluth, Georgia. The event came down to a duel between Phil Mickelson and David Toms, a 34-year-old journeyman pro from Bossier City, Louisiana, who had won five events during his nine years on the PGA Tour. In the third round on Saturday, Mickelson, who had yet to win a major during his nine years on the tour, held a two-stroke lead over Toms going into the 243-yard, par-three 15th hole. Mickelson, hitting first, missed the green with his tee shot and ultimately bogeyed the hole. Toms then unbelievably hit his tee shot into the cup for a hole-in-one and Mickelson's two-stroke lead became a one-stroke deficit.

Toms picked up another stroke later in the round and carried a two-stroke lead over Mickelson going into the final round on Sunday. Mickelson caught Toms early on the back nine, but Toms regained the lead when Mickelson three-putted the 16th green. Toms carried a one-stroke lead into the final hole, which was a relatively short par-four with a green guarded in front by a large water hazard. Toms's drive found the rough and he elected to lay up short of the water hazard with his second shot. When Mickelson's second shot cleared the water hazard and landed safely on the green, his first win in a major seemed assured.

With Mickelson's ball safely on the green and the tournament on the line, Toms pitched his third shot 90 yards over water to within 10 feet of the cup and then sank the 10-footer to match Mickelson's two-putt par and claim the Wanamaker Trophy with an amazing 265. It was Toms's first and only win in a major and his 265 is still the lowest score ever posted in the PGA Championship. It was an incredible performance by a little-known pro and Mickelson's first win in a major would have to wait for another day. Tiger Woods finished tied for 29th place and his slide in the majors continued.

At the close of the 2001 season, the Official World Golf Ranking year-end list of the top ten players in the world had Tiger Woods number one, Phil Mickelson number two, David Duval number three, Ernie Els number four, Sergio Garcia number six, and Vijay Singh number eight. Of the eight promising young players who had joined the PGA Tour in the 1990s, only Jim Furyk and John Daly were not among the top 10 players in the world. These young players were now dominating the PGA Tour.

After getting his 2002 season on track by again winning the Bay Hill Invitational in mid-March, Tiger Woods arrived in Augusta in April with hopes of putting an end to his slide in the majors. The win at Bay Hill seemed to have gotten him on track, as he posted scores of 70, 69, and 66 in the first three rounds at the Masters and was tied for the lead with Retief Goosen going into the final round. However, Ernie Els, Vijay Singh, Phil Mickelson, Sergio Garcia, and Spain's Jose Maria Olazabal were all within striking distance.

In the final round on Sunday, Goosen bogeyed the first hole. Woods then birdied the second and third holes to take a three-stroke lead over the South African, who never recovered from his shaky start and dropped out of contention a few holes later. At the turn, only Vijay Singh and Ernie Els were within striking distance of Woods. Els trailed Woods by two strokes going into the par-five 13th hole, where he hit his ball into Rae's Creek and took a triple-bogey on the hole to drop out of contention. Singh was within two strokes of Woods going into the par-five 15th hole, when he hit two balls into the water and took a disastrous nine on the hole to drop out of contention.

Woods final-round 71 gave him a 276 for the tournament and a three-stroke victory over Retief Goosen, who made a couple of late birdies to finish in second place, a stroke ahead of Phil Mickelson, who matched Woods's 71 in the final round. In winning the event for the second straight year, Tiger Woods joined Jack Nicklaus and Nick Faldo as the only players to successfully defend a Masters title.

The venue for the 2002 US Open was significant for two reasons: at 7,214 yards, it was the longest course on which the event had ever been played, and it was the first time the US Open had ever been held on a public course. It was played on the Black Course at Bethpage State Park in Farmingdale, New York, in central Long Island. Owned by the state of New York, Bethpage Black was designed by A. W. Tillinghast and built during the Depression with WPA money.

Tiger Woods, the longest hitter on the tour when John Daly wasn't in the field, found the length of Bethpage Black to his liking and his first-round 67 gave him an early lead. His 68 and 70 in the next two rounds put him four strokes ahead of Phil Mickelson and Sergio Garcia going into the final round on Sunday. His final-round 72 gave him a three-stroke, wire-to-wire victory over runner-up Mickelson. Garcia faded in the final round and finished in fourth place.

The USGA's public-course experiment was a success; since then, the US Open has been held on public courses four more times—at Torrey Pines in San Diego, California, in 2008; at Bethpage Black again in 2009; at Chambers Bay in University Place, Washington, in 2015; and at Erin Hills in Erin, Wisconsin, in 2017.

The 2002 British Open was played at historic Muirfield Links, overlooking the Firth of Forth in Gullane, Scotland. The course was originally designed by Old Tom Morris in 1891. Tiger Woods, the odds-on favorite to win his third straight major, was in the hunt until the third round on Saturday, when, playing in bad weather, he bogeyed the first hole and was never able to get back on track. His third-round 81 was his worst round ever as a professional and it dropped him out of contention.

Playing in weather that had turned calm and dry overnight, Ernie Els had a one-stroke lead over Thomas Levet of France and Australians Stuart Appleby and Steve Elkington with three holes to play in the final round. On 16, Els missed the green with his approach shot, had trouble with his short game, and took a double-bogey, a misadventure that put him a stroke behind Appleby, Elkington, and Levet. However, Els regrouped on 17 and got the birdie he needed to catch the others. They all parred the final hole and the event moved to four-hole, total-score playoff.

In the playoff, Levet birdied the second hole to take a one-stroke lead over Els and the Australians. Els made a dramatic birdie on the final hole to catch Levet and the match moved to a sudden-death playoff between the two. In the first extra hole, both players hit their approach shots into green-side bunkers. Els claimed the silver claret jug by getting down in two from the sand, a feat that Levet was unable to match. His playoff victory gave the Big Easy his third win in a major and erased all doubts as to his mental toughness.

The 2002 PGA Championship was held at Hazeltine National Golf Club in Chaska, Minnesota, near Minneapolis. Going into the final round, Justin Leonard held a three-stroke lead over Rich Beem, a 32-year-old pro from El Paso, Texas, who had won two events during his three-year career on the PGA Tour. Beem took a one-stroke lead when Leonard double-bogeyed the eighth hole. Leonard dropped off after that and the event became a two-man affair between Beem and hard-charging Tiger Woods, who had recovered from a slow start and was playing like the Tiger of old.

Hitting one of the best fairway woods of his life, Beem eagled the 597-yard, par-five 11th hole to open up a three-stroke lead over Woods. His lead increased to five strokes when Woods bogeyed 13 and 14. However, Woods, playing four holes ahead of Beem, recovered and birdied the last four holes, leaving Beem with a one-stroke lead with three holes to play. Beem's tee-shot on the long, par-three 16th hole cleared the water hazard in front of the green but his ball wound up 50 feet from the pin. With his lead in jeopardy, he proceeded to sink the 50-footer and increase his lead over Woods to two strokes. He then parred 17 and his three-putt bogey on 18 gave the unranked pro who had made the cut in a major only four times in his career a one-stroke victory over the best player in the world.

At the close of the 2002 season, the Official World Golf Ranking year-end list of the top ten players in the world included six of the eight promising young players who had joined the tour in the 1990s. Tiger Woods was number one on the list for the fifth consecutive year and Phil Mickelson was number two for the second year in a row. Ernie Els was number three on the list, Sergio Garcia was number four, and Vijay Singh was number eight. Of the eight promising young players, only David Duval, Jim Furyk, and John Daly were not ranked among the top ten players in the world. However, at this time only Woods, with 39 PGA Tour wins and eight majors to his credit, was approaching superstardom. Only time and the fortunes of golf would determine which of these players would become the superstars that professional golf was looking for.

Fifteen years later, in 2017, the eight promising young players who joined the PGA Tour in the 1990s were nearing the end of their careers and whether any of them had attained superstardom could be determined. A brief assessment of the careers of each of these players through 2017 is set forth below.

Early in his career John Daly had come out of nowhere to win two majors—the PGA Championship in 1991 and the British Open in 1995. However, he has won only three other PGA Tour events, the last one coming in 2004 when he won the Buick Invitational and was named the PGA Tour Comeback Player of the Year. His comeback was short-lived, however, because since then he has been winless on the tour. He has failed to make the cut in 29 of the 52 majors he has entered since winning the British Open in 1995 and his highest finish in a major since then was a tie for 15th place in the 2005 British Open.

Daly is now in his fifties and no longer plays regularly on the PGA Tour. He did not become a superstar even though he possessed two of the most important qualities of superstardom—he was long off the tee and possessed a game and personality that attracted large galleries. He was the longest hitter on the tour for most of his career, and only Tiger Woods drew larger galleries than Long John Daly when he was on his game. Significantly, he is the only player in either the United States or Europe with two majors to his credit who has never been invited to play in the Ryder Cup.

During his 23 years in professional golf, Jim Furyk has won 17 PGA Tour events and one major—the 2003 US Open, which he won with a record low score of 272. He has been on the Official World Golf Ranking year-end list of the top ten players seven times, with highs of number two in 2006 and number three in 2007. His best season was 2006 when he won the Vardon Trophy and was the second leading money-winner with more than 7 million dollars in official winnings. In 2010, he won the FedEx Cup and was named the PGA Player of the Year. In 2016, at age 46, he became the first player to shoot a 58 in a PGA Tour event. A popular and sometimes brilliant player with a sizeable following and a fairly consistent winner on the tour, a lack of success in the majors has kept him from superstardom.

Sergio Garcia's ten career PGA Tour wins are the most ever by a Spanish player. However, his first win in a major didn't come until 2017, when, at age 37, he posted an emotional win at the Masters. Noted for his iron play, he is very popular on the European Tour, where he has had eleven wins. In the United States, he won the Vardon Trophy and the Byron Nelson Award in 2008, when he was number two on the Official World Golf Ranking year-end list of the top ten players. A superstar in Europe, his failure to win regularly on the PGA Tour and a lack of success in the majors have kept him from superstardom in the United States.

In 2002, David Duval sustained the first in a series of injuries to his back, wrists, and shoulders, and his game suffered. Prior to the injuries, he had won 13 PGA Tour events and one major—the 2001 British Open—since joining the tour in 1995. Unfortunately, his victory in the British Open was his last win. Restricted by injuries, he no longer plays regularly on the tour. His career, which started out so brilliantly, has been hampered by injuries and bad luck, and he did not become the superstar that many had predicted.

Vijay Singh has 34 PGA Tour wins and three majors to his credit. His majors include the 1998 and 2004 PGA Championships and the 2000 Masters. He was on the Official World Golf Ranking year-end list of the top ten players for eleven consecutive years beginning in 1998, peaking at number two in 2003 and number one in 2004, when he was named the PGA Player of the Year. His 34 career PGA Tour wins are the most ever by a player who is not an American. He was the leading money-winner on the PGA Tour in 2003, 2004, and 2008. In 2004, he won the Vardon Trophy and the Byron Nelson Award. Showing remarkable longevity, he has won 22 events on the tour since turning forty, breaking Sam Snead's record of 18. In 2008, he won the FedEx Cup at age 45 and became the second player (after Tiger Woods) to exceed 60 million dollars in career winnings. Although his 34 career PGA Tour wins and three majors are superstar numbers, his lack of charisma, coupled with not being an American and a failure to win the US Open, have kept him from superstardom in the United States.

Ernie Els has 19 PGA Tour wins, 16 wins on the Sunshine Tour, and 28 wins on the European Tour, where he is the second leading career money-winner, behind Lee Westwood. His four majors include US Open victories in 1994 and 1997 and British Open victories in 2002 and 2012. He was on the Official World Golf Ranking year-end list of the top-10 players for 15 years in a row beginning in 1994 and was number five or better in nine of those years. In the majors, in addition to his four wins, he has had six second-place finishes and 23 top-five finishes. An immensely talented player and a super-star on the European and Sunshine Tours, he did not become a superstar in the United States primarily because he didn't play here often enough.

Phil Mickelson has won 42 PGA Tour events and five majors since join-ing the tour in 1992. His five majors include victories in the 2004, 2006, and 2010 Masters, the 2005 PGA Championship, and the 2013 British Open. He has also had 11 second-place finishes and seven third-place finishes in the majors. Six of his second-place finishes have come in the US Open, which is the only major he has not won. He has been number five or better on the Official World Golf Ranking year-end list of the top ten players 11 times, peaking at number two on four occasions. However, he has never been the number-one-ranked player in the world, has never been named the PGA Player of the Year, and has never won the US Open. He also has never been the leading money-winner on the PGA Tour in any particular year, although he has been second five times and third four times, and his 81 million dollars in official career winnings is the second-most ever.

Mickelson's 42 PGA Tour wins and five majors are superstar numbers. However, in his case they were more a product of longevity and sustained good play than golfing brilliance. It has taken him 22 years to get his 42 PGA Tour wins and his five wins in majors were spread over a ten-year period. He has averaged about two PGA Tour wins a year and has never won more than one major in any year. His career peaked in 2004, 2005, and 2006, when he won three majors, but even then, he won only five other PGA Tour events during that three-year period, and after 2006 he did not win another major for four years. He has not won a PGA Tour event since 2013, when he won the British Open, and is now in the twilight of his career. Although he may have approached superstar status in 2005 and 2006, since then his star has faded. Throughout his career, he has been a very talented and highly respected player, but for many years he was viewed by the golfing public as a perpetual runner-up. He did not build up a sizeable following and has had the misfortune of playing most of his career in the huge shadow of Tiger Woods.

At the close of the 2003 season, Tiger Woods had accumulated 39 PGA Tour wins and eight majors. He had dominated the World Golf Champion-ships, winning eight of 16 events. He had been the leading money-winner on the PGA Tour five times and had been named the PGA Player of the Year six years in a row. He had also been ranked number one in the world by Of-ficial World Golf Ranking for a record 252 consecutive weeks and had won the Vardon Trophy and the Byron Nelson Award five years in a row. Most importantly, perhaps, sports fans were coming to golf tournaments and turn-ing on their television sets in record numbers to watch him play.

In 2004, Woods's performance fell off as he worked on rebuilding his swing to reduce the stress on his left knee, which had undergone arthroscopic surgery in 1994 and again in 2002. He won only one PGA Tour event and no majors that year, and in September he was replaced as the number-one-ranked player in the world by Vijay Singh. He recovered in 2005, however, and regained his number-one ranking by winning six PGA Tour events and two majors—the Masters and the British Open. In May 2006, his father, Earl, died and he left the tour for nine weeks to be with his family. The first event after his return was the 2006 US Open at Winged Foot, where, for the first time in his professional career, he failed to make the cut in a major. Two months later he returned to form and shot an 18-under-par 270 at Royal Liverpool to win the British Open by two strokes over Chris DiMarco. Four weeks later, he shot another 270 to win the PGA Championship at Medinah by five strokes over Shaun Micheel. He finished the season by winning six consecutive PGA Tour events for the second time in his career and remained the number-one ranked player in the world. In 2007, he was once again the number-one ranked player, winning seven PGA Tour events and one major—the PGA Championship. He also won the FedEx Cup that year and was the runner-up in both the Masters and the US Open.

In April 2008, he again had arthroscopic surgery on his left knee and withdrew from the tour for two months. He returned in time to play in the US Open at Torrey Pines Golf Club in San Diego, California, a public course he had played as a boy. Playing on one good leg, he won the event in an 18-hole playoff with Rocco Mediate. He called it his greatest win ever. The win gave him his third career Grand Slam, with three or more wins in each of the four modern majors. It is an honor he shares only with Jack Nicklaus. Two days after his win at Torrey Pines, he announced that he had sustained a torn ligament in his left knee and a stress fracture in his left tibia and would undergo surgery and miss the rest of the 2008 season.

During the first eight years of the twenty-first century, Tiger Woods was the most marketable athlete in the world. He signed endorsement contracts with General Motors, Nike, Titleist, American Express, General Mills, and several other major companies. In 2000, he signed a five-year, 105-million-dollar contract extension with Nike, which at the time was the biggest endorsement contract ever for an athlete. In 2004, he signed a five-year, 40-million-dollar endorsement contract with Buick. *Golf Digest* reported that he had grossed 769 million dollars during the first 12 years of his professional career. A few years later, *Forbes* reported that he was the first athlete in the world to have made a billion dollars in his career and that his net worth exceeded 600 million dollars.

When he returned to the PGA Tour in 2009, he won six PGA Tour events and his second FedEx Cup and was again the number-one-ranked

Torrey Pines golf course in San Diego, California, where Tiger Woods played as a boy and won his final major.
© iStock / Lborja

player in the world. However, for the first time in five years he did not win a major. In the 2009 PGA Championship at Hazeltine National Golf Club in Chaska, Minnesota, he had a two-stroke lead going into the final round and for the first time in his professional career failed to hold a third-round lead in a major. He lost the event by three strokes to Y. E. Yang of South Korea. Earlier that year, he had tied for sixth-place in both the Masters and the US Open and had failed to make the cut in the British Open. Although he was ranked number one in the world, it was becoming evident that he wasn't the same player he had been prior to his injuries. Despite the drop-off in his play, however, Woods remained very popular with the golfing public and millions still turned on their television sets and came to golfing events to watch him play, hoping he would recover and again become the incredible player he had been prior to his injuries.

In 2001, Swedish golfer Jesper Parnevik had introduced Woods to Elin Nordegren, a Swedish model whom Parnevik employed as an au pair. Woods and Nordegren began dating, became engaged in 2003, were married in October 2004, and later had a daughter and a son.

On November 25, 2009, the *National Enquirer* published a report claiming that Woods was having an extramarital affair with a woman in New York City. Two days later, at about 2:30 a.m., Woods was involved in an automobile accident on the street where he lived in Windermere, Florida, wherein his car collided with a fire hydrant and a tree. The local police investigated the accident, gave Woods a ticket for careless driving, and reported that he had some facial lacerations. Because of the recent report of Woods's extramarital affair and because it was not clear that his facial lacerations were incurred in the accident, there was intense media speculation about the incident. Woods responded by calling it a private matter and credited his wife with helping him from the car after the accident.

Five days later, Woods announced that because of his injuries he would not be appearing in any golfing events for the rest of the year. On December 2, following a report of his involvement with yet another woman and the release of a voicemail message he had left for the woman, Woods released a statement admitting his involvement and apologizing for his actions. Over the next few days, several other women publicly claimed to have had sexual affairs with Woods. On December 11, Woods released another statement admitting his infidelity and announcing that he was taking an indefinite break from professional golf to try and save his marriage.

His attempt to save his marriage failed and his wife subsequently filed for divorce. The divorce became final in August 2010, and he was hit with one of the biggest divorce settlements in the history of American jurisprudence. In addition, most of the companies with whom he had signed endorsement contracts cancelled the contracts because of his social misconduct.

In March 2010, Woods announced that he was returning to professional golf and would play in the Masters. He finished in a tie for fourth, failed to win any of the 11 PGA Tour events he played in, and did not contend in any of the other majors that year. In 2011, he failed to win any of the nine PGA Tour events he played in; his best showing in a major was another fourth-place finish in the Masters. For the first time in his professional career, he was not on Official World Golf Ranking's year-end list of the top-10 players.

After going winless in 2011, in 2012 he won three of the 19 PGA Tour events he played in and his ranking rose to number three. He tied for third in the British Open that year but was not a contender in the other majors. He improved again in 2013, when he won five of the 16 PGA Tour events he played in and again became Official World Golf Ranking's number one player. In the majors, he tied for fourth in the Masters, tied for sixth in the British Open, and was not a contender in either the US Open or the PGA Championship.

In April 2014, he had back surgery and was unable to play for several months and failed to win any of the seven PGA Tour events he played in that year. In September 2015, he again had back surgery and was unable to play on the tour for several months. He failed to win any of the 11 PGA Tour events he played in that year and his best finish in a major was a tie for 17th in the Masters. In 2016, he again did not win a PGA Tour event and did not play in any of the majors. On May 29, 2017 at 3:00 a.m., he was found asleep in his car and arrested near Jupiter, Florida, for allegedly driving under the influence of alcohol or drugs. He later said that he was taking prescription drugs for pain. The arrest was highly publicized and further damaged his image in the eyes of the public. He failed to make the cut in the one PGA Tour event he entered in 2017. He has not won a PGA Tour event since 2013 and is no longer a ranked player.

Tiger Woods turned forty-two on December 30, 2017, and his career as a superstar appears to be over. But what a career it was. His 79 career PGA Tour wins are the second-most ever, trailing only Sam Snead's 82, and his 14 career majors trail only the 18 won by Jack Nicklaus. Woods has also won 18 World Golf Championship events (no other player has won more than three) and his 30 wins on the European Tour are the third-most ever. He won the Vardon Trophy and the Byron Nelson Award each a record nine times and was the PGA Player of the Year a record eleven times. He was Official World Golf Ranking's year-end number-one-ranked player a record twelve times and was ranked number one in the world for a record 545 weeks. He was the leading money-winner on the PGA Tour ten times and his official career winnings total of over 110 million dollars is by far the most ever.

Although he has stated that he intends to make a comeback and is capable of winning a few more majors, he is now in his forties and has a surgically repaired knee and back. His chances of making a comeback are slim, and even if he does win a few more majors, he will never become the immensely popular superstar he was prior to the disclosure of his marital infidelities. It appears that injuries and a character flaw have combined to take down the most talented player since Young Tom Morris and in doing so have deprived professional golf of its only superstar in the twenty-first century.

The use of GPS distance-measuring devices became popular with recreational golfers in the early 2000s. Not long after the devices appeared, the USGA adopted a rule precluding their use in USGA-sanctioned events. The USGA apparently felt that a player's score should be determined by the skill of the player and not by the accuracy of his distance-measuring device. USGA Rule 14-3 provides that a player may not use any artificial device or unusual equipment for the purpose of gauging or measuring distance that might affect the player's play. However, the rule permits the use of such devices if a local rule is adopted permitting their use.

In 2014, the USGA retired both the men's and the women's US Amateur Public Links Championships. To replace them, they created the US Amateur Four-Ball Championship and the US Women's Amateur Four-Ball Championship. Both championships are held annually on venues selected by the USGA.

The number of Americans playing golf peaked at 30 million in 2005 following 57 years of continuous growth. The number then decreased for a few years, bottoming out at 24.7 million in 2013. Since then, the number has increased and was reported by the National Golf Foundation to be 29 million in 2017. The decrease after 2005 was thought to have been caused primarily by a downturn in the nation's economy.

More young people are playing golf today than ever before thanks to junior golf programs conducted by the PGA of America, the USGA, and First Tee, a program for inner-city children initiated in 1996 by Tiger and Earl Woods and funded by the Tiger Woods Foundation. In 2017, there were 2.5 million golfers in the United States between the ages of six and 17. Golf is also being played by a wider range of Americans than ever before. According to the National Golf Foundation, 20 percent of the Americans playing golf in 2017 were either African Americans, Asian Americans, or Hispanic Americans.

The National Golf Foundation reports that the number of golf courses in the United States peaked at 16,052 in 2010 and by 2017 had decreased to 15,014. It is thought that the decrease in the number of courses was the result of a market adjustment correcting an oversupply of courses built during the last 40 years of the 20th century.

Even though the number of Americans playing golf has decreased slightly since 2005, the state of recreational golf in the United States is sound, primarily because a wider range of people are playing the game on better courses than ever before. The state of professional golf is a bit more problematic. Although it is awash in prize money, the PGA Tour has not had a true superstar since the fall of Tiger Woods, and history has shown that the popularity of professional golf falls off without a superstar.

• 13 •

The Story of Women's
Golf in the United States

The first account of a woman playing golf occurred in 1567 when Mary, Queen of Scots, was seen playing golf with the Earl of Bothwell a few days after the murder of her husband. Unfortunately, another 300 years would pass before women other than royalty would take up the game.

In 1832, a golf club that included women in its activities was founded at North Berwick in Scotland. In 1867, a ladies' golf club was founded at St. Andrews. It was primarily a putting club, however, as their play was limited to the practice greens. In Scotland, ladies' golf courses were opened at North Berwick in 1867 and at Perth in 1870, and women started playing at Dunbar in 1870. In 1868, a ladies' medal competition was held at Westward Ho in southwest England.

Between 1872 and 1890, ladies' golf clubs were established at Musselburgh, Carnoustie, Troon, and North Berwick in Scotland and seven ladies' golf clubs were formed in England. A ladies' course was created at Pau in France in 1877, but there are pictures of ladies playing on the men's course at Pau as early as 1856. In 1893, the Ladies Golf Union was founded in England and the first British Ladies Amateur Championship was held. The winner was Lady Margaret Scott, whose father supplied the land and built the course where the event was held.

In 1891, Shinnecock Hills became the first golf club in the United States with women members. In 1893, the club added a nine-hole women's course to its complex. A few years later, however, the women's course was sacrificed to lengthen the men's 18-hole course. The first golf club in the United States that was founded and operated solely by women was the Morris County Golf Club in Morristown, New Jersey. Its nicely designed, 6,000-yard, 18-hole golf course opened for play in 1894.

In 1895, the USGA held its first US Women's Amateur Championship on a nine-hole course at the Meadow Brook Club in Hempstead, New York. Lucy Barnes Brown, from Shinnecock Hills, shot a 132 and defeated 17 other players to win the 18-hole event. It was the only Women's Amateur ever held at stroke play. The second US Women's Amateur Championship was held in 1896 at the Morris County Golf Club in Morristown, New Jersey. Sixteen-year-old Beatrix Hoyt, also from Shinnecock Hills, won the match-play event. She won the event again in 1897 and 1898.

For the first 50 years of women's golf in the United States, the US Women's Amateur Championship was their only national championship. The USGA, which held an open championship for men beginning in 1895, elected not to hold an open championship for women, probably because there were no professional women golfers at the time.

The best woman golfer in the United States at the turn of the twentieth century was Beatrix Hoyt. The granddaughter of Salmon P. Chase, the chief justice of the US Supreme Court and Abraham Lincoln's Treasury Secretary, she was the first woman golfer to shoot in the eighties consistently. She also broke custom on the golf course by raising the bottom of her skirt to the top of her ankles and wearing a blouse without frills. After winning three US Women's Amateur Championships as a teenager, she retired from tournament golf in 1899 at age 19 to pursue a career in sculpture and landscape painting.

The next notable American women golfers were the Curtis sisters, Harriet and Margaret. Born in Manchester, Massachusetts, a few miles northeast of Boston, they learned to play golf at an early age at their father's country club. They were early members of the Women's Golf Association of Massachusetts, the first state women's golf organization. In 1906, Harriet won the US Women's Amateur at Brae Burn Country Club near Boston. In 1907, she was defeated by her sister Margaret in the finals of the event. Margaret won US Women's Amateur titles again in 1911 and 1912. Margaret was also a superb tennis player and in 1908 she won the US Open Doubles Championship with another woman and became the only woman ever to simultaneously hold US Open Championships in both tennis and golf. Margaret retired from tournament golf during World War I and after the war moved to France, where she served as manager of the Red Cross's Bureau for Refugees.

The next great American woman golfer was Alexa Stirling from Atlanta, Georgia. The daughter of a doctor, she was born in 1897 and learned to play golf at an early age at the Atlanta Athletic Club's East Lake Golf Course, where she was a contemporary and longtime friend of Bobby Jones. She won three consecutive US Women's Amateur titles beginning in 1916 and was the runner-up in the event on three other occasions. In 1920, she won the Cana-

Katherine Harley. The 1908 U.S. Women's Amateur Champion in traditional golfing attire.
Library of Congress

dian Women's Amateur Championship and in 1925 she married a Canadian doctor and moved to Ottawa, Ontario.

The best American woman golfer during the Roaring Twenties was Glenna Collett, who won the US Women's Amateur Championship six times—four times during the 1920s and twice in the early 1930s. Born in New Haven, Connecticut, in 1903, she grew up in Providence, Rhode Island, where she took up golf at age 14 and was instructed by Alex Smith, a two-time winner of the US Open. In 1919, at age 16, she qualified for the US Women's Amateur, where she won her first-round match but was defeated in the second round. Two years later she was the low qualifier for the event but lost her first-round match. In 1922, she set a single-round scoring record in qualifying and won her first US Women's Amateur Championship. She won the event again in 1925 and three times in a row beginning in 1928. In 1931, she lost to Helen Hicks of New York in the finals of the event. Later that year, she married Edwin Vare and retired from competitive golf to start a family.

In 1934, after having two children, she returned to tournament golf as Glenna Collett Vare and lost in the semifinals of the US Women's Amateur to Virginia Van Wie of Chicago. In 1935, she won her sixth and final US Women's Amateur Championship, defeating Virginia Van Wie in the semifinals and 17-year-old Patty Berg in the finals.

Joyce Wethered of England was a contemporary of Glenna Collett. Still widely regarded as England's greatest woman golfer ever, Wethered won the British Ladies Amateur Championship four times during the 1920s and the English Ladies Open Championship five times in a row beginning in 1920. Bobby Jones, after playing a series of exhibition matches with her in the late 1920s, called her the best golfer he had ever played with, man or woman.

Joyce Wethered and Glenna Collett maintained a spirited rivalry throughout the 1920s that attracted a lot of interest and did much to popularize women's golf in their respective countries. Their most famous match was played on the Old Course at St. Andrews in the 36-hole final of the 1929 British Ladies Amateur Championship. Collett shot a brilliant 34 on the first nine holes, two under men's par, and built up a five-hole lead over her English rival in the match-play event. Wethered won three holes back on the second nine and trailed Collett by two holes going into the final 18. Collett suffered a surprising reversal of form on the front nine of the final 18 and lost six holes to Wethered. Four holes down at the turn, Collett rallied early on the final nine and trailed Wethered by two after 34 holes. Her rally ended, however, when she carded a double-bogey on the 35th hole and she lost the match, 3 and 1. It was Wethered's fourth and final British Ladies Amateur

Championship and for Collett, who would never win the event, it was the most disappointing loss of her career.

Virginia Van Wie was the best woman golfer in the United States during the early 1930s. Born and raised in Chicago, she took up the game at an early age at Chicago's Beverly Golf Club, where her father was a member. After losing to Glenna Collett in the finals of the US Women's Amateur in 1928 and 1930 and in the semifinals in 1931, she broke through in 1932, defeating Collett 10 and 8 in the final. She won the event again in 1933, and in 1934 she won for the third consecutive time, defeating Glenna Collett Vare 3 and 2 in the final. She was named the Associated Press Female Athlete of the Year in 1934 and was called the world's greatest female athlete. With nothing left to prove, she retired from tournament golf in 1935 and became a golf instructor, a profession she pursued with much success in the Chicago area for the next thirty years.

The winner of the US Women's Amateur in 1938 was a twenty-year-old tomboy from Minneapolis and the University of Minnesota named Patty Berg. A natural athlete, she was good at all sports and started playing golf at age 13 at the suggestion of her parents. As strong as most men, she once played quarterback on a football team that included Bud Wilkinson, the legendary football coach of the University of Oklahoma Sooners. In 1935, at age 17 and only four years after she first swung a golf club, she won the Minnesota State Amateur Championship and was the runner-up to Glenna Collett Vare in the US Women's Amateur.

The winner of the US Women's Amateur in 1939 and 1940 was 20-year-old Betty Jameson from the University of Texas. Born in Norman, Oklahoma, and raised in Dallas, Texas, she started playing golf at age 11 and won a couple of state tournaments in Texas during her middle teens. The last prewar winner of the US Women's Amateur was Betty Hicks Newell from Long Beach, California, who won it in 1941.

The US Women's Amateur was not held during the war years of 1942 through 1945. The first postwar winner of the event was Babe Didrikson. Named Mildred Ella Didrikson at birth, she was born in 1911 in Port Arthur, Texas, the sixth of seven children born to her Norwegian immigrant parents. She was raised in Beaumont, Texas, where her family moved when she was four. Encouraged by her sports-minded parents to play the seasonal boy's sports, she was more than a tomboy. She was an exceptional athlete who could more than hold her own against the boys she competed against. She was not a good student, however, and had to repeat the eighth grade and later dropped out of high school. While in high school, she played on the school's basketball team and after she dropped out she moved to Dallas to play basketball on an AAU women's team sponsored by a Dallas insurance company,

Patty Berg. Her 15 majors are the most ever by a woman golfer.
Library of Congress

who employed her as a typist. In her second year of AAU basketball, she led the team to the AAU national championship and was selected to the AAU All-American team.

In 1932, the insurance company sent her to Evanston, Illinois, to compete in the National AAU Track and Field Championships, where she won the javelin throw, the baseball throw, the shot put, the broad jump, and the 80-meter hurdles. She also tied for first place in the high jump and was fourth in the discus throw. Her performances at the AAU Championships caught the attention of the US Olympic Committee and she was selected to the US Olympic Team. At the 1932 Olympic Games, which were held in Los Angeles, she was the star of the American team, winning gold medals in the javelin throw and the 80-meter hurdles and a silver medal in the high jump.

The fame she gained at the Olympics enabled her to quit her job as a typist and join a vaudeville tour, where for $3,500 a week—which was more than big money during the Depression years of the 1930s—she sang, danced, and played the harmonica. She sang well enough to have several records produced on the Mercury label. In 1934, at age 23, she quit the vaudeville tour and, at the suggestion of friends, took up golf. By 1935, she was good enough to join Gene Sarazen on an exhibition tour where thousands came to see how far the superwoman from the Olympics could hit a golf ball. To improve the rest of her game, which wasn't nearly up to the level of her game off the tees, she took a series of lessons from Tommy Armour at the Boca Raton Golf Club in Florida. By 1937, her game had improved to the point where she began competing in charitable golfing events. She was unable to play in the US Women's Amateur, however, because the USGA had revoked her amateur status in 1935 because of the money she had made during her exhibition tour with Gene Sarazen.

In January 1938, while competing in the Los Angeles Open, a men's PGA Tour event where she shot an 81 and an 84 in the first two rounds and missed the cut, she met a professional wrestler name George Zaharias. Zaharias was from Pueblo, Colorado, and was known in wrestling circles as "the Cryin' Greek from Cripple Creek." Babe had the frame and muscles of a man and, because of her manliness, was not thought to be a pretty woman in the classic sense. Zaharias was a big garrulous man with cauliflower ears, huge thighs, and bulging muscles. Babe and Zaharias were attracted to one another and began dating. Eleven months later, they were married in St. Louis and Babe Didrikson became Babe Didrikson Zaharias or, more often, Babe Zaharias.

During the war years, Babe worked on her golf game and played at benefits with other celebrities, raising money for war bonds and charities. In 1943, she applied to the USGA for reinstatement of her amateur status and in 1944 it was granted. When the US Women's Amateur was resumed after the war, she was ready, at age 35, to begin competing against the best women golfers in the world for the first time in her life.

The 1946 US Women's Amateur Championship was held in September at Southern Hills Country Club in Tulsa, Oklahoma, whose golf course carried a women's par of 75. Babe shot a six-over-par 156 in the 36-hole qualifying round and easily qualified for the match-play portion of the event. She won her first two matches without difficulty and in the third round defeated veteran amateur Maureen Orcutt 5 and 4. In the semifinals, she posted a 3 and 2 victory over Helen Sigel, a veteran amateur from Philadelphia who had twice been the runner-up in the event. In the 36-hole final match against veteran Clara Sherman from Pasadena, California, Babe led from outset and closed out the match 11 and 9 on the 27th hole. It was the biggest final-round margin of victory in the 45-year history of the event.

After winning the US Women's Amateur, Babe posted 15 consecutive victories before traveling to Muirfield Links in Gullane, Scotland, in June 1947, to play in the British Ladies Amateur Championship, an event that had never been won by an American. The Scots at Muirfield came out by the thousands to watch the superwoman from across the sea and immediately took a liking to her. Babe, who loved crowds, conversed continuously with the huge galleries that followed her. When it became known that the clothing she had brought with her was not warm enough for the cold Scottish weather, well-wishers from all over Scotland sent her so many garments that they nearly filled the clubhouse at Muirfield.

Playing the finest golf of her career, she qualified and sailed through the first five matches, defeating her opponents so badly that a British sportswriter called it "cruel to send our girls out against a game like that."[1] In the semifinals, she defeated the Scottish champion, Jean Donald, 7 and 5, using only 21 putts over the 13 holes of the match. In the 36-hole final match against Jacqueline Gordon of England, her game fell off a little and she was two down after 13 holes. However, she rallied and pulled even with Gordon after 18 holes and then took four of the next six holes and closed out the match 5 and 4 on the 32nd hole. The Scots cheered her all the way to the clubhouse, where she accepted the trophy and became the first American winner of the prestigious event.

In writing about Babe Zaharias in 2007, sportswriter Charles McGrath of the *New York Times* wrote, "She broke the mold of what a lady golfer was supposed to be. The ideal in the '20s and '30s was Joyce Wethered, a willowy Englishwoman with a picture-book swing that produced elegant shots, but not especially long ones. Zaharias developed a grooved athletic swing reminiscent of Lee Trevino's, and she was so long off the tee that a fellow Texan,

Babe Didrickson Zaharias. An Olympic champion and a golfing legend.
Library of Congress

the great Byron Nelson, once said that he knew of only eight men who could outdrive her. 'It's not enough just to swing at the ball,' Babe said. 'You've got to loosen your girdle and really let the ball have it.'" McGrath also wrote, "Except perhaps for Arnold Palmer, no golfer has ever been so beloved by the gallery."

In 1944, Betty Hicks Newell, Hope Seignious, and Ellen Griffin, three prominent American women golfers, founded the Women's Professional Golf Association (the WPGA). Patty Berg, Betty Jameson, Marlene Bauer, Marilyn Smith, and several other leading women golfers joined the WPGA and a tour was established. In 1947, after winning the British Ladies Amateur Championship, Babe Zaharias accepted a $300,000 offer to make a series of movie shorts. When the movies were completed, she joined the WPGA.

One of the objectives of the WPGA was to establish a national championship, open to all women golfers, amateur and professional. In 1946, the WPGA organized and held the first US Women's Open Championship at the Spokane Country Club in Spokane, Washington, a match-play event with a purse of $19,700. Patty Berg won the event, beating Betty Jameson 5 and 4 in the final, and received $5,600 for doing so. In 1947, the US Women's Open was changed to a 72-hole, three-day, stroke-play event with 36 holes played on the final day. The purse was dropped to $7,500 because of a lack of sponsors. Betty Jameson won with a 295 and collected $1,200. Babe Zaharias played in the event for the first time in 1948 and her 300 made her an eight-stroke winner over runner-up Betty Hicks Newell.

In 1949, the championship again had a purse of only $7,500. A 25-year-old, first-year pro from Atlanta, Georgia, named Louise Suggs won the event by 14 strokes over runner-up Babe Zaharias. Suggs had won the US Women's Amateur in 1947 and a year later had become the second American woman to win the British Ladies Amateur Championship. The lithe, five-foot-six-inch ball-striker hit such consistently good shots that she was called the Ben Hogan of women's golf. It was clear that she would be a force in women's professional golf for years to come.

From the outset, the WPGA was plagued with inadequate financing and a lack of sponsors, which resulted in low purses and a scarcity of events. By the late 1940s, it was becoming apparent that the organization was doomed to failure. In 1948, Babe and George Zaharias met with Patty Berg and sports promoter Fred Corcoran and began making plans to replace the WPGA. They later persuaded several other WPGA members to join them in forming a new organization.

In the spring of 1950, 13 professional women golfers, including Babe Zaharias, Patty Berg, Louise Suggs, and Betty Jameson, founded the Ladies

Professional Golf Association (the LPGA). Patty Berg was its first president and Fred Corcoran was its tournament director. With financial assistance from Wilson Sporting Goods, the LPGA began organizing tournaments and obtaining sponsorships. In 1950, its initial year of operation, the LPGA held seven tournaments with prize money totaling $50,000. Babe Zaharias won six of the seven events, including the 1950 US Women's Open. The leading money-winner, she collected $14,800. She later served as president of the LPGA from 1952 to 1955.

Helped immensely during its early years by the presence of players like Babe Zaharias, Patty Berg, Louise Suggs, and Betty Jameson, the LPGA Tour rose steadily from its meager beginnings. By 1952, it had 21 events on its tour and by 1970 its total prize money had increased to $435,000. By the turn of the 21st century, the total prize money on the LPGA Tour had increased to $38,500,000. In 2016, there were 33 events in 14 countries with prize money in excess of $63,000,000.

When the WPGA folded in 1950, the LPGA took over the management of the US Women's Open Championship and ran the event until 1953, when, at the request of the LPGA, the event was taken over by the USGA. The USGA continued the 72-hole, stroke-play, three-day format until 1965, when it eliminated the 36-hole final day and converted the tournament to a four-day event with 18 holes played each day.

In 1951, the LPGA Tour welcomed a new star in the person of Betsy Rawls. Tall, attractive, and a product of the South, she was born in Spartanburg, South Carolina, raised in Arlington, Texas, and educated at the University of Texas. Playing as an amateur, she was the runner-up to Babe Zaharias in the 1950 US Women's Open. In 1951, playing as a professional, she won the event, finishing five strokes ahead of runner-up Louise Suggs. In 1952, she won eight LPGA Tour events and was the leading money-winner with $14,505 in official winnings. In 1953, she again won the US Women's Open, and the LPGA Tour had another great player to join the likes of Zaharias, Berg, and Suggs.

In 1953, the LPGA Tour began awarding a trophy to the player with the lowest-scoring average for the season. The LPGA named its trophy the Vare Trophy, in honor of Glenna Collett Vare, the great golfer of the 1920s and 1930s. The first two winners of the trophy were Patty Berg in 1953 and Babe Zaharias in 1954. Berg won the trophy again in 1955 and 1956, and Louise Suggs won it in 1957.

In 1955, the LPGA held its first LPGA Championship, a match-play event played at Orchard Ridge Country Club in Fort Wayne, Indiana. Beverly Hanson won the event, defeating Louise Suggs 4 and 3 in the final.

In 1956, it was converted to a 72-hole, stroke-play, four-day event, that Marlene Bauer won in a playoff with Patty Berg.

Babe Zaharias was diagnosed with colon cancer in 1953 and underwent extensive surgery. In 1954, she felt well enough to enter the US Women's Open, where, in an incredible display of courage and talent, she won the event by 12 strokes over Betty Hicks Newell. Weakened by the disease and the surgery, she played in only eight LPGA events that year, of which she won two, the second being the last victory of her magnificent career. In 1955, the cancer returned and she resigned as president of the LPGA in July. On September 27, 1956, she died at a hospital in Galveston, Texas. She was only 45 years old. Women's golf had lost one of its greatest champions and benefactors. Considered by many to be the greatest female athlete in the history of American sports, she was named the Associated Press Female Athlete of the Year a record six times between1932 and 1954.

During the first eight years of its existence, the LPGA Tour was dominated by Babe Zaharias, Patty Berg, Louise Suggs, and Betsy Rawls. That changed in 1958 when 23-year-old Mickey Wright won the US Women's Open, the LPGA Championship, and three other LPGA Tour events. The daughter of a lawyer, Mickey Wright was born in February 1935 in San Diego, California, and started playing golf at an early age. At age 17, she won the US Girls Junior Championship and at age 19, while attending Stanford University, she won the Women's World Amateur Championship. In 1955, she dropped out of Stanford, turned professional, and joined the LPGA Tour. From 1958 to the mid-1960s, she dominated the LPGA Tour, winning 59 LPGA events, including four US Women's Open Championships, four LPGA Championships, and five other majors. In 1963, she won a record 13 LPGA events. She won the Vare Trophy a record five times in a row beginning in 1960 and was the leading money-winner for four consecutive years beginning in 1961. Her last multiwin year came in 1968 when she won four LPGA events.

After 1968, she won only two more LPGA events, the last one coming in 1973 when she won the Dinah Shore Winner's Circle at age 38. One of the greatest players ever, she won 82 LPGA events during her 14-year professional career, the second-most ever, trailing only the 88 wins later posted by Kathy Whitworth. She also won 13 major championships, which is second all-time to the 15 majors won by Patty Berg.

In 1964, three years after Charlie Sifford broke the color line on the men's PGA Tour, 37-year-old Althea Gibson, the winner of five Grand Slam singles titles in tennis, became the first African American woman to play on the LPGA Tour. Although her best finish on the tour was a tie for second place in the Len Immke Buick Open in 1972, she was a highly respected

Mickey Wright. Her 82 tour wins and 13 majors made her a legend in women's golf.
Library of Congress

player on the tour for several years. Judy Rankin had this to say about her fellow professional: "Althea might have been a real player of consequence had she started when she was young. She came along during a difficult time in golf, gained the support of a lot of people, and quietly made a difference."[2] The second African American woman to join the LPGA Tour was Renee Powell from Canton, Ohio, who began in 1967 and played for 13 years. The third African American woman to join the LPGA Tour was LaRee Sugg from Petersburg, Virginia, who started in 1995.

The events on the LPGA Tour that are considered "majors" have changed over the years. Both the US Women's Open and the LPGA Championship have been majors continuously since their inceptions in 1946 and 1955 respectively. The US Women's Open is now the third major of the season and is played in early July on venues in the United States selected by the USGA, which manages the event. In 2015, management of the LPGA Championship was turned over to the PGA of America and the name of the event was changed to the Women's PGA Championship. It is now the second major of the season and is played in early June on venues in the United States selected by the PGA of America.

The Women's Western Open was a major until 1967, when it was discontinued. The Titleholders Championship was a major from 1937 until 1972, when it was discontinued. The du Maurier Classic was a major from 1979 until 2000, when it was discontinued. The British Women's Open Championship became a major in 2001 and is now the fourth major of the season. It is played in late July on venues in Great Britain.

The Nabisco Dinah Shore Championship became a major in 1983. In 2002, its name was changed to the Kraft Nabisco Championship and in 2015 it became the ANA Inspiration. It is now the first major of the season and is played in late March or early April at Mission Hills Country Club in Rancho Mirage, California. In 2013, the Evian Masters changed its name to the Evian Championship and became the fifth major of the season. It is played in mid-September at the Evian Resort Golf Club in Evian-les-Bains, France.

In the middle 1960s, when Mickey Wright's great run was coming to an end, another superstar in the person of Kathy Whitworth joined the LPGA Tour. Born in September 1939 in Monahans, Texas, Kathy Whitworth spent most of her youth in Jal, New Mexico, where her father owned a hardware store. She began playing golf at age 13 and three years later won the New Mexico State Women's Amateur Championship. She attended Odessa Junior College in Odessa, Texas, briefly before turning professional and joining the LPGA Tour in 1958 at age 19. Her first LPGA Tour win didn't come until July 8, 1962, when she won the Kelly Girls Open. Her second win came three months later when she won the Phoenix Thunderbird Open, defeating

Althea Gibson. She broke racial barriers in both tennis and golf.
Library of Congress

runner-up Mickey Wright by four strokes. Her break-out season came in 1963 when she won eight LPGA Tour events.

After an off-year in 1964, when she won but one event, she surged past Mickey Wright in 1965, when she won eight LPGA Tour events and was the tour's leading money-winner. This marked the beginning of an incredible nine-year run during which she won 60 LPGA Tour events, was the leading money-winner eight times, won seven Vare Trophies, led the tour in wins six times, won five majors, and was named the LPGA Player of the Year seven times.

The only blemish on her record was that she never won the US Women's Open. The closest she came was in 1971, when she was the runner-up to JoAnne Carner. Her 88 career tour wins are the most ever by any professional golfer, man or woman. Sam Snead and Mickey Wright are tied for the second most with 82. In 1981, she became the first woman golfer to win a million dollars in official career prize money. The last of her six career majors came in 1975 when she won the LPGA Championship for the third time. The final LPGA Tour win of her career came on May 12, 1985, when she won the United Virginia Bank Classic at age 45. She is thought by many to be the best putter in the history of women's golf.

Kathy Whitworth. Her 88 tour wins are the most ever by either a woman or a man.
Library of Congress

Judy Rankin had great years in 1976 and 1977, during which she won a total of eleven LPGA Tour events. In both years, she won the Vare Trophy, was the leading money-winner, and was named LPGA Player of the Year. However, she never won a major and after 1977 she won only two more LPGA tour events. She retired in 1983 because of chronic back problems.

A force in women's professional golf during the 1970s was Sandra Palmer. Born in Fort Worth, Texas, in 1943, she was raised and first played golf in Bangor, Maine. She attended North Texas State University in Denton, Texas, where she was the Homecoming Queen, a cheerleader for the football team, and the star of the women's golf team. A four-time winner of the West Texas Amateur, she turned professional and joined the LPGA Tour in 1964. However, her first win on the tour didn't come until 1971, when she won the Sealy LPGA Classic. In 1972, she won her first major—the Titleholders Championship, which she won by ten strokes over Judy Rankin and Mickey Wright. During the decade of the '70s, she won 16 LPGA Tour events and two majors. Her best year came in 1975 when she won the US Women's Open and was the LPGA Tour's leading money-winner and Player of the Year. During her career she won 19 LPGA Tour events and two majors. She won her last LPGA Tour event at age 43 in 1986.

Another force in women's golf during the 1970s and '80s was JoAnne Carner. She was born in 1939 in Kirkland, Washington, and, like most professional golfers, began playing the game at an early age. In 1956, as JoAnne Gunderson, her maiden name, she won the US Junior Girls Championship at age 17. A graduate of Arizona State University, she was the dominant amateur in women's golf for ten years beginning in 1957. Her five US Women's Amateur Championships rank her second only to the six won by Glenna Collett Vare. She was the runner-up on two other occasions.

Called "Big Mama" by sportswriters, she didn't turn professional until 1970, when, at age thirty, she was the LPGA Rookie of the Year. A year later, she won the US Women's Open by seven strokes over Kathy Whitworth. She won the event again in 1976, defeating Sandra Palmer in an 18-hole playoff. For her career, she won 43 LPGA events, claimed five Vare Trophies, was the leading money-winner three times, and was the LPGA Player of the Year three times. Even though she won over a million dollars in career prize money, she and her husband, who was also her coach and business manager, customarily traveled by automobile from tournament to tournament and lived in an Airstream trailer that they towed with their automobile. In 2004, at age 65, she became the oldest player ever to make the cut in an LPGA Tour event.

The most successful and popular woman golfer during the late 1970s and 1980s was Nancy Lopez. Attractive and the possessor of a charming smile, she did much to boost the popularity of women's professional golf during her time. Born in January 1957 in Torrance, California, and raised in Roswell, New Mexico, she was good at golf from the day she first swung a club. She won the New Mexico Women's Amateur Championship at age 12 and the US Junior Girls Championship at age 15. In 1975, at age 18, she played as an amateur in the US Women's Open and was the runner-up to Sandra Palmer. She attended Tulsa University on a golf scholarship and was an NCAA All-American as a freshman. During her sophomore year, she dropped out of college to play professional golf. In 1977, before joining the LPGA Tour, she played in the US Women's Open as a professional and was the runner-up to Hollis Stacy.

She joined the LPGA Tour in late 1977 and was an immediate sensation. In 1978, she became the first player to be named LPGA Rookie of the Year, LPGA Player of the Year, and win the Vare Trophy, all in the same year. She led the tour in wins that year with nine, including five wins in a row at one point. She also won her first LPGA Championship that year and was the leading money-winner, collecting a record $189,814 in official winnings. In 1979, she did a repeat performance, again winning the Vare Trophy, leading the tour in wins with eight and official money-winnings with a record $197,489, and was again named the LPGA Player of the Year. No player since Babe Zaharias had joined the LPGA Tour with such success and fanfare.

In late 1979, she married Houston sportscaster Tim Mellon and her success on the tour took a hit. She won only three events in 1980 and three again in 1981. In 1982, she divorced Mellon and married baseball player Ray Knight and a year later gave birth to her first child. Her next successful season came in 1985, when she led the LPGA Tour with five wins and a record $416,472 in official winnings. She also won her third Vare Trophy and her second LPGA Championship and was named LPGA Player of the Year. She was winless in 1986, when she had her second child, and won only two events in 1987. She rebounded again in 1988, when she won three LPGA Tour events and was named the LPGA Player of the Year for the fourth time.

In 1989, she again won three LPGA events and won her final major—her third LPGA Championship. She won six more LPGA events before retiring in 2002 with 48 career LPGA Tour wins and three majors to her credit. In 2007, at age 50, she attempted a comeback but failed to make the cut in any of the six events she entered. She tried again in 2008 and again failed to make the cut in her three events.

The one blemish on her amazing career is that she never won the US Women's Open. She was runner-up in the event four times, the final one coming in 1997, when, at age 40, she lost to England's Alison Nicholas by a stroke and became the first player to shoot four rounds in the 60s and not win the event.

Another popular and successful player in the late twentieth century and beyond was Julie Inkster. Born in June 1960 in Santa Cruz, California, she attended nearby San Jose State University, where, as a member of the golf team, she was a three-time All-American. She won three consecutive US Women's Amateur titles beginning in 1980 and became the first player since Virginia Van Wie in 1932–1934 to do so.

She turned professional and joined the LPGA Tour in 1983. In 1984, she won two events, both of which were majors, and was the LPGA Rookie of the Year. She slowed down after her rookie season and won only 17 LPGA events during her first 15 years on the LPGA Tour, but was seemingly always near the top of the leaderboard. Peaking late, she had her best year in 1999, when, at age 39, she won five LPGA events and two majors, including her first US Women's Open Championship. She also won her first LPGA Championship that year, shooting a 16-under-par 272, still the lowest score to par in the history of the event.

She won three events in 2000, including her second LPGA Championship, where she defeated Stefania Croce of Italy in a playoff. In 2002, at age 42, she won her second US Women's Open Championship, defeating Annika Sörenstam of Sweden by two strokes. Her final LPGA win came on March 19, 2006, when, at age 45, she won the Safeway International by two strokes. She won 31 events and seven majors during her 23-year professional career, but she was never named the LPGA Player of the Year, was never the leading money-winner, and never won the Vare Trophy. However, her career prize money total of nearly 14 million dollars is the sixth-highest ever and the second highest by an American woman.

The 1994 and 1995 seasons marked the end of an era in women's professional golf and the beginning of another. Prior to 1995, the only non-American player named LPGA Player of the Year was Ayako Okamoto of Japan in 1987. After 1995, the only American LPGA Player of the Year was Stacy Lewis in 2012 and 2014. Prior to 1995, every winner of the Vare Trophy was an American, but since then the only American to win the trophy was Stacy Lewis in 2013 and 2014. Prior to 1994, every leading money-winner on the LPGA Tour was an American. Since then, the only American to claim that honor was Stacy Lewis in 2014.

At about the same time, foreign women also began dominating the major American championships. Prior to 1995, American women had won 46 of the 49 US Women's Open Championships and 35 of the 40 LPGA Championships. Since then, foreign women have won 13 of the 21 US Women's Open Championships and 17 of the 21 LPGA Championships. Since 1995, the only American women who have won more than one of these majors are Julie Inkster, who won four, and Cristie Kerr, who won two.

The first foreign player to have success on the LPGA Tour was Laura Davies, England's greatest professional woman player. She joined the LPGA Tour in 1994 and was a dominant player from 1994 to 1996, winning nine LPGA events and three majors. She was also the leading money-winner in 1994, the LPGA Player of the Year in 1996, and won the LPGA Championship in 1994 and 1996.

The next great foreign player was Annika Sörenstam of Sweden. She joined the LPGA Tour in 1994 after playing collegiately at the University of Arizona, where, in 1991, she became the first non-American to win an NCAA Individual Championship. One of the greatest players ever, she won 69 LPGA events and ten majors during an 11-year period that began in 1995. During her incredible 11-year run, she won 10 majors, was the leading money-winner and LPGA Player of the Year eight times, and won the Vare Trophy six times. She won the US Women's Open and the LPGA Championship three times apiece during her great run. When she retired in 2008, she was the all-time leading career money-winner on the LPGA Tour with over 22 million dollars in official winnings. Her 72 career wins are the third-most ever.

Next came Karrie Webb, Australia's greatest professional woman player. The winner of 25 LPGA events and six majors during a five-year period that began in 1996, she was the LPGA Player of the Year and leading money-winner three times and won three Vare Trophies and two US Open Championships. She is the second all-time leading career money-winner on the LPGA Tour with over 20 million dollars in official winnings.

The next great foreign player was Lorena Ochoa of Mexico, who joined the LPGA Tour in 2003, after playing collegiately at the University of Arizona, where she was an NCAA All-American. The winner of 24 LPGA events and two majors during a four-year period that began in 2006, she led the tour in wins and was the leading money-winner three years in a row beginning in 2006. She was also the LPGA Player of the Year and won the Vare Trophy four years in a row beginning in 2006. She is the fourth all-time leading career money-winner on the LPGA Tour with nearly 15 million dollars in official winnings.

After Lorena Ochoa's four-year run ended in 2009, a group of Asian women combined to dominate the LPGA Tour as never before. Included in this group were Inbee Park, Jiyai Shin, Na Yeon Choi, Hyo-joo Kim, So-

Yean Ryu, Sun-Young Yoo, and In-gee Chun of South Korea; Yani Tseng of Taiwan; Ariya Jutanugarn of Thailand; Lydia Ko of New Zealand; Ai Miyazato of Japan; and Shanshan Feng of China. During a seven-year period beginning in 2009, Asian players captured five LPGA Player of the Year awards, five Vare Trophies, seven Rookie of the Year awards, and six money-winning titles. They also won four US Women's Open Championships, five LPGA Championships, and 15 other majors during that seven-year period.

The American players who have enjoyed the most success on the LPGA Tour since 1995 are Cristie Kerr, Stacy Lewis, and Paula Creamer. Cristie Kerr was born in 1977 in Miami, Florida. A natural lefthander who plays golf right-handed, she had an outstanding junior golf career before turning professional and joining the LPGA Tour in 1997 at age 18. She started slowly on the LPGA Tour and did not win her first event until 2002. In 2006, she won three LPGA Tour events and was the only American to win more than one. Her first win in a major came in 2007, when she won the US Women's Open by two strokes over Lorena Ochoa and Angela Park of Brazil.

During her 19-year professional career, she has won 18 events and two majors. One of her majors was the 2010 LPGA Championship, where she became the first American winner of the event since Juli Inkster in 2000. At the close of the 2016 season, she had accumulated nearly 18 million dollars in career winnings, a total that ranks her third all-time on the LPGA Tour and first among American women.

Stacy Lewis was born in 1985 in Toledo, Ohio, and grew up in the Woodlands, near Houston, Texas. She attended the University of Arkansas, where, as a member of the women's golf team, she was a four-time All-American and won an NCAA Individual Championship in 2007. After graduating in 2008, she turned professional and joined the LPGA Tour.

She struggled early and didn't get her first win until 2011, when she won the Kraft Nabisco Championship, a major, by three strokes over Yani Tseng of Taiwan, the defending champion and the number-one ranked player in the world. In 2012, she found her stroke and led the LPGA Tour with four wins and was the LPGA Player of the Year, beating out Inbee Park for the honor. She continued to play well in 2013, when she won the Vare Trophy and three LPGA events, including the Women's British Open. In 2014, she again won three LPGA Tour events, was the tour's leading money-winner, won the Vare Trophy for the second straight year, and was the LPGA Player of the Year for the second time in three years, beating out Lydia Ko for the honor. She fell off after 2014 and did not win another LPGA Tour event until 2017. However, she had nine second-place finishes during those years and won nearly 3 million dollars in prize money.

The only child of an airline pilot father and a stay-at-home mother, Paula Creamer was born in 1986 in the Bay Area city of Mountain View, California. Raised in nearby Pleasanton, she was introduced to golf at age 10 and at age 13 was the top-ranked female junior golfer in California. Following an amateur career wherein she won 19 national junior golf events, she turned professional in 2004, at age 17. She joined the LPGA Tour in 2005 and was the LPGA Rookie of the Year and the second leading money-winner, collecting more than 1.5 million dollars in official winnings. By the close of the 2017 season, she had won ten LPGA events, including the 2010 US Women's Open, and had collected 12 million dollars in career winnings, a total that ranks her ninth all-time and fourth among American women.

In 2006, the World Congress of Women's Golf adopted a system of ranking women players called Women's World Golf Rankings. It is similar to the Official World Golf Rankings system adopted by the men. Rankings are based on the points players receive for finishes in sanctioned events over a two-year period. The number of points a player receives in an event depends on the player's finish and the strength of the field, which, in turn, is determined by the rankings of the players in the event. The only exception is that the five LPGA majors have a fixed-point allocation. There is no minimum event requirement for obtaining a ranking, but a player's ranking number is determined by dividing her point total by the greater of 35 or the number of sanctioned events she has played in over a two-year period. A player's point total is adjusted by a formula that gives more weight to recent events. Rankings are announced weekly by Women's World Golf Rankings, which also issues a year-end list of the top ten players in the world.

The first number-one ranked player in the world announced by Women's World Golf Rankings was Annika Sörenstam of Sweden, who was ranked number one in the world for 60 consecutive weeks beginning on February 21, 2006. She was followed by Lorena Ochoa of Mexico, who was ranked number one for a record 158 consecutive weeks beginning on April 23, 2007. After Ochoa, no player was ranked number one for more than a few weeks until February 14, 2011, when Yani Tseng of Taiwan began a run of 109 consecutive weeks at number one. Inbee Park of South Korea has been ranked number one on two occasions for a total of 92 weeks. Lydia Ko of New Zealand has been ranked number one twice, the most recent of which ended on June 1, 2017. She has had a total of 104 weeks at number one in the world.

The only American women who have been ranked number one by Women's World Golf Rankings are Cristie Kerr, who was ranked number one on three occasions in 2010 for a total of five weeks and Stacy Lewis, who was ranked number one for four weeks beginning on March 18, 2013, and for 21 weeks beginning on June 2, 2014.

Although the twenty-year dominance of the LPGA Tour by foreign women may have dampened the enthusiasm of American sports fans for women's professional golf somewhat, their disinterest is not shared by the tournament sponsors because the purses of LPGA events have grown steadily since 1995. The purse of the US Women's Open, for example, has grown from $1,000,000 in 1995 to $5,000,000 in 2017 and the winner's share has increased from $175,000 in 1995 to $900,000 in 2017. The purse of the LPGA Championship (now the Women's PGA Championship) has grown from $1,200,000 in 1995 to $3,500,000 in 2017 and the winner's share has increased from $180,000 in 1995 to $525,000 in 2017. Like the men's PGA Tour, the LPGA Tour is awash in prize money but does not have a superstar that American sports fans can relate to.

On the recreational side, women's golf has grown phenomenally over the years. Most private membership golf and country clubs now have women members and most municipal and privately owned public courses have women's clubs that sponsor tournaments for women golfers. The National Golf Foundation reports that the number of adult women golfers in the United States reached a high of 6.5 million in 2006. In addition, there were 600,000 girls between the ages of six and 17 playing golf in the United States at that time. Although the numbers have decreased slightly since then, the percentage of all recreational golfers in the United States who are female has remained at a constant 23 percent.

• *14* •

The Major Team Competitions

*A*merican golfers participate in five major team competitions, all of which are for cups. The men compete for the Walker Cup, the Ryder Cup, and the President's Cup, and the women compete for the Curtis Cup and the Solheim Cup. The Walker Cup and the Curtis Cup matches are played by amateur golfers, while the Ryder Cup, the President's Cup, and the Solheim Cup matches are played by professional golfers.

THE WALKER CUP

The Walker Cup Match is a competition between two ten-man teams of amateur men golfers, one from the United States and the other from Great Britain and Ireland. It is managed jointly by the USGA and the R&A and is played biennially in the odd-numbered years in alternate countries on courses selected by the host organization. It is played in match play over three days and consists of eight alternate-shot foursome matches and 18 singles matches. All matches are 18 holes in length.

In the spring of 1921, a group of leading American amateur golfers that included Francis Ouimet, Chick Evans, and Bobby Jones, traveled to England to play in the British Amateur at Royal Liverpool. While in England, they engaged a group of leading British amateurs in an informal competition as a warm-up for the British Amateur. The competition consisted of four foursome matches and eight singles matches and was won convincingly by the Americans, nine matches to three.

When USGA officials heard of the informal competition, they decided that the possibility of arranging a formal competition of this type should be looked into. The competition was organized and implemented largely through the efforts of USGA president George Herbert Walker, who donated a trophy to be awarded to the winning team in the competition. Walker is the maternal grandfather and namesake of George H. W. Bush, the 41st president of the United States, and the great-grandfather of George W. Bush, the 43rd president of the United States. The trophy was later named the Walker Cup in his honor.

The first official Walker Cup Match was held in 1922 at National Golf Links of America, Charlie Macdonald's creation in Southampton, New York. The American team, led by Bobby Jones, won the inaugural competition, eight matches to four. The second Walker Cup Match was played in 1923 on the Old Course at St. Andrews, where the American team again prevailed, this time 6-1/2 to 5-1/2. The competition was held annually for the first three years, but after 1924 it was held biennially in the even-numbered years until 1947, when it was changed to the odd-numbered years. No competitions were held from 1939 to 1946 because of World War II.

The competition originally consisted of four alternate-shot foursome matches and eight singles matches. All matches were held in match play and were 36 holes in length. In 1963, the matches were shortened to 18 holes and the format was changed to eight alternate-shot foursome matches and 16 singles matches. In 2009, the number of singles matches was increased to 18. For the first 67 years, American teams dominated the competitions, winning 29 of the first 31 Walker Cups, often by one-sided scores. Since 1989, however, the matches have been much closer. The results of all Walker Cup matches held through 2017 are set forth in appendix C.

THE RYDER CUP

The Ryder Cup Match is a competition between two twelve-man teams of professional golfers, one from the United States and the other from Europe. It is managed jointly by the PGA of America and Ryder Cup Europe and is held biennially in the even-numbered years in alternating countries on venues selected by the host organization. It is played in match play over three days and consists of eight four-ball matches, eight alternate-shot foursome matches, and twelve singles matches. All matches are 18 holes in length.

In the spring of 1926, a group of professional golfers from the United States that included Walter Hagen traveled to England to play in the British Open at Royal Lytham. A few days prior to the British Open, Hagen organized a team of ten American professionals to play a team of ten British professionals in an informal match as a warm-up. The British prevailed 13 matches to one in the informal competition and Samuel Ryder, a British seed merchant and golf nut, heard of the competition and thought it should become a regular event. He subsequently organized the competition, drew up a set of rules governing its play, and donated a trophy, later called the Ryder Cup, to be awarded to the winning team in the competition.

The first official Ryder Cup match was held in 1927 at the Worcester Country Club in Worcester, Massachusetts. The contestants were a ten-man team of professional golfers from the United States selected by the PGA of America and a ten-man team of British professionals. In the inaugural match, the American team, led by Captain Walter Hagen, defeated the British team, led by Captain Ted Ray, 9-1/2 matches to 2-1/2.

Although it was not required by the rules of the competition at the time, the PGA of America restricted membership on the American team to golfers born in the United States, thus eliminating Tommy Armour and the other Scottish immigrants who had contributed so much to professional golf in the United States. In 1929, the rules of the event were formally revised to include a requirement that all players be born and reside in the country they are representing and be members of their country's professional golf organization.

After the 1927 matches, it was decided to hold the competitions biennially in the odd-numbered years beginning in 1929. The competitions were not held during the war years of 1939 to 1945, and in 2002 the competitions were switched to the even-numbered years, where they have since remained.

The format of the competitions has changed over the years. The inaugural competition in 1927 was a two-day event consisting of four 36-hole alternate-shot foursome matches and eight 36-hole singles matches. That format was continued until 1961 when the matches were shortened to 18 holes in length and the number of matches was increased to eight alternate-shot foursome matches and 16 singles matches, all of which were played in two days. In 1963, the event was expanded to three days, and eight four-ball matches were added to the competition. In 1969, the size of the teams was increased from ten to twelve players. In 1973, the British team was enlarged to include Irish players and the name of their team was changed to Great Britain and Ireland. In 1977, the number of matches was changed to five alternate-shot foursome matches, five four-ball matches, and ten singles matches. In 1979, the number of matches was increased to eight alternate-shot foursome matches, eight four-ball matches, and twelve singles matches for a total of 28 matches, where it has since remained.

The first five Ryder Cup competitions were won by the host team. After World War II, however, the competitions were dominated by the United States teams, which won 15 of the next 17, usually by one-sided scores. To make the competitions more competitive, in 1979 the British-Irish team was enlarged to include all of Europe and the name of their team was changed to Team Europe. Since then the competitions have been much more even. The increase in the competitiveness of the matches has increased the popularity of the matches, and both the media coverage and the revenue generated by the matches have increased significantly.

The twelve-man US Ryder Cup team is selected under a system devised by the PGA of America whereby eight players are chosen through a complicated money-winning formula and four are chosen by the team captain (the so-called wild cards or captain's picks). The matches are now played over three days and include twelve singles matches, eight alternate-shot foursome matches wherein the two players on each team play a single ball and hit alternate shots, with the team posting the low score on a hole winning the hole, and eight four-ball matches wherein each player on each two-man team plays his own ball and the player with the low score on a hole wins the hole for his team. Those chosen to play in the matches do so for the honor of representing their team and country, as no prize money is awarded to the players. The results of all Ryder Cup matches held through 2016 are set forth in appendix C.

THE PRESIDENTS CUP

The President's Cup matches are a series of competitions between a twelve-man team of professional golfers from the United States and a similarly composed team from the rest of the world, excluding Europe. It was created by the PGA Tour in 1994 and has been held biennially since then. It was originally held in the even-numbered years but was switched to the odd-numbered years in 2003. It is held alternately in the United States, on a course selected by the PGA Tour, and in a country represented on the International Team. The president or prime minister of the host country traditionally serves as the honorary chairman of the event.

The matches are held in match play in a format that is similar to that of the Ryder Cup matches. It was originally a three-day event consisting of ten alternate-shot foursome matches, ten four-ball matches, and twelve singles matches. In 2000, the event was lengthened to four days, and in 2003 the format was changed to 11 alternate-shot foursome matches, 11 four-ball matches, and 12 singles matches played on the final day. In 2015, the number of foursome and four-ball matches was reduced from 11 to nine. No prize money is awarded, and the proceeds of the events are given to charities selected by the players and nonplaying captains of the teams. The first 10 President's Cup matches raised over 32 million dollars for charities around the world. The results of all Presidents Cup matches held through 2017 are set forth in appendix C.

THE CURTIS CUP MATCHES

The Curtis Cup Matches are a competition between a team of amateur women golfers from the United States and a similarly composed team from Great Britain and Ireland. The matches are played biennially in the even-numbered years in alternate countries. Each team consists of eight amateur women golfers and the matches are administered jointly by the USGA and the Ladies Golf Union of Great Britain. The format of the matches originally included three alternate-shot foursome matches and six singles matches, all of which were played in a single day. In 1964, the format was changed to six alternate-shot foursome matches and 12 singles matches played over two days. In 2008, the format was changed to six alternate-shot foursome matches, six four-ball matches, and eight singles matches, and the length of the event was increased to three days. All matches are played in match play and are 18 holes in length.

In 1905, Harriet and Margaret Curtis and several other leading American women golfers traveled to England to play in the British Ladies Amateur Championship. While in England they engaged some British women in a series of informal team competitions. In 1909, four of the British women came to the United States to continue the informal competitions. The informal competitions were continued periodically until 1932, when the Curtis sisters formalized them by donating a cup, later called the Curtis Cup, to be awarded to the winning team. As inscribed on the cup, the purpose of the Curtis Cup matches is to "stimulate friendly rivalry among the women golfers of many lands."

The inaugural Curtis Cup competition was played in 1932 at the Wentworth Club in Wentworth, England, and was won by the Americans, 5-1/2 matches to 3-1/2. The Americans won the first six competitions and, with a six-year interruption because of World War II, the first British victory came in 1952. The results of all Curtis Cup matches held through 2016 are set forth in appendix C.

THE SOLHEIM CUP MATCHES

The Solheim Cup matches are a competition between two teams of twelve professional women golfers, one from the United States and the other from

Europe. The matches were first held in 1990 and were organized largely through the efforts of Karsten Solheim, a Norwegian-American golf club manufacturer for whom the cup is named. The matches are played over three days and consist of eight alternate-shot foursome matches, eight four-ball matches, and twelve singles matches. All matches are played in match play and are 18 holes in length. The matches are played biennially in alternate countries in the odd-numbered years. They were played in the even-numbered years until 2003, when they were switched to the odd-numbered years. The American players are selected on a points system based on finishes in LPGA Tour events. European players are chosen via a system based on their finishes in both the Ladies European Tour and the LPGA. Both teams are supplemented by a number of captain's picks. The team captains are usually recently retired professional women golfers with Solheim Cup experience. The results of all Solheim Cup matches held through 2017 are set forth in appendix C.

· 𝒜 ·

A Timeline of Golf History

Date	Event
1300	The game of *het kolven* is invented by the Dutch
1400	*Het kolven* is introduced in Scotland, where the Scots revise the game to fit their links playing fields and invent the game of golf
1450	The first record of golf being played on the links at St. Andrews
1457	The Parliament of King James II of Scotland bans the playing of golf
1502	King James IV of Scotland lifts the ban on golf and purchases a set of golf clubs
1553	The archbishop of St. Andrews posts a notice advising his parishioners of their right to play golf on the links at St. Andrews
1567	Mary, Queen of Scots, is seen playing golf soon after the murder of her husband
1603	Golf is introduced in England by King James I of England, who has Scottish roots
1608	The first golf course outside of Scotland is established: a five-hole course at Blackheath, near London
1618	The feathery golf ball is invented
1621	Golf is first played at Dornoch in northern Scotland
1682	The Duke of York and John Patersone, a shoemaker from Edinburgh, defeat two English noblemen in the first known international golf match
1738	The Burgess Golfing Society, the first membership golf club, is founded in Edinburgh
1744	The first written rules of golf are drawn up by the Gentlemen Golfers of Leith

Date	Event
1754	A golf club called the Society of St. Andrews Golfers is founded in St. Andrews
1759	Stroke play is established for the first time by the Society of St. Andrews Golfers
1764	The layout of the Old Course at St. Andrews is changed from 22 holes to 18 holes
1776	The first golf club outside of Scotland is established at Blackheath in England
1826	Hickory replaces ash as the wood used to make shafts for golf clubs
1832	The first golf club that includes women is founded in North Berwick, Scotland
1833	Royal patronage is bestowed on the Perth Golfing Society
1834	Royal and Ancient patronage is bestowed on the Society of St. Andrews Golfers, and it becomes the Royal and Ancient Golf Club of St. Andrews (the R&A)
1837	A ladies' golf club is founded at St. Andrews and a ladies' course is opened at North Berwick
1848	The gutta-percha golf ball is invented
1850	Mechanical grass cutters are first used on golf courses
1851	Old Tom Morris builds a 12-hole golf course at Prestwick
1856	The Pau Golf Club is founded in France—the first golf club on the continent of Europe
1858	Allan Robertson shoots a 79 on the Old Course at St. Andrews and becomes the first golfer to break 80 in tournament play
1860	The first Open Championship (the British Open) is held at Prestwick
1867	Old Tom Morris wins the British Open at age 46—the oldest winner ever
1868	Young Tom Morris wins the British Open at age 17—the youngest winner ever
1872	Young Tom Morris wins his fourth consecutive British Open
1873	The Royal Montreal Golf Club is founded—the first golf club in North America
1875	Young Tom Morris dies at age 24
1884	The Edgewood Club of Tivoli in Tivoli, New York, opens a two-hole golf course and becomes the first golf club in the United States

Date	Event
1890	The concept of a par score for each hole and round of golf is first conceived
1891	The R&A standardizes the size of the hole at 4.25 inches in diameter
1893	The Shinnecock Hills Golf Club becomes the first club to admit women members and builds the first women's golf course in the United States
1894	The Morris County Golf Club, the first women's golf club in the United States, is founded in Morristown, New Jersey
1894	The United States Golf Association (the USGA) is founded
1895	The first US Open, US Amateur, and US Women's Amateur Championships are held by the USGA
1899	The rubber-wound golf ball is invented and patented by Coburn Haskell
1899	The wooden golf tee is invented by George Grant
1900	Par scores for holes and rounds of golf are adopted universally
1904	Walter Travis becomes the first American to win the British Amateur
1911	Johnny McDermott becomes the first American-born winner of the US Open
1913	Francis Ouimet wins the US Open, defeating Harry Vardon and Ted Ray of England, and popularizes golf in the United States
1916	The PGA of America is founded and the first PGA Championship is held
1916	Alexa Stirling wins the first of her three straight US Women's Amateur titles
1921	Walter Hagen becomes the first American-born winner of the PGA Championship
1922	Walter Hagen becomes the first American to win the British Open
1922	The first Walker Cup match is held
1922	Glenna Collett Vare wins the first of her four US Women's Amateur titles
1923	The number of Americans playing golf exceeds two million; there are more people playing golf in the United States than in the rest of the world combined
1924	The USGA approves the use of steel-shafted golf clubs
1925	The United Golfers Association (the UGA) is founded by African American golfers

Date	Event
1926	The UGA sponsors the first Negro National Open Golf Championship
1927	The first Ryder Cup matches are held
1929	The number of Americans playing golf exceeds five million
1930	Bobby Jones wins the US Open, the US Amateur, the British Open, and the British Amateur Championships in the same year
1932	Virginia Van Wie wins the first of her three straight US Women's Amateur titles
1932	The first Curtis Cup matches are held
1932	Gene Sarazen invents the sand iron and wins the US and British Opens
1933	Johnny Goodman becomes the last amateur to win the US Open
1933	The Augusta National Golf Club is founded by Bobby Jones and Clifford Roberts
1934	The first Masters Golf Tournament is held
1934	The PGA of America restricts membership in the organization to professional golfers of the Caucasian race
1935	Gene Sarazen wins the Masters with a double eagle on the 15th hole in the final round and becomes the first player to complete a Career Grand Slam
1938	The USGA imposes a bag limit of 14 golf clubs
1942	All major golf tournaments are discontinued for the duration of World War II
1942	The manufacture of golf clubs and balls is discontinued for the duration of the war
1944	The Women's Professional Golf Association (the WPGA) is founded and holds the first US Women's Open Championship
1945	Byron Nelson wins a record 19 PGA Tour events and wins 11 events in a row
1946	Ben Hogan wins 13 PGA Tour events—the second-most ever
1947	Babe Didrikson Zaharias becomes the first American to win the British Ladies Amateur Championship
1947	The USGA revises and simplifies the rules of golf
1949	Ben Hogan is severely injured in an automobile accident
1950	Sam Snead wins 11 PGA Tour events—the third-most ever
1950	The Ladies Professional Golf Association (the LPGA) is founded and replaces the WPGA
1950	Motorized golf carts become available to recreational golfers

Date	Event
1951	The USGA and the R&A adopt uniform rules of golf and abolish the stymie
1953	Ben Hogan wins the Masters, the US Open, and the British Open and completes a career Grand Slam
1953	The Tam O'Shanter World Championship in Chicago becomes the first televised PGA Tour event
1955	The US Supreme Court orders the desegregation of all municipal golf courses in the city of Atlanta, Georgia
1958	The PGA Championship changes from match play to stroke play
1960	The Tam O'Shanter Golf Club replaces its caddies with motorized golf carts
1960	Arnold Palmer wins the Masters and the US Open and a new era in golf begins
1961	The PGA of America removes its "Caucasians only" membership requirement and Charlie Sifford becomes the first African American to play on the PGA Tour
1961	Gary Player defeats Arnold Palmer in the Masters and becomes a superstar
1962	Jack Nicklaus defeats Arnold Palmer in the US Open and becomes a superstar
1963	Mickey Wright wins a record 13 LPGA events
1964	Pete Brown becomes the first African American to win a PGA Tour event
1965	Gary Player wins the US Open and completes a career Grand Slam
1965	Kathy Whitworth wins eight of her record 88 career LPGA victories
1966	Jack Nicklaus wins the British Open and completes his first career Grand Slam
1968	The US Open abolishes "Open Saturday" and becomes a four-day event
1968	The PGA of America reorganizes and creates a Tournament Players Division
1968	Solid-core golf balls become commercially available
1971	Jack Nicklaus completes his second career Grand Slam
1971	Lee Trevino wins the US Open, the Canadian Open, and the British Open in a 20-day span
1973	Johnny Miller shoots a final-round 63 to win the US Open
1974	The first Players Championship is held

Date	Event
1975	Tom Watson defeats Jack Nicklaus to win the Masters and becomes a superstar
1978	Jack Nicklaus wins the British Open and completes his third career Grand Slam
1978	Nancy Lopez is the LPGA Rookie of the Year and the LPGA Player of the Year
1979	Metal woods become commercially available
1979	Sam Snead, at age 67, shoots his age in a PGA Tour event
1980	The Senior PGA Tour is established (it is now called the Champions Tour)
1982	Tom Watson chips in on the 71st hole at Pebble Beach to defeat Jack Nicklaus in the US Open
1986	The Official World Golf Rankings system of ranking men golfers is adopted
1986	Jack Nicklaus becomes the oldest player to win the Masters when he wins his sixth Masters and his eighteenth and final major
1990	Golf clubs with graphite shafts become commercially available
1990	The first Solheim Cup matches are held
1990	Hale Irwin wins his third US Open at age 45 and becomes the oldest player to win the event
1991	Oversized drivers become commercially available
1994	Foreign women begin their domination of women's golf in the United States
1994	The first Presidents Cup matches are held
1997	Tiger Woods wins the Masters by 12 strokes and becomes the first African American to win a major
1999	The first World Golf Championships are held
1999	Julie Inkster shoots a record 16-under-par 272 to win the LPGA Championship
2000	Tiger Woods wins the US Open at Pebble Beach by 15 strokes and breaks or ties nine US Open records
2000	Tiger Woods wins three majors and completes a career Grand Slam at age 24
2001	Tiger Woods wins the Masters and holds all four major professional golf titles
2002	The US Open is held on a public course for the first time
2003	The number of Americans playing golf exceeds 30 million
2004	Phil Mickelson wins his first major—the Masters

Date	Event
2005	Tiger Woods wins the British Open and completes his second career Grand Slam
2006	The Women's World Golf Rankings system of ranking women golfers is adopted
2007	The first FedEx Cup competitions are held
2008	Tiger Woods wins the US Open and completes his third career Grand Slam
2010	Tiger Woods incurs knee and back injuries, admits marital infidelity, and ceases to be a ranked player

· *ℬ* ·

Winners of Major Professional
and Amateur Golf Championships

Table A2.1.   The United States Open Championship

Year	Winner	Score	Runner(s)-Up	Venue
1895	Horace Rollins	173#	Willie Dunn (175)	Newport Golf Club, Newport, RI
1896	James Foulis	152#	Horace Rollins (155)	Shinnecock Hills Golf Club, Southampton, NY
1897	Joe Lloyd	162#	Willie Anderson (163)	Chicago Golf Club, Wheaton, IL
1898	Fred Herd	328	Alex Smith (335)	Myopia Hunt Club, South Hamilton, MA
1899	Willie Smith	315	George Low, Bert Way & Val Fitzjohn (326)	Baltimore Country Club, Baltimore, MD
1900	Harry Vardon	313	J.H. Taylor (315)	Chicago Golf Club, Wheaton, IL
1901	Willie Anderson*	331	Alex Smith (331)	Myopia Hunt Club, South Hamilton, MA
1902	Laurie Auchterlonie	307	Stewart Gardner (313)	Garden City Golf Club, Garden City, NY
1903	Willie Anderson*	307	David Brown (307)	Baltusrol Golf Club, Springfield, NJ
1904	Willie Anderson	303	Gilbert Nicholls (308)	Glen View Golf Club, Golf, IL
1905	Willie Anderson	314	Alex Smith (316)	Myopia Hunt Club, South Hamilton, MA
1906	Alex Smith	295	Willie Smith (302)	Onwentsia Club, Lake Forest, IL
1907	Alec Ross	302	Gilbert Nicholls (304)	Philadelphia Cricket Club, Chestnut Hill, PA
1908	Fred McLeod*	322	Willie Smith (322)	Myopia Hunt Club, South Hamilton, MA
1909	George Sargent	290	Tom McNamara (294)	Englewood Golf Club, Englewood, NJ
1910	Alex Smith*	298	Macdonald Smith & John McDermott (298)	Philadelphia Cricket Club, Chestnut Hill, PA
1911	John McDermott*	307	George Simpson & Mike Brady (307)	Chicago Golf Club, Wheaton, IL
1912	John McDermott	294	Tom McNamara (296)	Country Club of Buffalo, Buffalo, NY
1913	Francis Ouimet@*	304	Harry Vardon & Ted Ray (304)	The Country Club, Brookline, MA
1914	Walter Hagen	290	Chick Evans@ (291)	Midlothian Country Club, Midlothian, IL
1915	Jerome Travers@	297	Tom McNamara (298)	Baltusrol Golf Club, Springfield, NJ
1916	Chick Evans@	286	Jock Hutchison (288)	The Minikahda Club, Minneapolis, MN
1917–1918	Event not held because of World War I			

Year	Winner	Score	Runner(s)-up	Location
1919	Walter Hagen*	301	Mike Brady (301)	Brae Burn Country Club, West Newton, MA
1920	Ted Ray	295	Jock Hutchison, Jack Burke, Leo Diegel & Harry Vardon (296)	Inverness Club, Toledo, OH
1921	Jim Barnes	289	Walter Hagen & Fred McLeod (298)	Columbia Country Club, Chevy Chase, MD
1922	Gene Sarazen	288	Bobby Jones@ & John Black (289)	Skokie Country Club, Glencoe, IL
1923	Bobby Jones@*	296	Bobby Cruickshank (296)	Inwood Country Club, Inwood, NY
1924	Cyril Walker	297	Bobby Jones@(300)	Oakland Hills Country Club, Birmingham, MI
1925	Willie Mcfarlane*	291	Bobby Jones@ (291)	Worcester Country Club, Worcester, MA
1926	Bobby Jones@	293	Joe Turnesa (294)	Scioto Country Club, Columbus, OH
1927	Tommy Armour*	301	Harry Cooper (301)	Oakmont Country Club, Oakmont, PA
1928	Johnny Farrell*	294	Bobby Jones@(294)	Olympia Fields Country Club, Olympia Fields, IL
1929	Bobby Jones@*	294	Al Espinosa (294)	Winged Foot Golf Club, Mamaroneck, NY
1930	Bobby Jones@	287	Macdonald Smith (289)	Interlachen Country Club, Edina, MN
1931	Billy Burke*	292	George Von Elm (292)	Inverness Club, Toledo, OH
1932	Gene Sarazen	286	Bobby Cruickshank & Phil Perkins (289)	Fresh Meadows Country Club, Queens, NY
1933	Johnny Goodman@	287	Ralph Guldahl (288)	North Shore Golf Club, Glenview, IL
1934	Olin Dutra	293	Gene Sarazen (294)	Merion Cricket Club, Ardmore, PA
1935	Sam Parks, Jr.	299	Jimmy Thomson (301)	Oakmont Country Club, Oakmont, PA
1936	Tony Monero	282	Harry Cooper (284)	Baltusrol Golf Club, Springfield, NJ
1937	Ralph Guldahl	281	Sam Snead (283)	Oakland Hills Country Club, Birmingham, MI
1938	Ralph Guldahl	284	Dick Metz (290)	Cherry Hills Country Club, Denver, CO
1939	Byron Nelson*	284	Craig Wood (284)	Philadelphia Country Club, Gladwyne, PA
1940	Lawson Little*	287	Gene Sarazen (287)	Canterbury Golf Club, Beachwood, OH

(continued)

Table A2.1. *(continued)*

Year	Winner	Score	Runner(s)-Up	Venue
1941	Craig Wood	284	Denny Shute (287)	Colonial Country Club, Fort Worth, TX
1942–1945	Event not held because of World War II			
1946	Lloyd Mangrum*	284	Byron Nelson & Vic Ghezzi (284)	Canterbury Golf Club, Beachwood, OH
1947	Lew Worsham*	282	Sam Snead (282)	St. Louis Country Club, Ladue, MO
1948	Ben Hogan	276	Jimmy Demaret (278)	Riviera Country Club, Pacific Palisades, CA
1949	Cary Middlecoff	286	Clayton Heafner & Sam Snead (287)	Medinah Country Club, Medinah, IL
1950	Ben Hogan*	287	Lloyd Mangrum (287)	Merion Golf Club, Ardmore, PA
1951	Ben Hogan	287	Clayton Heafner (289)	Oakland Hills Country Club, Bloomfield Hills, MI
1952	Julius Boros	281	Porky Oliver (285)	Northwood Club, Dallas, TX
1953	Ben Hogan	283	Sam Snead (289)	Oakmont Country Club, Oakmont, PA
1954	Ed Furgol	284	Gene Littler (285)	Baltusrol Golf Club, Springfield, NJ
1955	Jack Fleck*	287	Ben Hogan (287)	Olympic Country Club, San Francisco, CA
1956	Cary Middlecoff	281	Ben Hogan & Julius Boros (282)	Oak Hill Country Club, Rochester, NY
1957	Dick Mayer*	282	Cary Middlecoff (282)	Inverness Club, Toledo, OH
1958	Tommy Bolt	283	Gary Player (287)	Southern Hills Country Club, Tulsa, OK
1959	Billy Casper	282	Bob Rosburg (283)	Winged Foot Golf Club, Mamaroneck, NY
1960	Arnold Palmer	280	Jack Nicklaus@(282)	Cherry Hills Country Club, Denver, CO
1961	Gene Littler	281	Doug Sanders & Bob Goalby (282)	Oakland Hills Country Club, Bloomfield Hills, MI
1962	Jack Nicklaus*	283	Arnold Palmer (283)	Oakmont Country Club, Oakmont, PA
1963	Julius Boros*	293	Arnold Palmer & Jacky Cupit (293)	The Country Club, Brookline, MA
1964	Ken Venturi	278	Tommy Jacobs (282)	Congressional Country Club, Bethesda, MD
1965	Gary Player*	282	Kel Nagle (282)	Bellerive Country Club, St. Louis, MO
1966	Billy Casper*	278	Arnold Palmer (278)	Olympic Country Club, San Francisco, CA

1967	Jack Nicklaus	275	Arnold Palmer (279)	Baltusrol Golf Club, Springfield, NJ
1968	Lee Trevino	275	Jack Nicklaus (279)	Oak Hill Country Club, Rochester, NY
1969	Orville Moody	281	Al Geiberger, Deane Beman & Bob Rosburg (282)	Champions Golf Club, Houston, TX
1970	Tony Jacklin	281	Dave Hill (288)	Hazeltine National Golf Club, Chaska, MN
1971	Lee Trevino*	280	Jack Nicklaus (280)	Merion Golf Club, Ardmore, PA
1972	Jack Nicklaus	290	Bruce Crampton (293)	Pebble Beach Golf Links, Pebble Beach, CA
1973	Johnny Miller	279	John Schlee (280)	Oakmont Country Club, Oakmont, PA
1974	Hale Irwin	287	Forrest Fezler (289)	Winged Foot Golf Club, Mamaroneck, NY
1975	Lou Graham*	287	John Mahaffey (287)	Medinah Country Club, Medinah, IL
1976	Jerry Pate	277	Al Geiberger & Tom Weiskopf (279)	Atlanta Athletic Club, Duluth, GA
1977	Hubert Green	278	Lou Graham (279)	Southern Hills Country Club, Tulsa, OK
1978	Andy North	285	Dave Stockton & J.C. Snead (286)	Cherry Hills Country Club, Denver, CO
1979	Hale Irwin	284	Gary Player & Jerry Pate (286)	Inverness Club, Toledo, OH
1980	Jack Nicklaus	272	Isao Aoki (274)	Baltusrol Golf Club, Springfield, NJ
1981	David Graham	273	George Burns & Bill Rogers (276)	Merion Golf Club, Ardmore, PA
1982	Tom Watson	282	Jack Nicklaus (284)	Pebble Beach Golf Links, Pebble Beach, CA
1983	Larry Nelson	280	Tom Watson (281)	Oakmont Country Club, Oakmont, PA
1984	Fuzzy Zoeller*	276	Greg Norman (276)	Winged Foot Golf Club, Mamaroneck, NY
1985	Andy North	279	Dave Barr, Denis Watson & Chen Tze-chung (280)	Oakland Hills Country Club, Bloomfield Hills, MI
1986	Raymond Floyd	279	Lanny Wadkins & Chip Beck (281)	Shinnecock Hills Golf Club, Southampton, NY
1987	Scott Simpson	277	Tom Watson (278)	Olympic Club, San Francisco, CA
1988	Curtis Strange*	278	Nick Faldo (278)	The Country Club, Brookline, MA
1989	Curtis Strange	278	Chip Beck, Ian Woosnam & Mark McCumber (279)	Oak Hill Country Club, Rochester, NY

(continued)

Table A2.1. *(continued)*

Year	Winner	Score	Runner(s)-Up	Venue
1990	Hale Irwin*	280	Mike Donald (280)	Medinah Country Club, Medinah, OH
1991	Payne Stewart*	282	Scott Simpson (282)	Hazeltine National Golf Club, Chaska, MN
1992	Tom Kite	285	Jeff Sluman (287)	Pebble Beach Golf Links, Pebble Beach, CA
1993	Lee Janzen	272	Payne Stewart (274)	Baltusrol Golf Club, Springfield, NJ
1994	Ernie Els*	279	Colin Montgomerie & Loren Roberts (279)	Oakmont Country Club, Oakmont, PA
1995	Corey Pavin	280	Greg Norman (282)	Shinnecock Hills Golf Club, Southampton, NY
1996	Steve Jones	278	Davis Love III & Tom Lehman (279)	Oakland Hills Country Club, Bloomfield Hills, MI
1997	Ernie Els	276	Colin Montgomerie (277)	Congressional Country Club, Bethesda, MD
1998	Lee Janzen	280	Payne Stewart (281)	Olympic Club, San Francisco, CA
1999	Payne Stewart	279	Phil Mickelson (280)	Pinehurst Resort, Course No. 2, Pinehurst, NC
2000	Tiger Woods	272	Miguel Angel Jimenez & Ernie Els (287)	Pebble Beach Golf Links, Pebble Beach, CA
2001	Retief Goosen	276	Mark Brooks (278)	Southern Hills Country Club, Tulsa, OK
2002	Tiger Woods	277	Phil Mickelson (280)	Bethpage State Park (Black), Farmingdale, NY
2003	Jim Furyk	272	Stephen Leaney (275)	Olympia Fields Country Club, Olympia Fields, IL
2004	Retief Goosen	276	Phil Mickelson (278)	Shinnecock Hills Golf Club, Southampton, NY
2005	Michael Campbell	280	Tiger Woods (282)	Pinehurst Resort, Course No. 2, Pinehurst, NC

Year	Winner	Score	Runners-up (scores)	Location
2006	Geoff Ogilvy	285	Jim Furyk, Colin Montgomerie & Phil Mickelson (286)	Winged Foot Golf Club, Mamaroneck, NY
2007	Angel Cabrera	285	Jim Furyk & Tiger Woods (286)	Oakmont Country Club, Oakmont, PA
2008	Tiger Woods*	283	Rocco Mediate (283)	Torrey Pines Golf Course, San Diego, CA
2009	Lucas Glover	276	Phil Mickelson, David Duval & Ricky Barnes (278)	Bethpage State Park (Black), Farmingdale, NY
2010	Graeme McDowell	284	Gregory Havret (285)	Pebble Beach Golf Links, Pebble Beach, CA
2011	Rory McIlroy	268	Jason Day (276)	Congressional Country Club, Bethesda, MD
2012	Webb Simpson	281	Graeme McDowell & Michael Thompson (282)	Olympic Club, San Francisco, CA
2013	Justin Rose	281	Jason Day & Phil Mickelson (283)	Marion Golf Club, Ardmore, PA
2014	Martin Kaymer	271	Erik Compton & Rickie Fowler (279)	Pinehurst Resort, Course No. 2, Pinehurst, NC
2015	Jordan Spieth	275	Dustin Johnson & Louis Oosthuizen (276)	Chambers Bay Golf Course, University Place, WA
2016	Dustin Johnson	276	Jim Furyk, Shane Lowry & Scott Piercy (279)	Oakmont Country Club, Oakmont, PA
2017	Brooks Koepka	272	Hideki Matsuyama & Brian Harman (276)	Erin Hills Golf Course, Erin, WI

# denotes 36-hole event
* denotes playoff winner
@ denotes Amateur Golfer

Table A2.2.   The Open Championship (The British Open)

Year	Winner	Score	Runner(s)-Up	Venue
1860	Willie Park	174#	Old Tom Morris (176)	Prestwick Golf Club, Prestwick, Scotland
1861	Old Tom Morris	163#	Willie Park (167)	Prestwick Golf Club, Prestwick, Scotland
1862	Old Tom Morris	163#	Willie Park (176)	Prestwick Golf Club, Prestwick, Scotland
1863	Willie Park	168#	Old Tom Morris (170)	Prestwick Golf Club, Prestwick, Scotland
1864	Old Tom Morris	167#	Andrew Strath (169)	Prestwick Golf Club, Prestwick, Scotland
1865	Andrew Strath	162#	Willie Park (164)	Prestwick Golf Club, Prestwick, Scotland
1866	Willie Park	169#	David Park (171)	Prestwick Golf Club, Prestwick, Scotland
1867	Old Tom Morris	170#	Willie Park (172)	Prestwick Golf Club, Prestwick, Scotland
1868	Young Tom Morris	154#	Old Tom Morris (157)	Prestwick Golf Club, Prestwick, Scotland
1869	Young Tom Morris	157#	Bob Kirk (168)	Prestwick Golf Club, Prestwick, Scotland
1870	Young Tom Morris	149#	Bob Kirk & D. Strath (161)	Prestwick Golf Club, Prestwick, Scotland
1871	Event cancelled–No trophy available			
1872	Young Tom Morris	166#	Davie Strath (169)	Prestwick Golf Club, Prestwick, Scotland
1873	Tom Kidd	179#	Jamie Anderson (180)	The Old Course, St. Andrews, Scotland
1874	Mungo Park	159#	Young Tom Morris (161)	Musselburgh Golf Club, Scotland
1875	Willie Park	166#	Bob Martin (168)	Prestwick Golf Club, Prestwick, Scotland
1876	Bob Martin*	176#	Davie Strath (176)	The Old Course, St. Andrews, Scotland
1877	Jamie Anderson	160#	Bob Pringle (162)	Musselburgh Golf Club, Scotland
1878	Jamie Anderson	157#	Bob Kirk (159)	Prestwick Golf Club, Prestwick, Scotland
1879	Jamie Anderson	169#	Andrew Kirkaldy & James Allan (172)	The Old Course, St. Andrews, Scotland
1880	Bob Ferguson	162#	Peter Paxton (167)	Musselburgh Golf Club, Scotland
1881	Bob Ferguson	170#	Jamie Anderson (173)	Prestwick Golf Club, Prestwick, Scotland
1882	Bob Ferguson	171#	Willie Fernie (174)	The Old Course, St. Andrews, Scotland
1883	Willie Fernie*	159#	Bob Ferguson (159)	Musselburgh Golf Club, Scotland
1884	Jack Simpson	160#	Douglas Rolland & Willie Fernie (164)	Prestwick Golf Club, Prestwick, Scotland
1885	Bob Martin	171#	Archie Simpson (172)	The Old Course, St. Andrews, Scotland
1886	David Brown	157#	Willie Campbell (159)	Musselburgh Golf Club, Scotland

1887	Willie Park, Jr.	161#	Bob Martin (162)	Prestwick Golf Club, Prestwick, Scotland
1888	Jack Burns	171#	David Anderson & Ben Sayers (172)	The Old Course, St. Andrews, Scotland
1889	Willie Park, Jr.*	155#	Andrew Kirkaldy (155)	Musselburgh Golf Club, Scotland
1890	John Ball@	164#	Willie Fernie & Archie Simpson (167)	Prestwick Golf Club, Prestwick, Scotland
1891	Hugh Kirkaldy	166#	Andrew Kirkaldy & Willie Fernie (168)	The Old Course, St. Andrews, Scotland
1892	Harold Hilton@	305	Sandy Herd, John Ball@ & Hugh Kirkaldy (308)	Muirfield Links, Gullane, Scotland
1893	Willie Auchterlonie	322	Johnny Laidley@ (324)	Prestwick Golf Club, Prestwick, Scotland
1894	J.H. Taylor	326	Douglas Rolland (331)	Royal St. George's, Sandwich, England
1895	J.H. Taylor	322	Sandy Herd (326)	The Old Course, St. Andrews, Scotland
1896	Harry Vardon*	316	J.H. Taylor (316)	Muirfield Links, Gullane, Scotland
1897	Harold Hilton@	314	James Braid (315)	Royal Liverpool, Hoylake, England
1898	Harry Vardon	307	Willie Park, Jr. (308)	Prestwick Golf Club, Prestwick, Scotland,
1899	Harry Vardon	310	Jack White (315)	Royal St. George's, Sandwich, England
1900	J.H. Taylor	309	Harry Vardon (317)	The Old Course, St. Andrews, Scotland
1901	James Baird	309	Harry Vardon (312)	Muirfield Links, Gullane, Scotland
1902	Sandy Herd	307	Harry Vardon & James Baird (308)	Royal Liverpool, Hoylake, England
1903	Harry Vardon	300	Tom Vardon (306)	Prestwick Golf Club, Prestwick, Scotland
1904	Jack White	296	James Baird & J.H. Taylor (297)	Royal St. George's, Sandwich, England
1905	James Baird	318	J.H. Taylor & Rowland Jones (323)	The Old Course, St. Andrews, Scotland
1906	James Baird	300	J.H. Taylor (304)	Muirfield Links, Gullane, Scotland
1907	Arnaud Massy	312	J.H. Taylor (314)	Royal Liverpool, Hoylake, England
1908	James Baird	291	Tom Ball (299)	Prestwick Golf Club, Prestwick, Scotland
1909	J.H. Taylor	295	James Baird & Tom Ball (301)	Royal Cinque Ports, Deal, England
1910	James Baird	299	Sandy Herd (303)	The Old Course, St. Andrews, Scotland
1911	Harry Vardon*	303	Arnaud Massey (303)	Royal St. George's, Sandwich, England
1912	Ted Ray	295	Harry Vardon (299)	Muirfield Links, Gullane, Scotland
1913	J.H. Taylor	304	Ted Ray (312)	Royal Liverpool, Hoylake, England
1914	Harry Vardon	306	J.H. Taylor (309)	Prestwick Golf Club, Prestwick, Scotland

(continued)

Table A2.2.   *(continued)*

Year	Winner	Score	Runner(s)-Up	Venue
1915–1919	Event not held because of World War I			
1920	George Duncan	303	Sandy Herd (305)	Royal Cinque Ports, Deal, England
1921	Jock Hutchison*	296	Roger Wethered@ (296)	The Old Course, St. Andrews, Scotland
1922	Walter Hagen	300	George Duncan & Jim Barnes (301)	Royal St. George's, Sandwich, England
1923	Arthur Havers	295	Walter Hagen (296)	Royal Troon Golf Club, Troon, Scotland
1924	Walter Hagen	301	Ernest Whitcombe (302)	Royal Liverpool, Hoylake, England
1925	Jim Barnes	300	Archie Compston & Ted Ray (301)	Prestwick Golf Club, Prestwick, Scotland
1926	Bobby Jones@	291	Al Watrous (293)	Royal Lytham & St. Annes, Lancashire, England
1927	Bobby Jones@	285	Aubrey Boomer & Fred Robson (291)	The Old Course, St. Andrews, Scotland
1928	Walter Hagen	292	Gene Sarazen (294)	Royal St. George's, Sandwich, England
1929	Walter Hagen	292	Johnny Farrell (298)	Muirfield Links, Gullane, Scotland
1930	Bobby Jones@	291	Macdonald Smith & Leo Diegel (293)	Royal Liverpool, Hoylake, England
1931	Tommy Armour	296	Jose Jurado (297)	Carnoustie Golf Links, Carnoustie, Scotland
1932	Gene Sarazen	283	Macdonald Smith (288)	Prince's Golf Club, Sandwich, England
1933	Denny Shute*	292	Craig Wood (292)	The Old Course, St. Andrews, Scotland
1934	Henry Cotton	283	Sid Brews (288)	Royal St. George's, Sandwich, England
1935	Alfred Perry	283	Alfred Padgham (287)	Muirfield Links, Gullane, Scotland
1936	Alfred Padgham	287	Jimmy Adams (288)	Royal Liverpool, Hoylake, England
1937	Henry Cotton	290	Reginald Whitcombe (292)	Carnoustie Golf Links, Carnoustie, Scotland
1938	Reginald Whitcombe	295	Jimmy Adams (297)	Royal St. George's, Sandwich, England
1939	Dick Burton	290	Johnny Bulla (292)	The Old Course, St. Andrews, Scotland
1940–1945	Event not held because of World War II			
1946	Sam Snead	290	Bobby Locke & Johnny Bulla (294)	The Old Course, St. Andrews, Scotland
1947	Fred Daly	293	Frank Strenahan@ & Reg Horne (294)	Royal Liverpool, Hoylake, England
1948	Henry Cotton	284	Fred Daly (289)	Muirfield Links, Gullane, Scotland
1949	Bobby Locke*	283	Harry Bradshaw (283)	Royal St. George's, Sandwich, England
1950	Bobby Locke	279	Roberto de Vicenzo (281)	Royal Troon Golf Club, Troon, Scotland

Year	Winner	Score	Runner(s)-Up	Venue
1951	Max Faulkner	285	Tony Cerda (287)	Royal Portrush, Portrush, Ireland
1952	Bobby Locke	287	Peter Thomson (288)	Royal Lytham & St. Annes, Lancashire, England
1953	Ben Hogan	282	Frank Stranahan@, Dai Reese, Tony Certa & Peter Thomson (286)	Carnoustie Golf Links, Carnoustie, Scotland
1954	Peter Thomson	283	Syd Scott, Dai Reese & Bobby Locke (284)	Royal Birkdale, Southport, England
1955	Peter Thomson	281	John Fallon (283)	The Old Course, St. Andrews, Scotland
1956	Peter Thomson	286	Flory Van Donck (289)	Royal Liverpool, Hoylake, England
1957	Bobby Locke	279	Peter Thomson (282)	The Old Course, St. Andrews, Scotland
1958	Peter Thomson*	278	Dave Thomas (278)	Royal Lytham & St. Annes, Lancashire, England
1959	Gary Player	284	Flory Van Donck & Fred Bullock (286)	Muirfield Links, Gullane, Scotland
1960	Kel Nagle	278	Arnold Palmer (279)	The Old Course, St. Andrews, Scotland
1961	Arnold Palmer	284	Dai Reese (285)	Royal Birkdale, Southport, England
1962	Arnold Palmer	276	Kel Nagle (282)	Royal Troon Golf Club, Troon, Scotland
1963	Bob Charles*	277	Phil Rodgers (277)	Royal Lytham & St. Annes, Lancashire, England
1964	Tony Lema	279	Jack Nicklaus (284)	The Old Course, St. Andrews, Scotland
1965	Peter Thomson	285	Christy O'Connor & Brian Huggett (287)	Royal Birkdale, Southport, England
1966	Jack Nicklaus	282	Doug Sanders & Dave Thomas (283)	Muirfield Links, Gullane, Scotland
1967	Roberto De Vicenzo	278	Jack Nicklaus (280)	Royal Liverpool, Hoylake, England
1968	Gary Player	289	Jack Nicklaus & Bob Charles (291)	Carnoustie Golf Links, Carnoustie, Scotland
1969	Tony Jacklin	280	Bob Charles (282)	Royal Lytham & St. Annes, Lancashire, England
1970	Jack Nicklaus*	283	Doug Sanders (283)	The Old Course, St. Andrews, Scotland
1971	Lee Trevino	278	Lu Liang-Huan (279)	Royal Birkdale, Southport, England
1972	Lee Trevino	278	Jack Nicklaus (279)	Muirfield Links, Gullane, Scotland
1973	Tom Weiskopf	276	Johnny Miller & Neil Coles (279)	Royal Troon Golf Club, Troon, Scotland
1974	Gary Player	282	Peter Oosterhuis (286)	Royal Lytham & St. Annes, Lancashire, England
1975	Tom Watson*	279	Jack Newton (279)	Carnoustie Golf Links, Carnoustie, Scotland
Year	Winner	Score	Runner(s)-Up	Venue

(continued)

Table A2.2. *(continued)*

Year	Winner	Score	Runner(s)-Up	Venue
1976	Johnny Miller	279	Seve Ballesteros & Jack Nicklaus (285)	Royal Birkdale, Southport, England
1977	Tom Watson	268	Jack Nicklaus (269)	Turnberry Golf Links, Ayrshire, Scotland
1978	Jack Nicklaus	281	Tom Kite, Simon Owen, Raymond Floyd & Ben Crenshaw (283)	The Old Course, St. Andrews, Scotland
1979	Seve Ballesteros	283	Jack Nicklaus & Ben Crenshaw (286)	Royal Lytham & St. Annes, Lancashire, England
1980	Tom Watson	271	Lee Trevino (275)	Muirfield Links, Gullane, Scotland
1981	Bill Rogers	276	Bernhard Langer (280)	Royal St. George's, Sandwich, England
1982	Tom Watson	284	Peter Oosterhuis & Nick Price (285)	Royal Troon Golf Club, Troon, Scotland
1983	Tom Watson	275	Hale Irwin & Andy Bean (276)	Royal Birkdale, Southport, England
1984	Seve Ballesteros	276	Bernhard Langer & Tom Watson (278)	The Old Course, St. Andrews, Scotland
1985	Sandy Lyle	282	Payne Stewart (283)	Royal St. George's, Sandwich, England
1986	Greg Norman	280	Gordon Brand (285)	Turnberry Golf Links, Ayrshire, Scotland
1987	Nick Faldo	279	Paul Azinger & Rodger Davis (280)	Muirfield Links, Gullane, Scotland
1988	Seve Ballesteros	273	Nick Price (275)	Royal Lytham & St. Annes, Lancashire, England
1989	Mark Calcavecchia*	275	Greg Norman & Wayne Grady (275)	Royal Troon Golf Club, Troon, Scotland
1990	Nick Faldo	270	Payne Stewart & Mark McNulty (275)	The Old Course, St. Andrews, Scotland
1991	Ian Baker-Finch	272	Mike Harwood (274)	Royal Birkdale, Southport, England
1992	Nick Faldo	272	John Cook (273)	Muirfield Links, Gullane, Scotland
1993	Greg Norman	267	Nick Faldo (269)	Royal St. George's, Sandwich, England
1994	Nick Price	268	Jesper Parnevik (269)	Turnberry Golf Links, Ayrshire, Scotland
1995	John Daly*	282	Costantino Rocca (282)	The Old Course, St. Andrews, Scotland
1996	Tom Lehman	271	Mark McCumber & Ernie Els (273)	Royal Lytham & St. Annes, Lancashire, England
1997	Justin Leonard	272	Jesper Parnevik & Darren Clarke (275)	Royal Troon Golf Club, Troon, Scotland
1998	Mark O'Meara*	280	Brian Watts (280)	Royal Birkdale, Southport, England
1999	Paul Lawrie*	290	Justin Leonard & Jean Van de Velde (290)	Carnoustie Golf Links, Carnoustie, Scotland
2000	Tiger Woods	269	Thomas Bjorn & Ernie Els (277)	The Old Course, St. Andrews, Scotland

Year	Winner	Score	Runner-up(s)	Venue
2001	David Duval	274	Niclas Fasth (277)	Royal Lytham & St. Annes, Lancashire, England
2002	Ernie Els*	278	Thomas Levet, Stuart Appleby & Steve Elkington (278)	Muirfield Links, Gullane, Scotland
2003	Ben Curtis	283	Vijay Singh & Thomas Bjorn (284)	Royal St. George's, Sandwich, England
2004	Todd Hamilton*	274	Ernie Els (274)	Royal Troon Golf Club, Troon, Scotland
2005	Tiger Woods	274	Colin Montgomerie (279)	The Old Course, St. Andrews, Scotland
2006	Tiger Woods	270	Chris DiMarco (272)	Royal Liverpool, Hoylake, England
2007	Padraig Harrington*	277	Sergio Garcia (277)	Carnoustie Golf Links, Carnoustie, Scotland
2008	Padraig Harrington	283	Ian Poulter (287)	Royal Birkdale, Southport, England
2009	Stewart Cink*	278	Tom Watson (278)	Turnberry Golf Links, Ayrshire, Scotland
2010	Louis Oosthuizen	272	Lee Westwood (279)	The Old Course, St. Andrews, Scotland
2011	Darren Clarke	275	Dustin Johnson & Phil Mickelson (278)	Royal St. George's, Sandwich, England
2012	Ernie Els	273	Adam Scott (274)	Royal Lytham & St. Annes, Lancashire, England
2013	Phil Mickelson	281	Henrik Stenson (284)	Muirfield Links, Gullane, Scotland
2014	Rory McIlroy	271	Rickie Fowler & Sergio Garcia (273)	Royal Liverpool, Hoylake, England
2015	Zach Johnson*	273	Marc Leishman & Louis Oosthuizen (273)	The Old Course, St. Andrews, Scotland
2016	Henrik Stenson	264	Phil Mickelson (267)	Royal Troon Golf Club, Troon, Scotland
2017	Jordan Spieth	268	Matt Kuchar (271)	Royal Birkdale, Southport, England

# denotes 36-hole event
* denotes playoff winner
@ denotes Amateur Golfer

Table A2.3.   The Winners of the Players Championship

Year	Winner	Year	Winner	Year	Winner
1974	Jack Nicklaus	1989	Tom Kite	2004	Adam Scott
1975	Al Geiberger	1990	Jodie Mudd	2005	Fred Funk
1976	Jack Nicklaus	1991	Steve Elkington	2006	Stephen Ames
1977	Mark Hayes	1992	Davis Love III	2007	Phil Mickelson
1978	Jack Nicklaus	1993	Nick Price	2008	Sergio Garcia
1979	Lanny Wadkins	1994	Greg Norman	2009	Henrik Stenson
1980	Lee Trevino	1995	Lee Janzen	2010	Tim Clark
1981	Raymond Floyd	1996	Fred Couples	2011	K. J. Choi
1982	Jerry Pate	1997	Steve Elkington	2012	Matt Kuchar
1983	Hal Sutton	1998	Justin Leonard	2013	Tiger Woods
1984	Fred Couples	1999	David Duval	2014	Martin Kaymer
1985	Calvin Peete	2000	Hal Sutton	2015	Rickie Fowler
1986	John Mahaffey	2001	Tiger Woods	2016	Jason Day
1987	Sandy Lyle	2002	Craig Perks	2017	Kim Si-woo
1988	Mark McCumber	2003	Davis Love III		

Table A2.4.   The PGA Championship

Year	Winner	Score	Runner(s)-Up	Venue
1916	Jim Barnes	1-up	Jock Hutchison	Siwanoy Country Club, Bronxville, NY
1917–1918	Event not held because of World War I			
1919	Jim Barnes	6 & 5	Fred McLeod	Engineers Country Club, Roslyn, NY
1920	Jock Hutchison	1-up	J, Douglas Edgar	Flossmoor Country Club, Flossmoor, IL
1921	Walter Hagen	3 & 2	Jim Barnes	Inwood Country Club, Inwood, NY
1922	Gene Sarazen	4 & 3	Emmet French	Oakmont Country Club, Oakmont, PA
1923	Gene Sarazen	1-up	Walter Hagen	Pelham Country Club, Pelham, NY
1924	Walter Hagen	2-up	Jim Barnes	French Lick Resort, French Lick, IN
1925	Walter Hagen	6 & 5	Bill Mehlhorn	Olympia Fields Country Club, Olympia Fields, IL
1926	Walter Hagen	5 & 3	Leo Diegel	Salisbury Golf Club, East Meadow, NY
1927	Walter Hagen	1-up	Joe Turnesa	Cedar Crest Country Club, Dallas, TX
1928	Leo Diegel	6 & 5	Al Espinosa	Baltimore Country Club, Lutherville, MD
1929	Leo Diegel	6 & 4	John Farrell	Hillcrest Country Club, Los Angeles, CA
1930	Tommy Armour	1-up	Gene Sarazen	Fresh Meadow Country Club, Queens, NY
1931	Tom Creavy	2 & 1	Denny Shute	Wannamoisett Country Club, Rumford, RI
1932	Olin Dutra	4 & 3	Frank Walsh	Keller Golf Club, Maplewood, MN
1933	Gene Sarazen	5 & 4	Willie Goggin	Blue Mound Country Club, Wauwatosa, WI
1934	Paul Runyan	1-up	Craig Wood	Park Country Club, Williamsville, NY
1935	Johnny Revolta	5 & 4	Tommy Armour	Twin Hills Country Club, Oklahoma City, OK
1936	Denny Shute	3 & 2	Jimmy Thomson	Pinehurst Resort, Course No. 2, Pinehurst, NC
1937	Denny Shute	1-up	Harold McSpaden	Pittsburgh Field Club, Aspinwall, PA
1938	Paul Runyan	8 & 7	Sam Snead	Shawnee Golf Resort, Shawnee, PA
1939	Henry Picard	1-up	Byron Nelson	Pomonok Country Club, Flushing, NY
1940	Byron Nelson	1-up	Sam Snead	Hershey Country Club, Hershey, PA
1941	Vic Ghezzi	1-up	Byron Nelson	Cherry Hils Country Club, Denver, CO

(continued)

Table A2.4. *(continued)*

Year	Winner	Score	Runner(s)-Up	Venue
1942	Sam Snead	2 & 1	Jim Turnesa	Seaview Country Club, Atlantic City, NJ
1943	Event not held because of World War II			
1944	Bob Hamilton	1-up	Byron Nelson	Manito Golf & Country Club, Spokane, WA
1945	Byron Nelson	4 & 3	Sam Byrd	Moraine Country Club, Dayton, OH
1946	Ben Hogan	6 & 4	Porky Oliver	Portland Golf Club, Portland, OR
1947	Jim Ferrier	2 & 1	Chick Harbert	Plum Hollow Country Club, Detroit, MI
1948	Ben Hogan	7 & 6	Mike Turnesa	Norwood Hills Country Club, St. Louis, MO
1949	Sam Snead	3 & 2	Johnny Palmer	Hermitage Country Club, Richmond, VA
1950	Chandler Harper	4 & 3	Henry Williams, Jr.	Scioto Country Club, Columbus, OH
1951	Sam Snead	7 & 6	Walter Burkemo	Oakmont Country Club, Oakmont, PA
1952	Jim Turnesa	1-up	Chick Harbert	Big Spring Country Club, Louisville, KY
1953	Walter Burkemo	2 & 1	Felice Torza	Birmingham Country Club, Birmingham, MI
1954	Chick Harbert	4 & 3	Walter Burkemo	Keller Golf Club, Maplewood, MN
1955	Doug Ford	4 & 3	Cary Middlecoff	Meadowbrook Country Club, Detroit, MI
1956	Jack Burke, Jr.	3 & 2	Ted Kroll	Blue Hill Country Club, Canton, MA
1957	Lionel Hebert	2 & 1	Dow Finsterwald	Miami Valley Golf Club, Dayton, OH
1958	Dow Finsterwald	276	Billy Casper (278)	Llanerch Country Club, Havertown, PA
1959	Bob Rosburg	277	Jerry Barber & Doug Sanders (278)	Minneapolis Golf Club, St. Louis Park, MN
1960	Jay Hebert	281	Jim Ferrier (282)	Firestone Country Club, Akron, OH
1961	Jerry Barber*	277	Don January (277)	Olympia Fields Country Club, Olympia Fields, IL
1962	Gary Player	278	Bob Goalby (279)	Aronimink Golf Club, Newtown Square, PA
1963	Jack Nicklaus	279	Dave Ragan (281)	Dallas Athletic Club, Dallas, TX
1964	Bobby Nichols	271	Jack Nicklaus & Arnold Palmer (274)	Columbus Country Club, Columbus, OH
1965	Dave Marr	280	Jack Nicklaus & Billy Casper (282)	Laurel Valley Golf Club, Ligonier, PA
1966	Al Geiberger	280	Dudley Wysong (284)	Firestone Country Club, Akron, OH
1967	Don January*	281	Don Massengale (281)	Columbine Country Club, Littleton, CO

Year	Winner	Score	Runner(s)-up	Venue
1968	Julius Boros	281	Arnold Palmer & Bob Charles (282)	Pecan Valley Golf Club, San Antonio, TX
1969	Raymond Floyd	276	Gary Player (277)	NCR Country Club, Kettering, OH
1970	Dave Stockton	279	Arnold Palmer & Bob Murphy (281)	Southern Hills Country Club, Tulsa, OK
1971	Jack Nicklaus	281	Billy Casper (283)	PGA National Golf Club, Palm Beach Gardens, FL
1972	Gary Player	281	Jim Jamieson & Tommy Armour (283)	Oakland Hills Country Club, Bloomfield Hills, MI
1973	Jack Nicklaus	277	Bruce Crampton (281)	Canterbury Golf Club, Beachwood, OH
1974	Lee Trevino	276	Jack Nicklaus (277)	Tanglewood Park, Clemmons, NC
1975	Jack Nicklaus	276	Bruce Crampton (278)	Firestone Country Club, Akron, OH
1976	Dave Stockton	281	Don January & Raymond Floyd (282)	Congressional Country Club, Bethesda, MD
1977	Lanny Wadkins*	282	Gene Littler (282)	Pebble Beach Golf Links, Pebble Beach, CA
1978	John Mahaffey*	276	Jerry Pate & Tom Watson (276)	Oakmont Country Club, Oakmont, PA
1979	David Graham*	272	Ben Crenshaw (272)	Oakland Hills Country Club, Bloomfield Hills, MI
1980	Jack Nicklaus	274	Andy Bean (281)	Oak Hill Country Club, Rochester, NY
1981	Larry Nelson	273	Fuzzy Zoeller (277)	Atlanta Athletic Club, Duluth, GA
1982	Raymond Floyd	272	Lanny Wadkins (275)	Southern Hills Country Club, Tulsa, OK
1983	Hal Sutton	274	Jack Nicklaus (275)	Riviera Country Club, Pacific Palisades, CA
1984	Lee Trevino	273	Lanny Wadkins & Gary Player (277)	Shoal Creek Golf & Country Club, Birmingham, AL
1985	Hubert Green	278	Lee Trevino (280)	Cherry Hills Country Club, Denver, CO
1986	Bob Tway	276	Greg Norman (278)	Inverness Club, Toledo, OH
1987	Larry Nelson*	287	Lanny Wadkins (287)	PGA National Golf Club, Palm Beach Gardens, FL
1988	Jeff Sluman	272	Paul Azinger (275)	Oak Tree Golf Club, Edmond, OK
1989	Payne Stewart	276	Andy Bean, Mike Reid & Curtis Strange (277)	Kemper Lakes Golf Club, Hawthorn Woods, IL

(continued)

Table A2.4. *(continued)*

Year	Winner	Score	Runner(s)-Up	Venue
1990	Wayne Grady	282	Fred Couples (285)	Shoal Creek Golf & Country Club, Birmingham, AL
1991	John Daly	276	Bruce Lietzke (279)	Crooked Stick Golf Club, Carmel, IN
1992	Nick Price	278	Nick Faldo, John Cook, Jim Gallagher & Gene Sauers (281)	Bellerive Country Club, St. Louis, MO
1993	Paul Azinger*	272	Greg Norman (272)	Inverness Club, Toledo, OH
1994	Nick Price	269	Corey Pavin (275)	Southern Hills Country Club, Tulsa, OK
1995	Steve Elkington*	267	Colin Montgomerie (267)	Riviera Country Club, Pacific Palisades, CA
1996	Mark Brooks*	277	Kenny Perry (277)	Valhalla Golf Club, Louisville, KY
1997	Davis Love III	269	Justin Leonard (274)	Winged Foot Golf Club, Mamaroneck, NY
1998	Vijay Singh	271	Steve Stricker (273)	Sahalee Country Club, Redmond, WA
1999	Tiger Woods	277	Sergio Garcia (278)	Medinah Country Club, Medinah, IL
2000	Tiger Woods*	270	Bob May (270)	Valhalla Golf Club, Louisville, KY
2001	David Toms	265	Phil Mickelson (266)	Atlanta Athletic Club, Duluth, GA
2002	Rich Beem	278	Tiger Woods (279)	Hazeltine National Golf Club, Chaska, MN
2003	Shaun Micheel	276	Chad Campbell (278)	Oak Hill Country Club, Rochester, NY
2004	Vijay Singh*	280	Chris DiMarco & Justin Leonard (280)	Whistling Straits Golf Course, Kohler, WI
2005	Phil Mickelson	276	Steve Elkington & Thomas Bjorn (277)	Baltusrol Golf Club, Springfield, NJ
2006	Tiger Woods	270	Shaun Micheel (275)	Medinah Country Club, Medinah, IL
2007	Tiger Woods	272	Woody Austin (274)	Southern Hills Country Club, Tulsa, OK
2008	Padraig Harrington	277	Ben Curtis & Sergio Garcia (279)	Oakland Hills Country Club, Bloomfield Hills, MI
2009	Yang Yong-eun	280	Tiger Woods (283)	Hazeltine National Golf Club, Chaska, MN
2010	Martin Kaymer*	277	Bubba Watson (277)	Whistling Straits Golf Course, Kohler, WI
2011	Keegan Bradley	272	Jason Dufner (272)	Atlanta Athletic Club, Johns Creek, GA
2012	Rory McIlroy	275	David Lynn (283)	Kiawah Island Golf Resort, Kiawah Island, SC

Year	Winner	Score	Winner	Venue
2013	Jason Dufner	270	Jim Furyk (272)	Oak Hill Country Club, Rochester, NY
2014	Rory McIlroy	268	Phil Mickelson (269)	Valhalla Golf Club, Louisville, KY
2015	Jason Day	268	Jordan Spieth (271)	Whistling Straits Golf Course, Kohler, WI
2016	Jimmy Walker	266	Jason Day (267)	Baltusrol Golf Club, Springfield, NJ
2017	Justin Thomas	276	Francesco Molinari, Louis Oosthuizen & Patrick Reed (278)	Quail Hollow Club, Charlotte, NC

* denotes playoff winner

Note: The event changed from match play to stroke play in 1958

Table A2.5.   The Masters. Played at the Augusta National Golf Club, Augusta, Georgia

Year	Winner	Score	Runner(s)-Up	Score
1934	Horton Smith	284	Craig Wood	285
1935	Gene Sarazen*	282	Craig Wood	282
1936	Horton Smith	285	Harry Cooper	286
1937	Byron Nelson	283	Ralph Guldahl	285
1938	Henry Picard	285	Ralph Guldahl & Harry Cooper	287
1939	Ralph Guldahl	279	Sam Snead	280
1940	Jimmy Demaret	280	Lloyd Mangrum	284
1941	Craig Wood	280	Byron Nelson	283
1942	Byron Nelson*	280	Ben Hogan	280
1943–1945	Event not held because of World War II			
1946	Herman Keiser	282	Ben Hogan	283
1947	Jimmy Demaret	281	Frank Stranahan & Byron Nelson	283
1948	Claude Harmon	279	Cary Middlecoff	284
1949	Sam Snead	282	Lloyd Mangrun & Johnny Bulla	285
1950	Jimmy Demaret	283	Jim Ferrier	285
1951	Ben Hogan	280	Skee Riegel	282
1952	Sam Snead	286	Jack Burke, Jr.	290
1953	Ben Hogan	274	Porky Oliver	279
1954	Sam Snead*	289	Ben Hogan	289
1955	Cary Middlecoff	279	Ben Hogan	286
1956	Jack Burke, Jr.	289	Ken Venturi	290
1957	Doug Ford	283	Sam Snead	286
1958	Arnold Palmer	284	Doug Ford & Fred Hawkins	285
1959	Art Wall, Jr.	284	Cary Middlecoff	285
1960	Arnold Palmer	282	Ken Venturi	283
1961	Gary Player	280	Arnold Palmer & Charles Coe@	281
1962	Arnold Palmer*	280	Dow Finsterwald & Gary Player	280

Year				
1963	Jack Nicklaus	286	Tony Lema	287
1964	Arnold Palmer	276	Jack Nicklaus & Dave Marr	282
1965	Jack Nicklaus	271	Arnold Palmer & Gary Player	280
1966	Jack Nicklaus*	288	Gay Brewer & Tommy Jacobs	288
1967	Gay Brewer	280	Bobby Nichols	281
1968	Bob Goalby	277	Roberto De Vicenzo	278
1969	George Archer	281	Billy Casper, George Knudson & Tom Weiskopf	282
1970	Billy Casper*	279	Gene Littler	279
1971	Charles Coody	279	Jack Nicklaus & Johnny Miller	281
1972	Jack Nicklaus	286	Bruce Crampton, Bobby Mitchell & Tom Weiskopf	289
1973	Tommy Armour	283	J.C. Snead	284
1974	Gary Player	278	Tom Weiskopf & Dave Stockton	280
1975	Jack Nicklaus	276	Johnny Miller & Tom Weiskopf	277
1976	Raymond Floyd	271	Ben Crenshaw	279
1977	Tom Watson	276	Jack Nicklaus	278
1978	Gary Player	277	Hubert Green, Rod Funseth & Tom Watson	278
1979	Fuzzy Zoeller*	280	Ed Sneed & Tom Watson	280
1980	Seve Ballesteros	275	Gibby Gilbert & Jack Newton	279
1981	Tom Watson	280	Jack Nicklaus & Johnny Miller	282
1982	Craig Stadler*	284	Dan Pohl	284
1983	Seve Ballesteros	280	Ben Crenshaw & Tom Kite	284
1984	Ben Crenshaw	277	Tom Watson	279
1985	Bernhard Langer	282	Curtis Strange, Seve Ballesteros & Raymond Floyd	284
1986	Jack Nicklaus	279	Greg Norman & Tom Kite	280
1987	Larry Mize*	285	Seve Ballesteros & Greg Norman	285
1988	Sandy Lyle	281	Mark Calcavecchia	282
1989	Nick Faldo*	283	Scott Hoch	283
1990	Nick Faldo*	278	Raymond Floyd	278
1991	Ian Woosnam	277	Jose Marie Olazabal	278

(continued)

Table A2.5. *(continued)*

Year	Winner	Score	Runner(s)-Up	Score
1992	Fred Couples	275	Raymond Floyd	277
1993	Bernhard Langer	277	Chip Beck	281
1994	Jose Maria Olazabal	279	Tom Lehman	281
1995	Ben Crenshaw	274	Davis Love III	275
1996	Nick Faldo	276	Greg Norman	281
1997	Tiger Woods	270	Tom Kite	282
1998	Mark O'Meara	279	Fred Couples & David Duval	280
1999	Jose Maria Olazabal	280	Davis Love III	282
2000	Vijay Singh	278	Ernie Els	281
2001	Tiger Woods	272	David Duval	274
2002	Tiger Woods	276	Retief Goosen	279
2003	Mike Weir*	281	Len Mattiace	281
2004	Phil Mickelson	279	Ernie Els	280
2005	Tiger Woods*	276	Chris DeMarco	276
2006	Phil Mickelson	281	Tim Clark	283
2007	Zach Johnson	289	Tiger Woods, Retief Goosen & Rory Sabbatini	291
2008	Trevor Immelman	280	Tiger Woods	283
2009	Angel Cabrera*	276	Kenny Perry & Chad Campbell	276
2010	Phil Mickelson	272	Lee Westwood	275
2011	Charl Schwartzel	274	Jason Day & Adam Scott	276
2012	Bubba Watson*	278	Louis Oosthuizen	278
2013	Adam Scott*	279	Angel Cabrera	279
2014	Bubba Watson	280	Jonas Blixt & Jordan Spieth	283
2015	Jordan Spieth	270	Phil Mickelson & Justin Rose	274
2016	Danny Willett	283	Jordan Spieth & Lee Westwood	286
2017	Sergio Garcia*	279	Justin Rose	279

* denotes playoff winner
@ denotes amateur

Table A2.6. The United States Women's Open Championship

Year	Winner	Score	Runner(s)-Up	Venue
1946	Patty Berg	5 & 4	Betty Jameson	Spokane Country Club, Spokane, WA
1947	Betty Jameson	295	Sally Sessions & Polly Riley (301)	Starmount Forest Country Club, Greensboro, NC
1948	Babe Zaharias	300	Betty Hicks Newell (308)	Atlantic City Country Club, Northfield, NJ
1949	Louise Suggs	291	Babe Zaharias (305)	Prince Georges Country Club, Landover, MD
1950	Babe Zaharias	291	Betsy Rawls@ (300)	Rolling Hills Country Club, Wichita, KS
1951	Betsy Rawls	293	Louise Suggs (298)	Druid Hills Golf Club, Atlanta, GA
1952	Louise Suggs	284	Marlene Hagge (291)	Bala Golf Club, Philadelphia, PA
1953	Betsy Rawls*	302	Jackie Pung (302)	Country Club of Rochester, Rochester, NY
1954	Babe Zaharias	291	Betty Hicks Newell (303)	Salem Country Club, Peabody, MA
1955	Fay Crocker	299	Mary Lena Faulk (303)	Wichita Country Club, Wichita, KS
1956	Kathy Cornelius*	302	Barbara McIntire (302)	Northland Country Club, Duluth, MN
1957	Betsy Rawls	299	Patty Berg (305)	Winged Foot Golf Club, Mamaroneck, NY
1958	Mickey Wright	290	Louise Suggs (295)	Forest Lake Country Club, Bloomfield Hills, MI
1959	Mickey Wright	287	Louise Suggs (289)	Churchill Valley Country Club, Pittsburgh, PA
1960	Betsy Rawls	292	Joyce Ziske (293)	Worcester Country Club, Worcester, MA
1961	Mickey Wright	293	Betsy Rawls (299)	Baltusrol Golf Club, Springfield, NJ
1962	Murie Lindstrom	301	JoAnne Prentice & Ruth Jessen (303)	Dunes Golf & Beach Club, Myrtle Beach, SC
1963	Mary Mills	289	Sandra Haynie & Louise Suggs (292)	Kenwood Country Club, Cincinnati, OH
1964	Mickey Wright*	290	Ruth Jessen (290)	San Diego Country Club, Chula Vista, CA
1965	Carol Mann	290	Kathy Cornelius (292)	Atlantic City Country Club, Northfield, NJ
1966	Sandra Spuzich	297	Carol Mann (298)	Hazeltine National Golf Club, Chaska, MN
1967	Catherine Lacoste@	294	Susie Maxwell & Beth Stone (296)	The Homestead, Hot Springs, VA
1968	Susie Berning	289	Mickey Wright (292)	Moselem Springs Golf Club, Fleetwood, PA
1969	Donna Caponi	294	Peggy Wilson (295)	Scenic Hills Country Club, Pensacola, FL
1970	Donna Caponi	287	Sandra Haynie (288)	Muskogee Country Club, Muskogee, OK

(continued)

Table A2.6. *(continued)*

Year	Winner	Score	Runner(s)-Up	Venue
1971	JoAnne Carner	288	Kathy Whitworth (295)	Kahkwa Country Club, Erie, PA
1972	Susie Berning	299	Kathy Ahern, Pam Barnett, & Judy Rankin (300)	Winged Foot Golf Club, Mamaroneck, NY
1973	Susie Berning	290	Gloria Ehret (295)	Country Club of Rochester, Rochester, NY
1974	Sandra Haynie	295	Carol Mann & Beth Stone (296)	LaGrange Country Club, LaGrange, IL
1975	Sandra Palmer	295	JoAnne Carner, Sandra Post, & Nancy Lopez@ (299)	Atlantic City Country Club, Northfield, NJ
1976	JoAnne Carner*	292	Sandra Palmer (292)	Rolling Green Country Club, Springfield, PA
1977	Hollis Stacy	292	Nancy Lopez (294)	Hazeltine National Golf Club, Chaska, MN
1978	Hollis Stacy	289	JoAnne Carner & Sally Little (290)	Country Club of Indianapolis, Indianapolis, IN
1979	Jerilyn Britz	284	Debbie Massey & Sandra Palmer (286)	Brooklawn Country Club, Fairfield, CT
1980	Amy Alcott	280	Hollis Stacy (289)	Richland Country Club, Nashville, TN
1981	Pat Bradley	279	Beth Daniel (280)	LaGrange Country Club, LaGrange, IL
1982	Janet Alex	283	Beth Daniel, Sandra Haynie, & Donna White (289)	Del Paso Country Club, Sacramento, CA
1983	Jan Stephenson	290	JoAnne Carner (291)	Cedar Ridge Country Club, Broken Arrow, OK
1984	Hollis Stacy	290	Rosie Jones (291)	Salem Country Club, Peabody, MA
1985	Kathy Baker	280	Judy Dickenson (283)	Baltusrol Golf Club, Springfield, NJ
1986	Jane Geddes*	287	Sally Little (287)	NCR Golf Club, Kettering, OH
1987	Laura Davies*	285	Ayako Okamoto & JoAnne Carner (285)	Plainfield Country Club, Edison, NJ
1988	Liselotte Neumann	277	Patty Sheehan (280)	Baltimore Country Club, Baltimore, MD
1989	Betsy King	278	Nancy Lopez (282)	Indianwood Country Club, Lake Orion, MI
1990	Betsy King	284	Patty Sheehan (285)	Atlanta Athletic Club, Duluth, GA
1991	Meg Mellon	283	Pat Bradley (285)	Colonial Country Club, Fort Worth, TX
1992	Patty Sheehan*	280	Julie Inkster (280)	Oakmont Country Club, Oakmont, PA
1993	Lauri Merten	280	Donna Andrews & Helen Alfredsson (281)	Crooked Stick Golf Club, Carmel, IN

Year	Winner	Score	Runner(s)-up	Venue
1994	Patty Sheehan	277	Tammie Green (278)	Indianwood Country Club, Lake Orion, MI
1995	Annika Sörenstam	278	Meg Mellon (279)	Broadmoor Golf Club, Colorado Springs, CO
1996	Annika Sörenstam	272	Kris Tschetter (278)	Pine Needles Golf Club, Southern Pines, NC
1997	Alison Nicholas	274	Nancy Lopez (275)	Pumpkin Ridge Golf Club, North Plains, OR
1998	Se Ri Pak*	290	Jenny Chuasiriporn @ (290)	Blackwolf Run, Kohler, WI
1999	Julie Inkster	272	Sherri Turner (277)	Old Waverly Golf Club, West Point, MS
2000	Karrie Webb	282	Cristie Kerr & Meg Mellon (287)	Merit Club, Libertyville, IL
2001	Karrie Webb	273	Se Ri Pak (281)	Pine Needles Golf Club, Southern Pines, NC
2002	Julie Inkster	276	Annika Sörenstam (278)	Prairie Dunes Country Club, Hutchinson, KS
2003	Hilary Lunke*	283	Angela Stanford & Kelly Robbins (283)	Pumpkin Ridge Golf Club, North Plains, OR
2004	Meg Mellon	274	Annika Sörenstam (276)	Orchards Golf Club, South Hadley, MA
2005	Birdie Kim	287	Brittany Lang@ & Morgan Pressel@ (289)	Cherry Hills Country Club, Denver, CO
2006	Annika Sörenstam*	284	Pat Hurst (284)	Newport Country Club, Newport, RI
2007	Cristie Kerr	279	Angela Park & Lorena Ochoa (281)	Pine Needles Golf Club, Southern Pines, NC
2008	Inbee Park	283	Helen Alfredsson (287)	Interlachen Country Club, Edina, MN
2009	Eun-Hee Ji	284	Candy Kung (285)	Saucon Valley Country Club, Bethlehem, PA
2010	Paula Creamer	281	Suzann Pettersen & Na Yean Choi (285)	Oakmont Country Club, Oakmont, PA
2011	Ryu So-yeon*	281	Hee Kyung Seo (281)	Broadmoor Golf Club, Colorado Springs, CO
2012	Choi Na-yeon	281	Amy Yang (285)	Blackwolf Run, Kohler, WI
2013	Inbee Park	280	I.K. Kim (284)	Sebonack Golf Club, Southampton, NY
2014	Michelle Wie	278	Stacy Lewis (280)	Pinehurst Resort, Pinehurst, NC
2015	In-gee Chun	272	Amy Yang (283)	Lancaster Country Club, Lancaster, PA
2016	Brittany Lang*	282	Anna Nordqvist (282)	Corde Valle Golf Club, San Martin, CA
2017	Park Sung-hyun	277	Choi Hye-jin@ (279)	Trump National Golf Club, Bedminster, NJ

* denotes playoff winner
@ denotes Amateur Golfer

Table A2.7.   The Women's PGA Championship

Year	Winner	Score	Runner(s)-Up	Venue
1955	Beverly Hanson	4 & 3	Louise Suggs	Orchard Ridge Country Club, Ft. Wayne, IN
1956	Marlene Hagge*	291	Patty Berg (291)	Forest Lake Country Club, Detroit, MI
1957	Louise Suggs	285	Wifii Smith (288)	Churchill Valley Country Club, Pittsburgh, PA
1958	Mickey Wright	288	Fay Crocker (294)	Churchill Valley Country Club, Pittsburgh, PA
1959	Betsy Rawls	288	Patty Berg (289)	Sheraton Hotel Country Club, French Lick, IN
1960	Mickey Wright	292	Louise Suggs (295)	Sheraton Hotel Country Club, French Lick, IN
1961	Mickey Wright	287	Louise Suggs (296)	Stardust Country Club, Las Vegas, NV
1962	Judy Kimball	282	Shirley Spork (286)	Stardust Country Club, Las Vegas, NV
1963	Mickey Wright	294	Mary Lena Faulk & Mary Mills (296)	Stardust Country Club, Las Vegas, NV
1964	Mary Mills	278	Mickey Wright (280)	Stardust Country Club, Las Vegas, NV
1965	Sandra Haynie	279	Clifford Ann Creed (280)	Stardust Country Club, Las Vegas, NV
1966	Gloria Ehret	282	Mickey Wright (285)	Stardust Country Club, Las Vegas, NV
1967	Kathy Whitworth	284	Shirley Englehorn (285)	Pleasant Valley Country Club, Sutton MA
1968	Sandra Post*	294	Kathy Whitworth (294)	Pleasant Valley Country Club, Sutton MA
1969	Betsy Rawls	293	Susie Berning & Carol Mann (297)	Concord Golf Club, Kiamesha Lake, NY
1970	Shirley Englehorn*	285	Kathy Whitworth (285)	Pleasant Valley Country Club, Sutton MA
1971	Kathy Whitworth	288	Kathy Ahearn (292)	Pleasant Valley Country Club, Sutton MA
1972	Kathy Ahearn	293	Jane Blalock (299)	Pleasant Valley Country Club, Sutton MA
1973	Mary Mills	288	Betty Burfeindt (289)	Pleasant Valley Country Club, Sutton MA
1974	Sandra Haynie	287	JoAnne Carner (289)	Pleasant Valley Country Club, Sutton MA
1975	Kathy Whitworth	288	Sandra Haynie (289)	Pine Ridge Golf Course, Baltimore, MD
1976	Betty Burfeindt	287	Judy Rankin (288)	Pine Ridge Golf Course, Baltimore, MD
1977	Chako Higuchi	279	Pat Bradley, Sandra Post & Judy Rankin (282)	Bay Tree Golf Plantation, Myrtle Beach, SC
1978	Nancy Lopez	275	Amy Alcott (281)	Jack Nicklaus Sports Ctr., Kings Island, OH

Year	Winner	Score	Runner(s)-up	Location
1979	Donna Caponi	279	Jerilyn Britz (282)	Jack Nicklaus Sports Ctr., Kings Island, OH
1980	Sally Little	285	Jane Blalock (288)	Jack Nicklaus Sports Ctr., Kings Island, OH
1981	Donna Caponi	280	Jerilyn Britz & Pat Meyers (281)	Jack Nicklaus Sports Ctr., Kings Island, OH
1982	Jan Stephenson	279	JoAnne Carner (281)	Jack Nicklaus Sports Ctr., Kings Island, OH
1983	Patty Sheehan	279	Sandra Haynie (281)	Jack Nicklaus Sports Ctr., Kings Island, OH
1984	Patty Sheehan	272	Beth Daniel & Pat Bradley (282)	Jack Nicklaus Sports Ctr., Kings Island, OH
1985	Nancy Lopez	273	Alice Miller (281)	Jack Nicklaus Sports Ctr., Kings Island, OH
1986	Pat Bradley	277	Patty Sheehan (278)	Jack Nicklaus Sports Ctr., Kings Island, OH
1987	Jane Geddes	275	Betsy King (276)	Jack Nicklaus Sports Ctr., Kings Island, OH
1988	Sherri Turner	281	Amy Alcott (282)	Jack Nicklaus Sports Ctr., Kings Island, OH
1989	Nancy Lopez	274	Ayako Okamoto (277)	Jack Nicklaus Sports Ctr., Kings Island, OH
1990	Beth Daniel	280	Rosie Jones (281)	Bethesda Country Club, Bethesda, MD
1991	Meg Mellon	274	Pat Bradley & Ayako Okamoto (275)	Bethesda Country Club, Bethesda, MD
1992	Betsy King	267	JoAnne Carner, Karen Noble & Liselotte Neumann (278)	Bethesda Country Club, Bethesda, MD
1993	Patty Sheehan	275	Lauri Merten (276)	Bethesda Country Club, Bethesda, MD
1994	Laura Davies	279	Alice Ritzman (282)	DuPont Country Club, Wilmington, DE
1995	Kelly Robbins	274	Laura Davies (275)	DuPont Country Club, Wilmington, DE
1996	Laura Davies	213#	Julie Piers (214)	DuPont Country Club, Wilmington, DE
1997	Chris Johnson*	281	Leta Lindley (281)	DuPont Country Club, Wilmington, DE
1998	Se Ri Pak	273	Donna Andrews & Lisa Hackney (276)	DuPont Country Club, Wilmington, DE
1999	Juli Inkster	268	Liselotte Neumann (272)	DuPont Country Club, Wilmington, DE
2000	Juli Inkster*	281	Stefania Croce (281)	DuPont Country Club, Wilmington, DE
2001	Karrie Webb	270	Laura Diaz (272)	DuPont Country Club, Wilmington, DE
2002	Se Ri Pak	279	Beth Daniel (282)	DuPont Country Club, Wilmington, DE
2003	Annika Sorenstam*	278	Grace Park (278)	DuPont Country Club, Wilmington, DE
2004	Annika Sorenstam	271	Shi Hyun Ahn (274)	DuPont Country Club, Wilmington, DE
2005	Annika Sorenstam	277	Michelle Wie@ (280)	Bulle Rock Golf Course, Havre de Grace, MD

(continued)

Table A2.7. *(continued)*

Year	Winner	Score	Runner(s)-Up	Venue
2006	Se Ri Pak*	280	Karrie Webb (280)	Bulle Rock Golf Course, Havre de Grace, MD
2007	Suzann Pettersen	274	Karrie Webb (275)	Bulle Rock Golf Course, Havre de Grace, MD
2008	Yani Tseng	276	Maria Hjorth (276)	Bulle Rock Golf Course, Havre de Grace, MD
2009	Anna Nordqvist	273	Lindsey Wright (277)	Bulle Rock Golf Course, Havre de Grace, MD
2010	Cristie Kerr	269	Song-Hee Kim (281)	Locust Hill Country Club, Rochester, NY
2011	Yani Tseng	269	Morgan Pressel (279)	Locust Hill Country Club, Rochester, NY
2012	Shanshan Feng	282	Mika Miyazato, Stacy Lewis, Suzann Pettersen & Eun-Hee Ji (284)	Locust Hill Country Club, Rochester, NY
2013	Inbee Park*	283	Catriona Matthew (283)	Locust Hill Country Club, Rochester, NY
2014	Inbee Park*	277	Brittany Lincicone (277)	Monroe Golf Club, Pittsford, NY
2015	Inbee Park	273	Sei Young Kim (278)	Westchester Country Club, Harrison, NY
2016	Brooke Henderson*	278	Lydia Ko (278)	Sahalee Country Club, Sammamish, WA
2017	Danielle Kang	271	Brooke Henderson (272)	Olympia Fields Country Club, Olympia Fields, IL

\# denotes 54-hole event
* denotes playoff winner
@ denotes Amateur Golfer

Table A2.8.   The Senior PGA Championship

Year	Winner	Year	Winner	Year	Winner
1937	Jock Hutchison	1964	Sam Snead	1990	Gary Player
1938	Fred McLeod	1965	Sam Snead	1991	Jack Nicklaus
1939	Not held	1966	Fred Haas	1992	Lee Trevino
1940	Otto Hackbarth	1967	Sam Snead	1993	Tom Wargo
1941	Jack Burke, Sr.	1968	Chandler Harper	1994	Lee Trevino
1942	Eddie Willaims	1969	Tommy Bolt	1995	Raymond Floyd
1943	Not held–WW II	1970	Sam Snead	1996	Hale Irwin
1944	Not held–WW II	1971	Julius Boros	1997	Hale Irwin
1945	Eddie Williams	1972	Sam Snead	1998	Hale Irwin
1946	Eddie Williams	1973	Sam Snead	1999	Allen Doyle
1947	Jock Hutchison	1974	Roberto De Vicenzo	2000	Doug Tewell
1948	Charles McKenna	1975	Charlie Sifford	2001	Tom Watson
1949	Marshall Crichton	1976	Pete Cooper	2002	Fuzzy Zoeller
1950	Al Watrous	1977	Julius Boros	2003	John Jacobs
1951	Al Watrous	1978	Joe Jiminez	2004	Hale Irwin
1952	Ernest Newnham	1979 (Feb.)	Jack Fleck	2005	Mike Reid
1953	Harry Schwab	1979 (Dec.)	Don January	2006	Jay Haas
1954	Gene Sarazen	1980	Arnold Palmer	2007	Denis Watson
1955	Mortie Dutra	1981	Miller Barber	2008	Jay Haas
1956	Pete Burke	1982	Don January	2009	Michael Allen
1957	Al Watrous	1983	Not held	2010	Tom Lehman
1958	Gene Sarazen	1984 (Jan.)	Arnold Palmer	2011	Tom Watson
1959	Willie Goggin	1984(Dec.)	Peter Thomson	2012	Roger Chapman
1960	Dick Metz	1985	Not held	2013	Koki Idoki
1961	Paul Runyon	1986	Gary Player	2014	Colin Montgomerie
1962	Paul Runyon	1987	Chi Chi Rodriguez	2015	Colin Montgomerie
1963	Herman Barron	1988	Gary Player	2016	Rocco Mediate
		1989	Larry Mowry	2017	Bernhard Langer

Table A2.9. The United States Senior Open Championship

Year	Winner	Year	Winner	Year	Winner
1980	Roberto De Vicenzo	1993	Jack Nicklaus	2006	Allen Doyle
1981	Arnold Palmer	1994	Simon Hobday	2007	Brad Bryant
1982	Miller Barber	1995	Tom Weiskopf	2008	Eduardo Romero
1983	Billy Casper	1996	Dave Stockton	2009	Fred Funk
1984	Miller Barber	1997	Graham Marsh	2010	Bernhard Langer
1985	Miller Barber	1998	Hale Irwin	2011	Olin Browne
1986	Dale Douglas	1999	Dave Eichelberger	2012	Roger Chapman
1987	Gary Player	2000	Hale Irwin	2013	Kenny Perry
1988	Gary Player	2001	Bruce Fleisher	2014	Colin Montgomerie
1989	Orville Moody	2002	Dan Pooley	2015	Jeff Maggert
1990	Lee Trevino	2003	Bruce Lietzke	2016	Gene Sauers
1991	Jack Nicklaus	2004	Peter Jacobsen	2017	Kenny Perry
1992	Larry Laoretti	2005	Allen Doyle		

Table A2.10. The Senior Players Championship

Year	Winner	Year	Winner	Year	Winner
1983	Miller Barber	1995	J.C. Snead	2007	Loren Roberts
1984	Arnold Palmer	1996	Raymond Floyd	2008	D.A. Weibring
1985	Arnold Palmer	1997	Larry Gilbert	2009	Jay Haas
1986	Chi Chi Rodriguez	1998	Gil Morgan	2010	Mark O'Mera
1987	Gary Player	1999	Hale Irwin	2011	Fred Couples
1988	Billy Casper	2000	Raymond Floyd	2012	Joe Daley
1989	Orville Moody	2001	Allen Doyle	2013	Kenny Perry
1990	Jack Nicklaus	2002	Stewart Ginn	2014	Bernhard Langer
1991	Jim Albus	2003	Craig Stadler	2015	Bernhard Langer
1992	Dave Stockton	2004	Mark James	2016	Bernhard Langer
1993	Jim Colbert	2005	Peter Jacobsen		
1994	Dave Stockton	2006	Bobby Wadkins		

Table A2.11. The Senior Open Championship (The Senior British Open)

Year	Winner	Year	Winner	Year	Winner
1987	Neil Coles	1998	Brian Huggett	2008	Bruce Vaughan
1988	Gary Player	1999	Christy O'Connor, Jr.	2009	Loren Roberts
1989	Bob Charles	2000	Christy O'Connor, Jr.	2010	Bernhard Langer
1990	Gary Player	2001	Ian Stanley	2011	Russ Cochran
1991	Bobby Verwey	2002	Noboru Sugai	2012	Fred Couples
1992	John Fourie	2003	Tom Watson	2013	Mark Wiebe
1993	Bob Charles	2004	Pete Oakley	2014	Bernhard Langer
1994	Tom Wargo	2005	Tom Watson	2015	Marco Dawson
1995	Brian Barnes	2006	Loren Roberts	2016	Paul Broadhurst
1996	Brian Barnes	2007	Tom Watson	2017	Bernhard Langer
1997	Gary Player				

Table A2.12. The Tradition

Year	Winner	Year	Winner	Year	Winner
1989	Don Bies	1999	Graham Marsh	2009	Mike Reid
1990	Jack Nicklaus	2000	Tom Kite	2010	Fred Funk
1991	Jack Nicklaus	2001	Doug Tewell	2011	Tom Lehman
1992	Lee Trevino	2002	Jim Thorpe	2012	Tom Lehman
1993	Tom Shaw	2003	Tom Watson	2013	David Frost
1994	Raymond Floyd	2004	Craig Stadler	2014	Kenny Perry
1995	Jack Nicklaus	2005	Loren Roberts	2015	Jeff Maggert
1996	Jack Nicklaus	2006	Eduardo Romero	2016	Bernhard Langer
1997	Gil Morgan	2007	Mark McNulty	2017	Bernhard Langer
1998	Gil Morgan	2008	Fred Funk		

Table A2.13.   The United States Amateur Championship

Year	Winner	Year	Winner	Year	Winner
1895	Charles Macdonald	1936	John Fischer	1977	John Fought
1896	H.J. Whigham	1937	John Goodman	1978	John Cook
1897	H.J. Whigham	1938	William Turnesa	1979	Mark O'Meara
1898	Findlay Douglas	1939	Bud Ward	1980	Hal Sutton
1899	Herbert Harriman	1940	Richard Chapman	1981	Nathaniel Crosby
1900	Walter Travis	1941	Bud Ward	1982	Jay Sigel
1901	Walter Travis	1942	Not held–WWII	1983	Jay Sigel
1902	Louis James	1943	Not held–WWII	1984	Scott Verplank
1903	Walter Travis	1944	Not held–WWII	1985	Sam Randolph
1904	Chandler Egan	1945	Not held–WWII	1986	Buddy Alexander
1905	Chandler Egan	1946	Ted Bishop	1987	Billy Mayfair
1906	Eben Byers	1947	Skee Riegel	1988	Eric Meeks
1907	Jerry Travers	1948	William Turnesa	1989	Chris Patton
1908	Jerry Travers	1949	Charles Coe	1990	Phil Mickelson
1909	Robert Gardner	1950	Sam Urzetta	1991	Mitch Voges
1910	William Fownes, Jr.	1951	Billy Maxwell	1992	Justin Leonard
1911	Harold Hilton	1952	Jack Westland	1993	John Harris
1912	Jerry Travers	1953	Gene Littler	1994	Tiger Woods
1913	Jerry Travers	1954	Arnold Palmer	1995	Tiger Woods
1914	Frances Ouimet	1955	Harvie Ward	1996	Tiger Woods
1915	Robert Gardner	1956	Harvie Ward	1997	Matt Kuchar
1916	Chick Evans	1957	Hillman Robbins	1998	Hank Kuehne
1917	Not held–WWI	1958	Charles Coe	1999	David Gossett
1918	Not held–WWI	1959	Jack Nicklaus	2000	Jeff Quinney
1919	Davidson Herron	1960	Deane Beman	2001	Bubba Dickerson
1920	Chick Evans	1961	Jack Nicklaus	2002	Ricky Barnes
1921	Jesse Guilford	1962	Labron Harris	2003	Nick Flanagan
1922	Jess Sweetser	1963	Deane Beman	2004	Ryan Moore
1923	Max Martson	1964	Bill Campbell	2005	Edoardo Molinari
1924	Bobby Jones	1965	Bob Murphy	2006	Richie Ramsay
1925	Bobby Jones	1966	Gary Cowan	2007	Colt Knost
1926	George Von Elm	1967	Bob Dickson	2008	Danny Lee
1927	Bobby Jones	1968	Bruce Fleisher	2009	An Byeong-hun
1928	Bobby Jones	1969	Steve Melnyk	2010	Peter Uihlein
1929	Harrison Johnston	1970	Lanny Wadkins	2011	Kelly Kraft
1930	Bobby Jones	1971	Gary Cowan	2012	Steven Fox
1931	Francis Ouimet	1972	Vinny Giles	2013	Matthew Fitzpatrick
1932	Ross Somerville	1973	Craig Stadler	2014	Gunn Yank
1933	George Dunlap	1974	Jerry Pate	2015	Bryson DeChambeau
1934	Lawson Little	1975	Fred Ridley	2016	Curtis Luck
1935	Lawson Little	1976	Bill Sander	2017	Doc Redman

Table A2.14.   The United States Women's Amateur Championship

Year	Winner	Year	Winner	Year	Winner
1895	Lucy Barnes Brown	1936	Pamela Barton	1977	Beth Daniel
1896	Beatrix Hoyt	1937	Estelle Lawson Page	1978	Cathy Sherk
1897	Beatrix Hoyt	1938	Patty Berg	1979	Carolyn Hill
1898	Beatrix Hoyt	1939	Betty Jameson	1980	Juli Inkster
1899	Ruth Underhill	1940	Betty Jameson	1981	Juli Inkster
1900	Frances Griscom	1941	Betty Hicks Newell	1982	Juli Inkster
1901	Genevieve Hecker	1942	Not held–WWII	1983	Joanne Pacillo
1902	Genevieve Hecker	1943	Not held–WWII	1984	Deb Richard
1903	Bessie Anthony	1944	Not held–WWII	1985	Michiko Hattori
1904	Georgianna Bishop	1945	Not held–WWII	1986	Kay Cockerill
1905	Pauline Mackay	1946	Babe Zaharias	1987	Kay Cockerill
1906	Harriot Curtis	1947	Louise Suggs	1988	Pearl Sinn
1907	Margaret Curtis	1948	Grace Lenczyk	1989	Vicki Goetze
1908	Katherine Harley	1949	Dorothy Porter	1990	Pat Hurst
1909	Dorothy Campbell	1950	Beverley Hanson	1991	Amy Fruhwirth
1910	Dorothy Campbell	1951	Dorothy Kirby	1992	Vicki Goetze
1911	Margaret Curtis	1952	Jacqueline Pung	1993	Jill McGill
1912	Margaret Curtis	1953	Mary Lena Faulk	1994	Wendy Ward
1913	Gladys Ravenscroft	1954	Barbara Romack	1995	Kelli Kuehne
1914	Katherine Harley	1955	Patricia Lesser	1996	Kelli Kuehne
1915	Florence Vanderbeck	1956	Marlene Stewart	1997	Silvia Cavalleri
1916	Alexa Stirling	1957	JoAnne Gunderson	1998	Grace Park
1917	Not held–WWI	1958	Anne Quast	1999	Dorothy Delasin
1918	Not Held–WWI	1959	Barbara McIntire	2000	Marcy Newton
1919	Alexa Stirling	1960	JoAnne Gunderson	2001	Meredith Duncan
1920	Alexa Stirling	1961	Anne Quast Decker	2002	Becky Lucidi
1921	Marion Hollins	1962	JoAnne Gunderson	2003	Virada Nirapathpongporn
1922	Glenna Collett	1963	Ann Quast Welts	2004	Jane Park
1923	Edith Cummings	1964	Barbara McIntire	2005	Morgan Pressel
1924	Dorothy Campbell Hurd	1965	Jean Ashley	2006	Kimberly Kim
1925	Glenna Collett	1966	JoAnne Gunderson	2007	Mariajo Uribe
1926	Helen Stetson	1967	Mary Lou Dill	2008	Amanda Blumenherst
1927	Miriam Burns Horn	1968	JoAnne Gunderson	2009	Jennifer Song
1928	Glenna Collett	1969	Catherine Lacoste	2010	Danielle Kang
1929	Glenna Collett	1970	Martha Wilkinson	2011	Danielle Kang
1930	Glenna Collett	1971	Laura Baugh	2012	Lydia Ko
1931	Helen Hicks	1972	Mary Budke	2013	Emma Talley
1932	Virginia Van Wie	1973	Carol Semple	2014	Kristen Gillman
1933	Virginia Van Wie	1974	Cynthia Hill	2015	Hannah O'Sullivan
1934	Virginia Van Wie	1975	Beth Daniel	2016	Seong Eun-jeong
1935	Glenna Collett Vare	1976	Donna Horton	2017	Sophia Schubert

· 𝒞 ·

Winners of Major
Team and Cup Competitions

Table A3.1. Ryder Cup Matches

Year	Winner	Year	Winner	Year	Winner
1927	USA 9 ½ to 2 ½	1961	USA 14 ½ to 9 ½	1989	Draw 14 to 14
1929	Great Britain 7 to 5	1963	USA 23 to 9	1991	USA 14 ½ to 13 ½
1931	USA 9 to 3	1965	USA 19 ½ to 12 ½	1993	USA 15 to 13
1933	Great Britain 6 ½ to 5 ½	1967	USA 23 ½ to 8 ½	1995	Europe 14 ½ to 13 ½
1935	USA 9 to 3	1969	Draw 16 – 16	1997	Europe 14 ½ to 13 ½
1937	USA 8 to 4	1971	USA 18 ½ to 13 ½	1999	USA 14 ½ to 13 ½
1939–1945	Not held – WWII	1973	USA 19 to 13	2002	Europe 15 ½ to 12 ½
1947	USA 11 to 1	1975	USA 21 to 11	2004	Europe 18 ½ to 9 ½
1949	USA 7 to 5	1977	USA 12 ½ to 7 ½	2006	Europe 18 ½ to 9 ½
1951	USA 9 ½ to 2 ½	1979	USA 17 to 11	2008	USA 16 ½ to 11 ½
1953	USA 6 ½ to 5 ½	1981	USA 18 ½ to 9 ½	2010	Europe 14 ½ to 13 ½
1955	USA 8 to 4	1983	USA 14 ½ to 13 ½	2012	Europe 14 ½ to 13 ½
1957	Great Britain 7 ½ to 4 ½	1985	Europe 16 ½ to 11 ½	2014	Europe 16 ½ to 11 ½
1959	USA 8 ½ to 3 ½	1987	Europe 15 to 13	2016	USA 17 to 11

Table A3.2. Walker Cup Matches

Year	Winner	Year	Winner	Year	Winner
1922	USA 8 to 4	1957	USA 8 ½ to 3 ½	1989	Britain & Ireland 12 ½ to 11 ½
1923	USA 6 ½ to 5 ½	1959	USA 9 to 3	1991	USA 14 to 10
1924	USA 9 to 3	1961	USA 11 to 1	1993	USA 19 to 5
1926	USA 6 ½ to 5 ½	1963	USA 14 to 10	1995	Britain & Ireland 14 to 10
1928	USA 11 to 1	1965	Draw 12 to 12	1997	USA 18 to 6
1930	USA 10 to 2	1967	USA 15 to 9	1999	Britain & Ireland 15 to 9
1932	USA 9 ½ to 2 ½	1969	USA 13 to 11	2001	Britain & Ireland 15 to 9
1934	USA 9 ½ to 2 ½	1971	Britain & Ireland 13 to 11	2003	Britain & Ireland 12 ½ to 11 ½
1936	USA 10 ½ to 1 ½	1973	USA 14 to 10	2005	USA 12 ½ to 11 ½
1938	Britain & Ireland 7 ½ to 4 ½	1975	USA 15 ½ to 8 ½	2007	USA 12 ½ to 11 ½
1940–1946	Not held – WWII	1977	USA 16 to 8	2009	USA 16 ½ to 9 ½
1947	USA 8 to 4	1979	USA 15 ½ to 8 ½	2011	Britain & Ireland 14 to 12
1949	USA 10 to 2	1981	USA 15 to 9	2013	USA 17 to 9
1951	USA 7 ½ to 4 ½	1983	USA 13 ½ to 10 ½	2015	Britain & Ireland 16 ½ to 9 ½
1953	USA 9 to 3	1985	USA 13 to 11	2017	USA 19 to 7
1955	USA 10 to 2	1987	USA 16 ½ to 7 ½		

Table A3.3.   Presidents Cup Matches

Year	Winner	Year	Winner
1994	USA 20 to 12	2011	USA 19 to 15
1996	USA 16 ½ to 15 ½	2013	USA 18 ½ to 15 ½
1998	International 20 ½ to 11 ½	2015	USA 15 ½ to 14 ½
2000	USA 21 ½ to 10 ½	2017	USA 19 to 11
2003	Draw 17 to 17		
2005	USA 18 ½ to 15 ½		
2007	USA 19 ½ to 14 ½		
2009	USA 19 ½ to 14 ½		

Table A3.4.   FedEx Cup Winners

Year	Winner	Year	Winner
2007	Tiger Woods	2015	Jordan Spieth
2008	Vijay Singh	2016	Rory McIlroy
2009	Tiger Woods	2017	Justin Thomas
2010	Jim Furyk		
2011	Bill Haas		
2012	Brandt Snedeker		
2013	Henrik Stenson		
2014	Billy Horschel		

Table A3.5. Curtis Cup Matches

Year	Winner	Year	Winner	Year	Winner
1932	USA 5 ½ to 3 ½	1962	USA 8 to 1	1990	USA 14 to 4
1934	USA 6 ½ to 2 ½	1964	USA 10 ½ to 7 ½	1992	Britain & Ireland 10 to 8
1936	Draw 4 ½ to 4 ½	1966	USA 13 to 5	1994	Draw 9 to 9
1938	USA 5 ½ to 3 ½	1968	USA 10 ½ to 7 ½	1996	Britain & Ireland 11 ½ to 6 ½
1940	Not held – WWII	1970	USA 11 ½ to 6 ½	1998	USA 10 to 8
1942	Not held – WWII	1972	USA 10 to 8	2000	USA 10 to 8
1944	Not held – WWII	1974	USA 13 to 5	2002	USA 11 to 7
1946	Not held – WWII	1976	USA 11 ½ to 6 ½	2004	USA 10 to 8
1948	USA 6 ½ to 2 ½	1978	USA 12 to 6	2006	USA 11 ½ to 6 ½
1950	USA 7 ½ to 1 ½	1980	USA 13 to 5	2008	USA 13 to 7
1952	Britain & Ireland 5 to 4	1982	USA 14 ½ to 3 ½	2010	USA 12 ½ to 7 ½
1954	USA 6 to 3	1984	USA 9 ½ to 8 ½	2012	Britain & Ireland 10 ½ to 9 ½
1956	Britain & Ireland 5 to 4	1986	Britain & Ireland 13 to 5	2014	USA 13 to 7
1958	Draw 4 ½ to 4 ½	1988	Britain & Ireland 11 to 7	2016	Britain & Ireland 11 ½ to 8 ½
1960	USA 6 ½ to 2 ½				

Table A3.6. Solheim Cup

Year	Winner	Year	Winner	Year	Winner
1990	USA 11 ½ to 4 ½	2000	Europe 14 ½ to 11 ½	2009	USA 16 to 12
1992	Europe 11 ½ to 6 ½	2002	USA 15 ½ to 12 ½	2011	Europe 15 to 13
1994	USA 13 to 7	2003	Europe 17 ½ to 10 ½	2013	Europe 18 to 10
1996	USA 17 to 11	2005	USA 15 ½ to 12 ½	2015	USA 14 ½ to 13 ½
1998	USA 16 to 12	2007	USA 16 to 12	2017	USA 16 ½ to 11 ½

· 𝒟 ·

Number of Wins in
Professional Golf Events through 2017

Table A4.1. Players with 20 or More Wins in PGA Tour Events

Rank	Name	PGA Tour Wins	Wins in Majors	Span of Years
1	Sam Snead	82	7	1936–1965
2	Tiger Woods	79	14	1996–2013
3	Jack Nicklaus	73	18	1962–1986
4	Ben Hogan	64	9	1938–1959
5	Arnold Palmer	62	7	1955–1973
6	Byron Nelson	52	5	1935–1951
7	Billy Casper	51	3	1956–1975
8	Walter Hagen	45	11	1914–1936
9	Phil Mickelson	42	5	1991–2013
10	Cary Middlecoff	40	3	1945–1961
11	Gene Sarazen	39	7	1922–1941
	Tom Watson	39	8	1974–1998
13	Lloyd Mangrum	36	1	1940–1956
14	Vijay Singh	34	3	1993–2008
15	Horton Smith	32	2	1928–1941
16	Harry Cooper	31	0	1923–1939
	Jimmy Demaret	31	3	1938–1957
18	Leo Diegel	30	2	1920–1934
19	Gene Littler	29	1	1954–1977
	Paul Runyon	29	2	1930–1941
	Lee Trevino	29	6	1968–1984
22	Henry Picard	26	2	1932–1945
23	Tommy Armour	26	3	1920–1938
	Johnny Miller	25	2	1971–1994
25	Gary Player	24	9	1958–1978
	Macdonald Smith	24	0	1924–1936
27	Johnny Farrell	22	1	1921–1936
	Raymond Floyd	22	4	1963–1992

(continued)

Table A4.1. *(continued)*

Rank	Name	PGA Tour Wins	Wins in Majors	Span of Years
29	Jim Barnes	21	4	1916–1937
	Davis Love III	21	1	1987–2015
	Willie Macfarlane	21	1	1916–1936
	Lanny Wadkins	21	1	1972–1992
	Craig Wood	21	2	1928–1944
34	Hale Irwin	20	3	1971–1994
	Bill Mehlhorn	20	0	1923–1930
	Greg Norman	20	2	1984–1997
	Doug Sanders	20	0	1956–1972

Table A4.2.   Players with Four or More Wins in Men's Major Professional Championships

Rank	Name	U.S. Open	British Open	Masters	PGA	Total Wins in Majors
1	Jack Nicklaus	4	3	6	5	18
2	Tiger Woods	3	3	4	4	14
3	Walter Hagen	2	4	0	5	11
4	Ben Hogan	4	1	2	2	9
5	Gary Player	1	3	3	2	9
6	Tom Watson	1	5	2	0	8
7	Gene Sarazen	2	1	1	3	7
	Arnold Palmer	1	2	4	0	7
	Sam Snead	0	1	3	3	7
	Bobby Jones	4	3	0	0	7
	Harry Vardon	1	6	0	0	7
12	Lee Trevino	2	2	0	2	6
	Nick Faldo	0	3	3	0	6
14	Phil Mickelson	0	1	3	1	5
	Byron Nelson	1	0	2	2	5
	Seve Ballesteros	0	3	2	0	5
	James Braid	0	5	0	0	5
	John Henry Taylor	0	5	0	0	5
	Peter Thomson	0	5	0	0	5
20	Raymond Floyd	1	0	1	2	4
	Willie Anderson	4	0	0	0	4
	Ernie Els	2	2	0	0	4
	Jim Barnes	1	1	0	2	4
	Rory McIlroy	1	1	0	2	4
	Bobby Locke	0	4	0	0	4
	Tom Morris, Sr.	0	4	0	0	4
	Tom Morris, Jr.	0	4	0	0	4
	Willie Park, Sr.	0	4	0	0	4

Table A4.3.   Players with 20 or More Wins in LPGA Tour Events

Rank	Name	LPGA Tour Wins	Wins in Majors	Span of Years
1	Kathy Whitworth	88	6	1962–1985
2	Mickey Wright	82	13	1956–1973
3	Annika Sorenstam	72	10	1995–2008
4	Louise Suggs	61	11	1946–1962
5	Patty Berg	60	15	1937–1962
6	Betsy Rawls	55	8	1951–1972
7	Nancy Lopez	48	3	1978–1997
8	JoAnne Carner	43	2	1969–1985
9	Sandra Haynie	42	4	1962–1982
10	Babe Zaharias	41	10	1940–1955
	Karrie Webb	41	7	1995–2014
12	Carol Mann	38	2	1964–1975
13	Patty Sheehan	35	6	1981–1996
14	Betsy King	34	6	1984–2001
15	Beth Daniel	33	1	1979–2003
16	Pat Bradley	31	6	1976–1995
	Juli Inkster	31	7	1983–2006
18	Amy Alcott	29	5	1975–1991
19	Jane Blalock	27	0	1970–1985
	Lorena Ochoa	27	2	2004–2009
21	Marlene Hagge	26	1	1952–1972
	Judy Rankin	26	0	1968–1979
23	Se Ri Pak	25	5	1998–2010
24	Donna Caponi	24	4	1969–1981
25	Marilynn Smith	21	2	1954–1972
26	Laura Davies	20	4	1987–2001

Notes

CHAPTER 5

1. Herbert Warren Wind, *The Story of American Golf* (New York: Alfred A. Knopf, 1975), 82.

CHAPTER 6

1. John Garrity, *The Ultimate Golf Book*, ed. Charles McGrath and David McCormick (Boston: Houghton Mifflin, 2006), 57–58.
2. Garrity, *The Ultimate Golf Book*, 159.

CHAPTER 8

1. Herbert Warren Wind, *The Story of American Golf* (New York: Alfred A. Knopf, 1975), 356.
2. Wind, *The Story of American Golf*, 380.

CHAPTER 9

1. Curt Sampson, *The Eternal Summer* (Dallas, TX: Taylor, 1992), 180–81.
2. African American Registry, "Segregation of the Golf Course: *Holmes v. Atlanta* Ruled," aaregistry.org/historic_events/view/segregation_golf_course_holmes_v_atlanta_ruled.

CHAPTER 10

1. Curt Sampson, *The Eternal Summer* (Dallas, TX: Taylor, 1992), 40.
2. Sampson, *The Eternal Summer*, 50.
3. Sampson, *The Eternal Summer*, 139.

CHAPTER 11

1. Curt Sampson, *The Eternal Summer* (Dallas, TX: Taylor, 1992), 65.
2. Sampson, *The Eternal Summer*, 40.
3. Herbert Warren Wind, *The Story of American Golf* (New York, Alfred A. Knopf, 1975), 488.

CHAPTER 13

1. Herbert Warren Wind, *The Story of American Golf* (New York: Alfred A. Knopf, 1975), 332.
2. Francis Clayton and Yanik Rice Lamb, *Born to Win* (Hoboken, NJ: John Wiley & Sons, 2004), 152–53.

Bibliography

BOOKS

Chapman, Kenneth C. *The Rules of the Green: A History of the Rules of Golf.* Chicago: Triumph Books, 1997.

Cook, Kevin. *Tommy's Honor: The Story of Old Tom Morris and Young Tom Morris, Golf's Founding Father and Son.* New York: Gotham Books, 2007.

Feinstein, John, Dan Jenkins, and others. *The Ultimate Golf Book,* edited by Charles McGrath and David McCormick. Boston: Houghton Mifflin, 2006.

Frost, Mark. *The Greatest Game Ever Played: Harry Vardon, Francis Ouimet, and the Birth of Modern Golf.* New York: Hyperion, 2002.

Gray, Francis Clayton, and Yanik Rice Lamb. *Born to Win: The Authorized Biography of Althea Gibson.* Hoboken, NJ: John Wiley & Sons, 2004.

Harriet, Ramona. *A Missing Link in History: The Journey of African Americans in Golf,* 2nd ed. Wilberforce, OH: Ramona Harriet, 2015.

Jenchura, John R. *Golf—A Good Walk and Then Some.* Merion, PA: John R. Jenchura, 2010.

Jones, Robert T., Jr. *Golf Is My Game.* Garden City, NY: Doubleday, 1960.

MacKenzie, Alister. *The Spirit of St. Andrews.* Chelsea, MI: Sleeping Bear Press, 1995.

Nelson, Byron. *How I Played the Game.* New York: Dell, 1993.

Nicklaus, Jack, with Herbert Warren Wind. *The Greatest Game of All: My Life in Golf.* New York: Simon & Schuster, 1969.

Owen, David. "The Chosen One." In *The Best American Sports Writing,* edited by Bud Collins and Glenn Stout, 115–36. Boston: Houghton Mifflin, 2001.

Sampson, Curt. *The Eternal Summer: Palmer, Nicklaus and Hogan in 1960, Golf's Golden Year.* Dallas, TX: Taylor, 1992.

Sampson, Curt. *Hogan.* Nashville, TN: Rutledge Hill Press, 1996.

Wind, Herbert Warren. *The Story of American Golf,* 3rd ed., rev. New York: Alfred A. Knopf, 1975.

INTERNET SOURCES

"Bogey to Blow-Up." scottishgolfhistory.org (5 January 2016).

"Early Women's Golf Clubs, Part I." scottishgolfhistory.org (8 January 2016).

"Golf Ball from Hairy to Haskell." scottishgolfhistory.org (5 January 2016).

"Golf Carts—Profit Center or Not?" usga.org/green section (5 January 2016).

"Golf—Meaning of Word Golf." scottishgolfhistory.org (5 January 2016).

"History of PGA Championship." pga.com/events/pga championship history.

"Links Golf Course—meaning." scottishgolfhistory.org (5 January 2016).

"List of U.S. Open Champions." usopen.com/history/champions (3 January 2018).

"Lists of Winners of Major Golf Championships." topendsports.com/events/golf/majors (2 January 2018).

"New World: Oldest Golf Clubs and Courses." scottishgolfhistory.org (11 January 2016).

"Oldest Golf Clubs and Courses in America, Part II." scottishgolfhistory.org (28 February 2016).

"Records, U.S. Open" www.usopen.com/history/records.

"Segregation of Golf Course: Holmes v. Atlanta Ruled." African American Registry. aaregistry.org/historic events (7 December 2016).

"Wooden Golf Balls: An Assumption and a Fallacy." scottishgolfhistory.org (11 January 2016).

"18 Hole Round." scottishgolfhistory.org (5 January 2016).

"120 Years of the USGA (Part 1) 1894–1924." usga.org (12 January 2016).

"120 Years of the USGA (Part 2) 1925–1955." usga.org (15 January 2016).

"120 Years of the USGA (Part 3) 1955–1984." usga.org (15 January 2016).

"120 Years of the USGA (Part 4) 1985–Present." usga.org (20 January 2016).

Index

About the Author

John Williamson was born and raised in Argyle, a small town in upstate New York founded by Scottish immigrants in the 1760s. He studied mechanical engineering at Union College in Schenectady, New York, served a three-year hitch in the US Air Force, and studied law at the Cornell University Law School in Ithaca, New York. After finishing law school, he moved to Colorado, where he practiced law in Denver for 15 years before becoming a full-time writer. This is his ninth published book; the other eight consist of seven law books and *The Gray Walls of Hell*, the biography of a prisoner. His knowledge of golf comes from having played the game for over a half-century, mostly on public courses in the United States, Scotland, and Canada.